TRICIA MOON

Chicago Graphic Design

Chicago Graphic Design

The best of Contemporary Chicago Graphic Design, with essays on past and future trends.

Organized by
Robert Perlman

Editor
Rob Dewey

Essays by
Victor Margolin
Greg Samata
Rick Valicenti
Patrick Whitney

Designed by
VSA Partners, Inc.

Published by
RWP/RP Elite Editions
Resource World Publications Inc.
Rockport Publishers, Inc.

Elite Editions Library

Distributed by
North Light Books
Cincinnati, Ohio

Copyright ©1994 by Resource World Publications, Inc. and Rockport Publishers, Inc.

All rights reserved. No part of this book may be reproduced in any form without written permission of the copyright owners. All images in this book have been reproduced with the knowledge and prior consent of the designers concerned and no responsibility is accepted by the producer, publisher or printer for any infringement of copyright or otherwise arising from the contents of this publication. Every effort has been made to ensure that credits accurately comply with information applied.

First published in the United States by RWP/RP Elite Editions, a trade name of Resource World Publications, Inc. and Rockport Publishers, Inc.

Resource World Publications, Inc.
209 West Central Street Ste. 204
Natick, Massachusetts 01760
Telephone 508.651.7000
Fax 508.651.9950

Rockport Publishers, Inc.
146 Granite Street
Rockport, Massachusetts 01966
Telephone 508.546.9590
Fax 508.546.7141
Telex 518.601.9284
ROCKPORT PUB

Design & Coordination:
VSA Partners, Inc.

Editor:
Rob Dewey

Production Designer:
Geoffrey Mark

Printer:
Regent Publishing Services Limited, Hong Kong

Photo Credits:
Lawrence Okrent, page 7
Chicago Historical Society, page 8 left
Chicago Board of Trade, page 8 bottom
Chicago Historical Society, page 9
Chicago Historical Society, page 10 top

Distribution to the book trade and art trade in the United States by North Light, an imprint of F&W Publications
1507 Dana Avenue
Cincinnati, Ohio 45207
Telephone 613.531.2222

Distributed to the book trade and art trade throughout the rest of the world by:
Rockport Publishers, Inc.
Rockport, Massachusetts, 01966

ISBN 1-56496-071-4
Printed in Hong Kong

Table of Contents

7	Why Chicago? Rob Dewey
12	Chicago Graphic Design: A Brief History Victor Margolin
20	Murrie Lienhart Rysner & Associates
28	Kovach Design Co.
36	Michael Glass Design, Inc.
44	VSA Partners, Inc.
52	Segura Inc.
60	Nicholas Associates
68	Source/Inc.
76	Hayward Blake & Company
84	Concrete
92	The Mark of Your Time Greg Samata
94	Windy City Communications
102	Crosby Associates Inc.
110	Mark Oldach Design
118	Pressley Jacobs Design Inc.
126	H. Greene & Co.
134	Porter/Matjasich & Associates
142	Cagney+McDowell, Inc.
150	McMillan Associates
158	Michael Stanard, Inc.
166	Liska & Associates, Inc.
174	Business As Usual Rick Valicenti
180	Meta–4 Incorporated
188	Tanagram, Inc.
196	Strandell Design
204	Kym Abrams Design
212	Hafeman Design Group
220	Gerhardt & Clemons, Inc.
228	Thirst
236	Lipson·Alport·Glass & Associates
244	ComCorp, Inc.
252	Essex Two Incorporated
260	Is Theory of Any Use to Designers? Patrick Whitney & Kim Erwin
268	Index of Firms and Principals Acknowledgements

Acknowledgements

In the 20th century, Chicago became recognized around the world as a leading center of graphic design. While primarily known for its corporate style, the diversity of Chicago graphic design has grown in recent years to include work that is both extremely personal and experimental. This book will examine the historical forces which led to Chicago's status as a design center, explore the current work of 30 of Chicago's leading design offices, and consider how Chicago is continuing to shape the future of visual communications.

Chicago's place at the center of the nation forged it into a world center of commerce and culture. Its energy and vitality has been tempered over time, however, by traditional Midwestern pragmatism and rationality. Similarly, graphic design in Chicago has historically been informed by both the practical needs of business and the provocative ideas of design theorists who made the city their home.

Chicago has had a significant and disproportionate impact on the visual culture of our society. This power as a center of architecture, advertising, printing and publishing is directly attributable to its place at the center of the nation's water and rail systems in the late 19th century.

The completion of the Illinois and Michigan Canal in 1848 connected the Mississippi River and the bounty of the American West to the Great Lakes and the cities of the East. Railroads operating south of the Great Lakes made their western terminals in Chicago, while the various western railroads made their eastern terminals there. By 1869, with the linkup of the transcontinental railroad, the city had rail connections extending all the way to the Pacific Ocean.

Chicago became the clearinghouse for much of the nation's commodities and natural resources including grain, lumber and livestock. By the late 1860s, for example, over 50 million bushels of grain came in and out of Chicago each year. In 1872 alone, more than 9,000 vessels carrying lumber arrived in Chicago. The Union Stockyards, located several miles southwest of the city's center, were the largest in the world.

Chicago Exchanges
Chicago Board of Trade . . . . corn, oats, other grains
Chicago Board Options Exchange . . . . stock options
Chicago Mercantile Exchange . . . . meat, livestock
International Money Market . . . . treasury bonds and notes, currencies, precious metals
Chicago Rice and Cotton Exchange . . . rice, cotton
MidAmerica Commodity Exchange . . . financial futures

The Union Stockyards, c. 1910

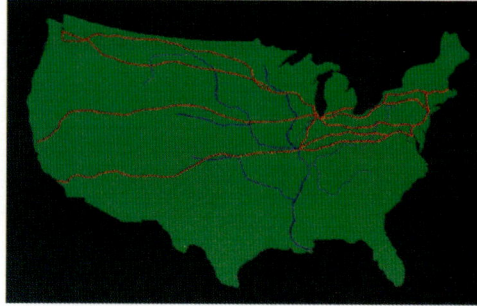

Late 19th Century U.S. Rail Lines and Waterways

The need to somehow manage the vast amount of buying and selling resulted in systems of grading the quality of commodities like grain and lumber. In a short time, the Chicago grading systems proliferated throughout the region, creating speculative markets, futures contracts, and eventually full-scale futures markets. Today, Chicago is home to several of the world's leading financial exchanges.

The combination of large-scale economic activity and massive transportation and distribution networks helped Chicago become a national center of the printing, publishing and advertising industries. Design scholar and historian Victor Margolin of the University of Illinois at Chicago details in his essay the development of graphic design in Chicago in this context.

Chicago was also the home of the country's largest merchandising companies of the period, Sears, Roebuck and Co. and Montgomery Ward. Sears' first general merchandise catalogue, published in 1896, featured 532 pages of goods. By 1945, Sears' annual sales exceeded $1 billion; sales grew to $1 billion per month by 1967. These awesome economic forces helped Chicago become a leader in scholarship and research as well. The University of Chicago, for example, has produced more than 60 Nobel Prize winners in the past century. A number of other outstanding universities including Northwestern, Roosevelt, DePaul and Loyola have contributed to the city's reputation as a world center for ideas. Chicago's economic and cultural richness was enhanced by the birth of such institutions as the Art Institute of Chicago and the Chicago Symphony Orchestra in the 1890s.

The Chicago Board of Trade

"A Busy Bee-Hive," color lithograph, 1900

View westward, The Great
Basin, World's Columbian
Exposition, 1893

**Congresses Held in Conjunction with
the World's Columbian Exposition of 1893**

World's Parliament of Religions
International Congress of Education
Congress of Authors
Congress of Architects
Philosophy Congress
Labor Congress
World's Congress of Representative Women
Congress of Evolution

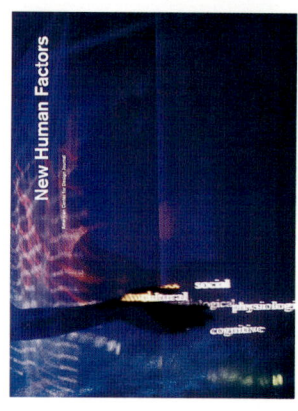

American Center for Design
Journal, vol. 7, no. 1, 1993,
Bridge Group

Chicago was also home of the World's Columbian Exposition of 1893, perhaps the most influential event of its type ever held. Nearly 28 million people – roughly 45% of the nation's population in 1893 – visited the fair during its six-month run. On a single day, October 9, more than 760,000 visitors jammed the grounds to mark the anniversary of the Great Chicago Fire. In addition to its appeal as unprecedented entertainment, the fair also made significant cultural and social contributions. A quarter million exhibits were brought to Chicago from over 60 nations. A series of congresses brought together 700,000 of the world's greatest minds. A number of reform movements, including those on behalf of women and labor, received significant attention at the fair.

The city's economic and cultural vitality became a beacon to scholars, writers, artists and designers in the early part of the 20th century, particularly in the 1930s, when the dark cloud of fascism was casting its shadow over Europe. It was during this period that the New Bauhaus was established in Chicago under the leadership of László Maholy-Nagy. Chicago design and architecture flourished in the middle part of this century.

Thanks largely to the influence of the New Bauhaus and the work of such individuals and firms as Richard Latham, Jay Doblin, Unimark and the Center for Advanced Research in Design (CARD) at Container Corporation of America, Chicago emerged as a global center for design theory and ideas. Institutions such as the Institute of Design and American Center for Design – and journals such as *Design Issues,* published by the University of Illinois at Chicago, and the *American Center for Design Journal* – continue this rich tradition. Patrick Whitney, director of the Institute of Design, shares in his essay a number of current and recent projects undertaken by I.D. students and alumni which give us a glimpse of the future of visual communications.

The portfolios of work by Chicago design offices which make up the heart of this volume provide clear evidence that today's graphic designers are applying the best of historical and current design thinking to work for an immense range of clients. Between their energy and the city's vital design and cultural institutions, Chicago's influence on our visual culture will continue in its scope and impact for many years to come.

Architects Associated with Chicago

Daniel H. Burnham
Louis Sullivan
Bertrand Goldberg
Mies van der Rohe
Frank Lloyd Wright
Walter Netsch
Harry Weese
Thomas Beeby
Stanley Tigerman
Helmut Jahn

Notable University of Chicago Nobel Prize Winners

Gary Becker, economics, 1992

Leon Lederman, physics, 1988

Herbert A. Simon, economics, 1978

Saul Bellow, literature, 1976

Milton Friedman, economics, 1976

James Dewey Watson, medicine, 1962

Enrico Fermi, physics, 1938

James Franck, physics, 1925

Logo for Chicago 93, the centennial celebration of the World's Columbian Exposition, Silvio Design

Will Denslow, poster for L. Frank Baum's "The Wonderful Wizard of Oz," 1890s. *Above*

Will Bradley, poster for the Stone & Kimball novel "When Hearts Are Trumps," 1894. *Right*

Claude Fayette Bragdon, poster for The Chap Book, c. 1897. *Above*

Oscar Hanson, poster for the North Shore Line, 1920s. *Right*

Commerce, always central to Chicago, has been a major factor in the development of the city's graphic design tradition. Essential to the rise of Chicago's commercial and typographic arts were its communication needs – represented by the newspapers, magazines, railroad timetables and promotional materials that had to appear regularly – and the exceptional growth of the printing industry which spawned a number of related enterprises such as publishing and advertising. Beginning in the late 19th century, these enterprises provided considerable work for commercial artists and layout men whose use of decorative alphabets and tightly-spaced layouts typified the job printing of the period.

In the 1890s, Chicago's burgeoning book publishing industry produced everything from textbooks to best sellers. The book publishers, as well as those who published magazines and newspapers, attracted commercial artists and typographers who began to specialize in publication design and illustration. One Chicago firm of the period, George M. Hill, published a best seller by a local writer, L. Frank Baum, who penned "The Wonderful Wizard of Oz." Illustrations for the book were drawn by Will Denslow, a Chicago newspaper artist, although subsequent volumes in the Oz series were, for the most part, illustrated by John R. Neill.

The most prominent Chicago literary publisher of the 1890s was Stone & Kimball, a firm that was started in Cambridge by two Harvard undergraduates. In 1894 Herbert Stone and Hannibal Ingalls Kimball moved their company to Chicago where Stone grew up and his father Melville had founded the Chicago Daily News in 1875. Shortly before leaving Cambridge, Stone & Kimball began to publish *The Chap Book*, which became the leading "little magazine" of the 1890s. It appeared twice a month and was a bargain at five cents an issue. Some of the finest American and European writers of the day wrote for the publication

ABCDEFGHIJKL
MNOPQRSTUVWXYZ &
abcdefghijklmnopq
rstuvwxyz
1234567890 $
‛·—.,':;!?[]

Oswald Cooper, Cooper Black Condensed, 1920s.
Far Left

Otis Shepard, Wrigley's Gum billboard, 1940s.
Above

Container Corporation of America truck with logotype by Egbert Jacobson, 1936.

László Moholy-Nagy, catalog cover for School of Design, c. 1943. *Top*

Robert Hunter Middleton, exhibition announcement for the STA, 1950. *Above*

Bruce Beck, promotional portfolio, 1952. *Below*

When the automobile became widespread, the billboard emerged as a major outdoor advertising vehicle. Chicago was the home of the Poster Advertising Association, the national organization for the billboard industry, which published an excellent monthly magazine, The Poster, that promoted the spread of billboard advertising in the United States.

Advertising created a need for lettering and layouts which produced a distinct type of commercial artist, the lettering man. Foremost among the lettering men in Chicago was Oswald Cooper who was extremely knowledgeable about advertising and printing. Besides using available display types in his ads, he did much display lettering himself and wrote copy as well. As with Bradley, type foundries were interested in casting some of his lettering faces. His best-known face is Cooper Black, which he completed in the early 1920s and which was widely used in advertising layouts.

Cooper learned his trade at Frank Holme's School of Illustration where Frederic Goudy taught briefly. But that was not the only place to study commercial art in Chicago. The School of the Art Institute also offered courses in poster and advertising design and a number of Chicago commercial artists and illustrators were students there.

Perhaps the classiest Chicago advertising campaign of the 1920s was mounted by the Chicago Rapid Transit Lines and the Chicago North Shore and Milwaukee Railroad. Each month for three or four years a new poster advertising the Elevated Lines, Rapid Transit, or South Shore Lines appeared on the train platforms. The posters were created by local illustrators including Willard Elmes, Rocco Navigato and Oscar Hanson. The flat colors, strong tones and hand lettering were reminiscent of the modern posters one might have seen in the German poster magazine Das Plakat.

In 1921 the School of the Art Institute established a Department of Printing Arts under Ernst Detterer. The curriculum included "printing, typesetting, design in relation to printed pages, lettering, composition, life and [the] story of processes of reproduction." This course, in which students engaged in such rarefied practices as laying gold leaf on a page, was an alternative to entering commercial art through a print shop or printing plant.

Detterer's department functioned for ten years during which time a number of graduates became outstanding local designers. Among them was Robert Hunter Middleton who went to work for the Ludlow Typograph Company in 1923 and became the company's Director of Typeface Design 10 years later. During his long

Chicago Graphic Design:
A Brief History

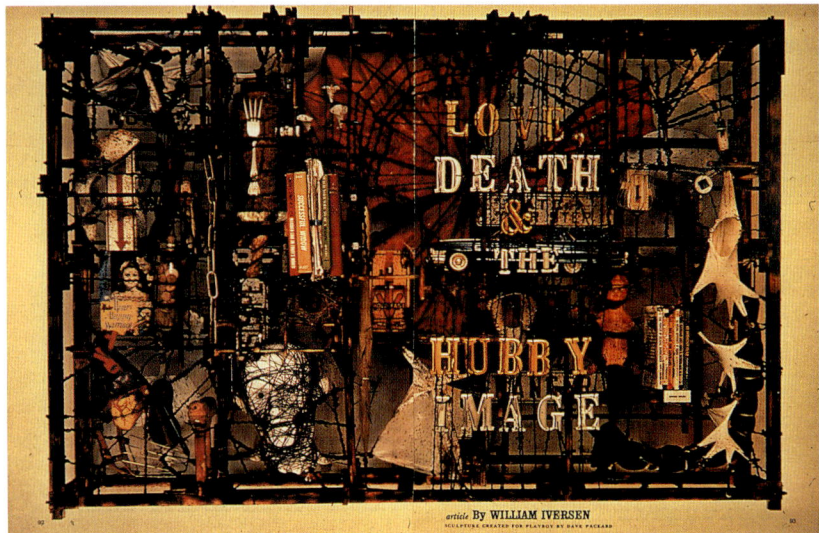

Art Paul, layout for Playboy, 1963. *Left*

Carl Regehr, cover of Chicago Magazine, 1965. *Above*

John Massey, art director (CARD), Graphic Standards Manual for Department of Labor, c. 1968. *Right*

Norman Perman, booklets for Continental Bank, 1966. *Below Left*

Massimo Vignelli, cover of Unimark's magazine Dot Zero, 1967. *Below Right*

tenure at Ludlow, Middleton designed almost 100 typefaces. In 1945 he established his own printing and publishing venture, the Cherryburn Press, where one of his major projects, undertaken for the Newberry Library, was to print a collection of blocks by the British wood engraver Thomas Bewick.

Middleton was among the founding members of the Society of Typographic Arts (STA) in 1927. Some designers in this group had belonged to the American Institute of Graphic Arts in New York but split off from that organization because they felt it was too strongly oriented toward its local members. The aim of the STA was to establish high standards in typography and elevate public taste in design matters. The organization's early members, besides Middleton, included Ray DaBoll, William Kittridge (whose Lakeside Press was the source of many finely produced and designed books), and Douglas McMurtrie, the printing scholar. McMurtrie's book "Modern Typography and Layout," published in 1929, explored the relation of abstract art to graphic design and argued anew for a modern typography in America that drew from the European avant-garde but was not completely influenced by it. By 1934, after Hitler came to power in Germany,

some European designers began to emigrate to the United Sates. That year the Austrian designer and illustrator Joseph Binder was invited by the Art Directors Club of Chicago to teach his now-famous course on graphic stylization and simplicity. Binder's most notable influence was on Otis Shepard, the art director of the Wrigley Company who adopted Binder's style for Wrigley billboards and car cards.

In 1936 a group called 27 Chicago Designers published the first book of work by its members. Among those included in the group's early volumes were John Averill, Rodney Chirpe, Egbert Jacobson, Robert Hunter Middleton, Ray DaBoll, Bert Ray, Paul Ressinger and Oswald Cooper. Since its beginning, 27 Chicago Designers has tried to publish a new volume every year, although this has not always been possible. Nonetheless the work of the group's changing membership continues to be a good reflection of significant trends in Chicago's graphic design practice.

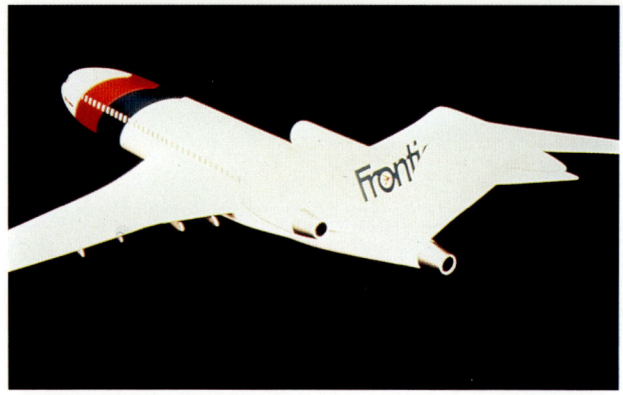

Unimark, visual identity for Frontier Airlines, c. 1970. *Top Right*

RVI Corporation, Fire Extinguishing Equipment Packaging 1972. *Above*

Bill Bonnell, poster for exhibition at Ryder Gallery, 1970s. *Below*

It was not until 1937, however, when László Moholy-Nagy came to Chicago to establish the New Bauhaus, that the advanced ideas in visual communication which had been developing in Europe since the end of World War I hit Chicago with full force and inaugurated a new, more sophisticated and international phase of the city's graphic design practice. Moholy-Nagy brought over Gyorgy Kepes, a fellow Hungarian who had studied at the Bauhaus-influenced design school in Budapest and then worked with him in Berlin and London. Kepes headed the Light Workshop at the School of Design, which Moholy-Nagy started after the New Bauhaus folded in 1938. This workshop included photography as well as typography, layout and serigraphy.

Many local designers were introduced to modern design ideas through a special course which Kepes gave in 1938 under the sponsorship of the Chicago Art Directors Club. He also influenced many students in his courses at the School of Design where he remained until 1943. Designers who took either day or night classes with Kepes or Moholy-Nagy included Mort and Millie Goldsholl, Elsa Kula, Bruce Beck and Herb Pinzke.

In 1944 Paul Theobald and Company, a Chicago publisher specializing in books on modern design and architecture, brought out Kepe's "Language of Vision," a book which extended his ideas to a wider audience. This volume provided a completely new approach to visual design, one based more on the principles of Gestalt psychology and the forms of modern art than on the traditional book and layout arts. In 1947 Paul Theobald published Moholy-Nagy's last book, "Vision in Motion," a summation of his philosophy of education and design, which he completed shortly before he died.

The initial step in Chicago's development as a major center of corporate design occurred in 1936 when Walter Paepcke, president of Container Corporation of America, hired Egbert Jacobson as the company's first design director. Jacobson was not only responsible for the company's logos, stationery, invoices, annual reports and advertising but also its offices, interiors, factories and trucks. One of his first projects was to develop a series of corporate advertisements and he turned over the assignment to Charles Coiner at the N.W. Ayer advertising agency in Philadelphia. Coiner hired

Chicago Graphic Design: A Brief History

the French poster artist A.M. Cassandre to do a group of innovative newspaper ads; then, during the war, other well-known artists and designers including Herbert Bayer, Man Ray, Fernand Léger, Herbert Matter and Matthew Leibowitz produced advertisements for the company. Bayer later became a design consultant to Container Corporation.

In 1951 Paepcke supported the first International Design Conference at Aspen; several years later the Aspen meeting assumed its own administration, though Container Corporation continued to contribute financially. The initiative taken by the STA in organizing subsequent Aspen conferences was a fitting context for a number of important design firms that emerged in the 1950s.

Bert Ray, who had been an art director at Abbott Laboratories, opened an office around 1950 and one thinks as well of firms such as Whitaker-Guernsey and Tempo. Other designers who became active at this time were Everett McNear, Norman Perman, Ed Bedno, Bruce Beck, Randall Roth, Ann Long, Rhodes Patterson, Susan Jackson Keig and Carl Regehr. In 1951 Phoebe Moore became the first woman elected to the 27 Chicago Designers to be followed not long after by Elsa Kula.

Another important event of the 1950s was the founding of Playboy in 1953 with Arthur Paul as art director. Paul hired some of the best artists and illustrators in the country to define Playboy's visual identity and created many exciting layouts himself. Following the founding of Esquire in 1933, Playboy became one of the few stylish magazines published in Chicago for a mass market.

One of the early Chicago firms to concentrate on corporate design was the RVI Corporation founded by Robert Vogele. Like Ralph Eckerstrom and John Massey, who followed Egbert Jacobson as successive design directors of Container Corporation, Vogele came from the art department of the University of Illinois Press in Champaign-Urbana where he had worked under Eckerstrom.

Eckerstrom, who arrived at Container Corporation in 1955, left there in 1964 to join a group of partners in founding Unimark, a graphic and product design office that was intended to operate on a worldwide scale. Others involved in the venture were Jim Fogelman, Massimo Vignelli, Larry Klein and Jay Doblin, who came to Chicago in 1955 from Raymond Loewy's New York office to serve as director of the Institute of Design.

After succeeding Eckerstrom as design director at Container Corporation, Massey started the Center for Advanced Research in Design (CARD), a studio within the company that was set up to work with outside clients. These included Atlantic Richfield, the U.S. Department of Labor and the Mayor's Committee on Economic and Cultural Development, located in Chicago's City Hall. For this committee, CARD designers created a set of banners and posters to brighten up the city center.

Robert Vogele, Ansul Chemical Company 1957 Annual Report

STA Design Journal cover, 1985, Kovach Design.

Chris Garland, cover for Zoetrope, 1979. *Above*

Rick Valicenti and Michael Giammanco, poster for the Lyric Opera of Chicago, 1988. *Below*

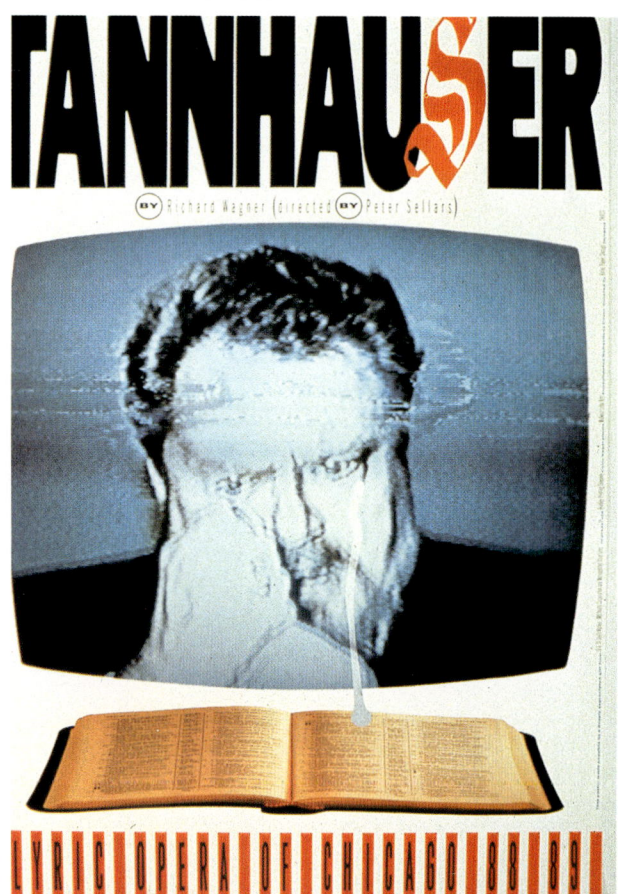

Another designer who worked for the Mayor's Committee was Carl Regehr, the first art director of Chicago Magazine, a publication that was intended to enhance Chicago's public image. Subsequently Regehr left Chicago for the University of Illinois in Champaign-Urbana where he became a key figure in the graphic design program there. Among the program's recognized graduates was Bill Bonnell, who first established a Chicago reputation at Container Corporation before moving on to New York to open his own office.

By the late 1960s, RVI Corporation, Unimark and CARD, as well as other firms such as Goldsholl Associates, Design Consultants Inc. and the Design Partnership, gave Chicago a national profile as a center of corporate design. But the city also had a graphic underground in the 1960s comparable to cities like Berkeley and New York. A notable figure in this movement was Skip Williamson whose free-lance work included covers for the Chicago Seed, an underground newspaper. Between 1968 and 1973, Williamson and some friends published Bijou, the only underground comic book to originate in Chicago.

By the time Unimark dissolved around 1979, it had become a training ground for many designers who continued to work in Chicago after they left the firm. Among these were John Greiner. Designers who had first trained at RVI Corporation before going out on their own included Wayne Webb, Jim Lienhart, Bill Cagney, Bill McDonald, Pat Whitney and Bart Crosby. During the 1960s and 1970s many other designers in the city were doing innovative work as well. One thinks, for example, of Norman Perman, Randall Roth, Ed and Jane Bedno, Michael Reid and David Burke.

In 1972 Doblin established his own firm where he developed a focus on corporate planning. He emphasized this approach in his work for major clients such as J.C. Penney and Xerox. After Doblin's death in 1989, the work of the firm continued under the leadership of Larry Keeley who had worked with Doblin to develop a multi-disciplinary focus for complex problem-solving.

Chicago Graphic Design: A Brief History

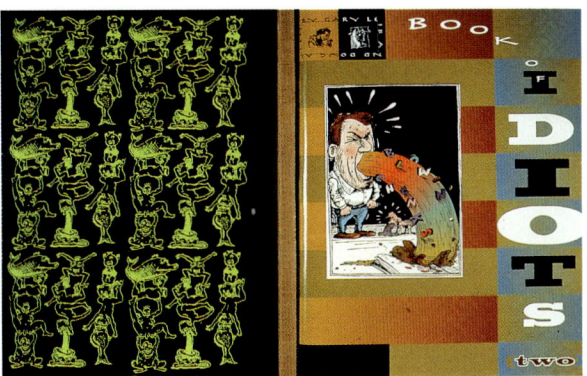

Anthony Ma, comic book cover, 1991.

VSA Partners Inc., poster for a Harley-Davidson, Inc. MDA event, 1992.

The emphasis on corporate design and planning that developed in the 1960s and 1970s also helped broaden the orientation of STA. The STA in 1978 undertook the planning for the biennial international congress convened by the International Council of Graphic Design Associations (ICOGRADA). The ICOGRADA congress was organized around the theme of "Design That Works" and tried to give more emphasis to research and theory than previous congresses had. The same year Women in Design was founded in Chicago. This organization has sought more equitable working conditions and recognition for women designers and mounted a major exhibit on women graphic designers for its 10th anniversary.

STA's interest in research was pursued in a new publication, the *Design Journal,* which first appeared in the fall of 1979. STA was also one of the first design organizations to take an interest in design history. Supported by a National Endowment for the Humanities grant, it sponsored a conference in June 1981 on "The History of Graphic Design in Chicago." In 1989 it changed its name to American Center for Design (ACD) to reflect its broader outlook and include other design disciplines. In the meantime the American Institute for Graphic Arts became a national organization and a Chicago chapter was formed to complement the graphic design activities of the ACD.

Despite a thriving contemporary art scene that has drawn consistently on popular culture since the 1960s, very few of Chicago's graphic designers have made use of this source to the degree that the city's artists have. One of the first to do so was Chris Garland, whose studio Xeno introduced a new wave look from California in the early 1980s. Others who have at times practiced a freer, more experimental style as a counterpart to the predominance of corporate and business graphics in the city include Rick Valicenti's firm Thirst; Concrete, the office of Jilly Simons; Dana Arnett and Maria Grillo of VSA Partners, Inc.; Anthony Ma's firm, Tanagram; and Carlos Segura of Segura, Inc.

Although the national graphic design scene today is pluralistic and difficult to characterize, the corporate legacy of the 1960s still remains the strongest influence in Chicago even though a host of small experimental firms have gained wide reputations. Whether or not they will have a stronger presence in the future remains to be seen.

are unique graphics and a signature "wave" trademark, Design: Jim Lienhart. *Top Left*

Murrie White Drummond Lienhart & Associates' 25th anniversary announcement wine bottle, Design: Wayne Krimston. *Bottom Left*

for the Quaker Oats Company's Gatorade brand, Design: Linda Voll. *Top Right*

Bold graphics highlight the new designs for Parsons Technology's computer software line, Design: Wayne Krimston. *Bottom Right*

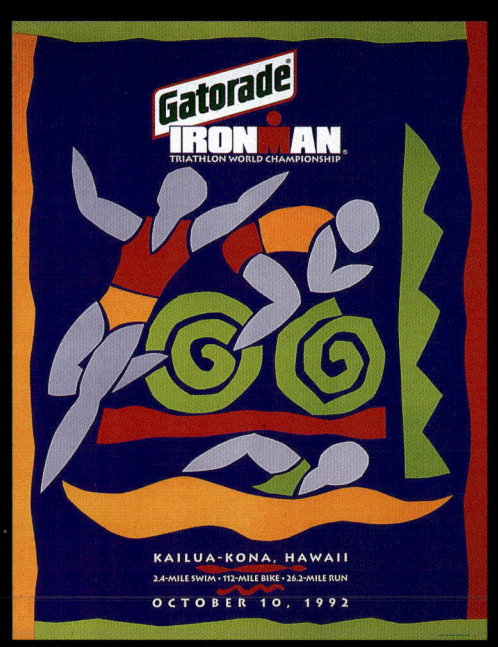

Miles Laboratories, Inc.
Nestle Beverage Co.
Ore-Ida Foods, Inc.
Oscar Mayer Foods Corp.
The Procter & Gamble Co.
The Quaker Oats Co.
SmithKline Beecham
Thomas J. Lipton Co.

Creating successful, long-lasting brand images in the highly competitive marketplace is the key to Murrie Lienhart Rysner & Associates' success since 1965. Their expertise lies in all aspects of packaging, from marketing analysis and strategic planning to industrial and graphic design and implementation.

MLR has developed a team of over forty professionals that form a partnership with each of its clients to achieve their many and diverse goals. As Herbert L. Murrie, President, says: "The market-place demand for unique and powerful images which reflect the product's personality has never been greater."

Murrie Lienhart Rysner & Associates

Contemporary elegance with a traditional flair helped launch Fiddlehead Cellars' Pinot Noir wine, Design: Kate McSherry. *Top Left*

Eye-appealing packaging has proven to be a successful marketing tool for Kaytee Products, Inc., Design: Kate McSherry. *Top Right*

Murrie Lienhart Rysner & Associates' 1993 New Year's card and name change announcement, Design: Adrienne Muryn. *Center Right*

Effective January 1, 1993, Murrie Lienhart Rysner & Associates' new corporate identity, Design: Jim Lienhart. *Bottom*

Murrie Lienhart Rysner & Associates

Savings Institutions Magazine, covers, Design: Jim Lienhart, Annie Donlin. *Right*

New product packaging for the Gerber Products Company's line of child-care products, Design: Kate McSherry. *Above*

A new, proprietary branded image for Bausch & Lomb disposable contact lenses, Design: Adrienne Muryn, Jacque Kelly. *Left*

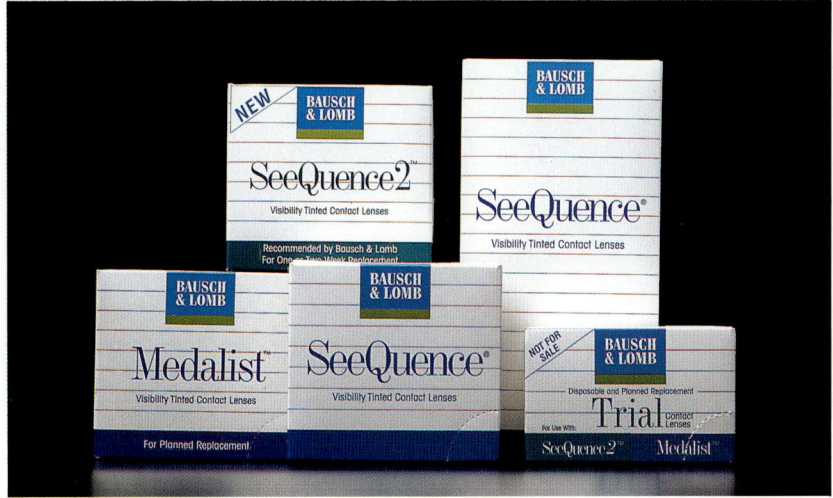

New packaging to appeal to the modern mother, for the William Carter Company's product line, Design: Jim Lienhart. *Left*

William Carter Company's new identity communicates love, care and growth, Design: Jim Lienhart. *Below*

A more contemporary, appetizing and quality look for a line of spices from Tone Bros., Inc., Design: Amy Leppert. *Center*

Fresh, new designs for the Oscar Mayer Foods Corporation's Claussen brand pickles, Design: Amy Leppert. *Bottom*

Murrie Lienhart Rysner & Associates

Updated packaging designs for the Starkist Seafood Company, Design: Adrienne Muryn, Sue Killian. *Top Left*

A polished, new image for S.C. Johnson & Son, Inc.'s Behold furniture polish, Design: Kate McSherry. *Bottom Right*

A bold, new presence for the Product & Gamble Company's well-known Comet cleaner, Design: Wayne Krimston. *Top Right*

New packaging to reinforce the leadership of One-A-Day vitamins from Miles Laboratories, Inc., Design: Wayne Krimston. *Bottom Right*

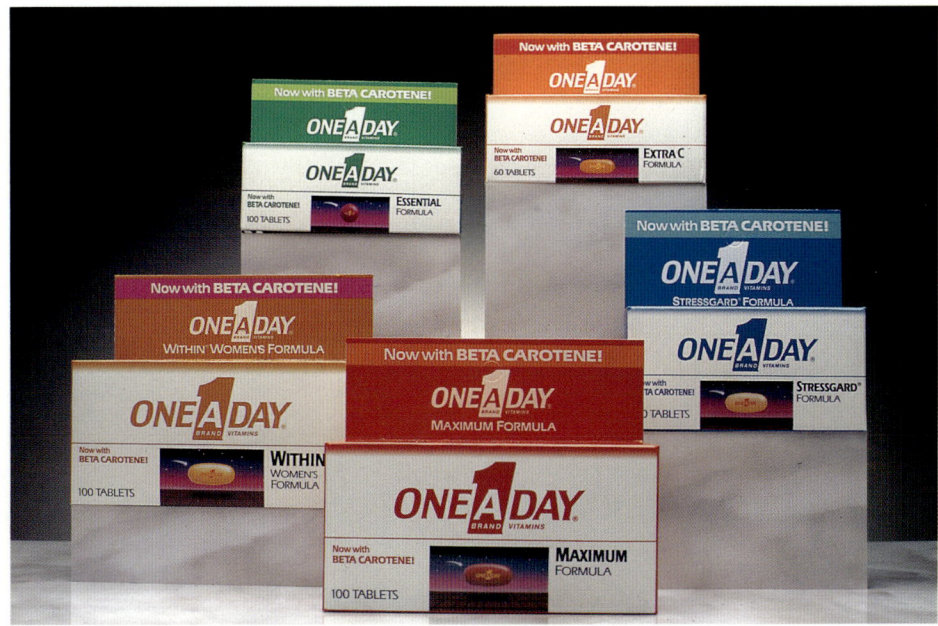

New design provides a more contemporary personality for Lipton's Golden Sauté brand, Design: Jayce Schmidt. *Left*

A modern, yet classic, Italian image for the Kraft General Foods, Inc.'s, DiGiorno pasta and sauce, Design: Kate McSherry. *Center Left*

Package design for Pillsbury, Inc.'s Bake Tops communicates a unique selling point, Design: Linda Voll. *Center Right*

Updated designs for Kraft General Foods, Inc.'s Butter Mints depict higher product quality, Design: Jayce Schmidt. *Bottom Left*

Chicago-based Montana Street Cafe restaurant's new identity projects a modern cafe ambience, Design: Linda Voll. *Bottom Right*

Murrie Lienhart Rysner & Associates

Updated identity gives Ore-Ida Foods Inc. a stronger brand umbrella, Design: Kate McSherry, Luis Izaguirre. *Bottom Left*

Critical to the redesign, Kraft General Foods Inc.'s Miracle Whip brand name has more impact, Design: Jim Lienhart. *Right*

Ore-Ida Food's Harvest Fries packaging positions the product as more natural, Design: Linda Voll. *Center*

Packaging designs that helped launch General Mills, Inc.'s new cereal/snack concept, Fingos, Design: Jayce Schmidt. *Bottom Right*

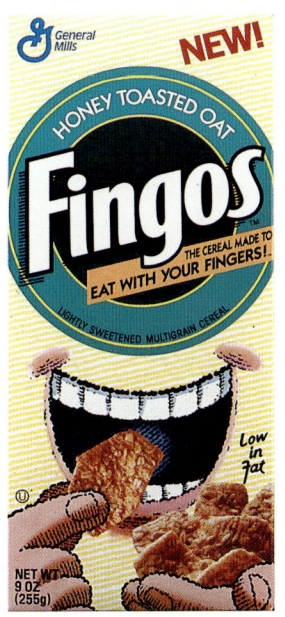 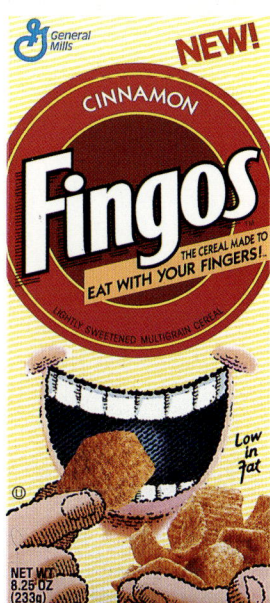

Miglin-Beitler, 1991, a construction barricade featuring "the boys." *Leo Burnett USA,* 1991, another barricade displays the company's unofficial symbol, the fat black pencils used by its founder. Part of a complete marketing program. *Chicago Board Options Exchange,* 1984, the visitors exhibit in their new building and trading floor.

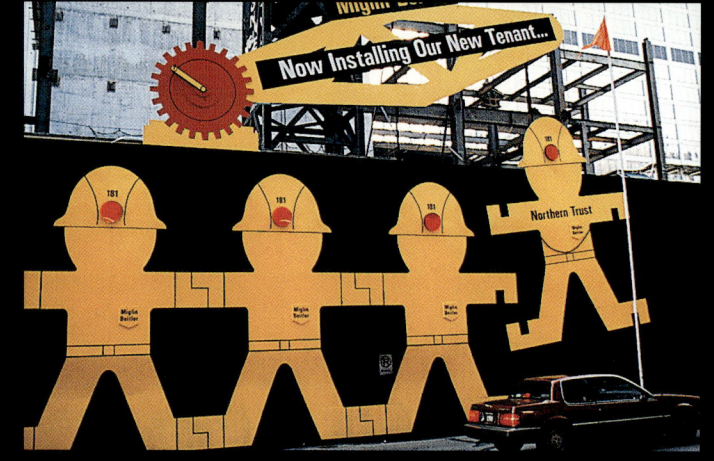

Date Founded: 1992. Ron Kovach has been a principal or partner since 1975. Collaborating designers, artists, photographers acknowledged within this project retrospective: Marie Laure Abrioux, Mark Anderson, Steven Bagby, Teresa Costantini, Kwok Chan, Kelli Evans, Kerry Grady, Lois Grimm, Eric Hausman, Jerzy Kucinski, Lee Madden, Robert Natkin, Jason Penny, Masha Reshetnikova, François Robert, LN Vallaincort, Angie Weiss Chapin.

Kovach Design Co.

Ron Kovach, like many effective problem solvers, followed a circuitous journey to bring a big picture perspective to the project table. His search for self-identity included the Marine Corps (discipline and passion); pre-med (a scientific method); a degree in product design (the manufacturing process); design education (the search for fresh ideas); corporate vice president (strategy and business plans); and many hours of volunteer work on professional boards (leadership). Today he is part of a consortium of peers offering an impressive creative, marketing and strategic planning capability.

Since each project is unique, the solutions take many forms. The process is subtractive, to collect everything that seems important and then whittle down and refine. What you wind up with is disarmingly simple solutions. Naturally, a strong influence on this ethos are the Beatles. "Their clever and refreshing tunes stimulated your intellect, but more importantly, your emotions. They pushed buttons. You could easily relate."

Today, summarizing all the experience, collaboration and search for a better way, the projects are limited only by time and budgets.

American Institute of Graphic Arts, 1991, initiated an explosive array of color and ideas via these individually designed banners along Michigan Avenue for the national design conference. *The Professional Golfers' Association of America*, 1993, logo redesigned for new product applications.

Kovach Design Co.

RR Donnelley & Sons Company, 1991, a subtle market-driven strategy and redesign of printing giant RR Donnelley & Sons Company "corporate" mark, transformed into a "printer's" mark, suitable for use with all of the information technologies available today. The past is linked with the future, while a comprehensive identity manual assures the redesigned mark's clear, consistent use. Introducing a new childcare program for company employees, as well as, *Choices*, the new flex-benefits healthcare program.

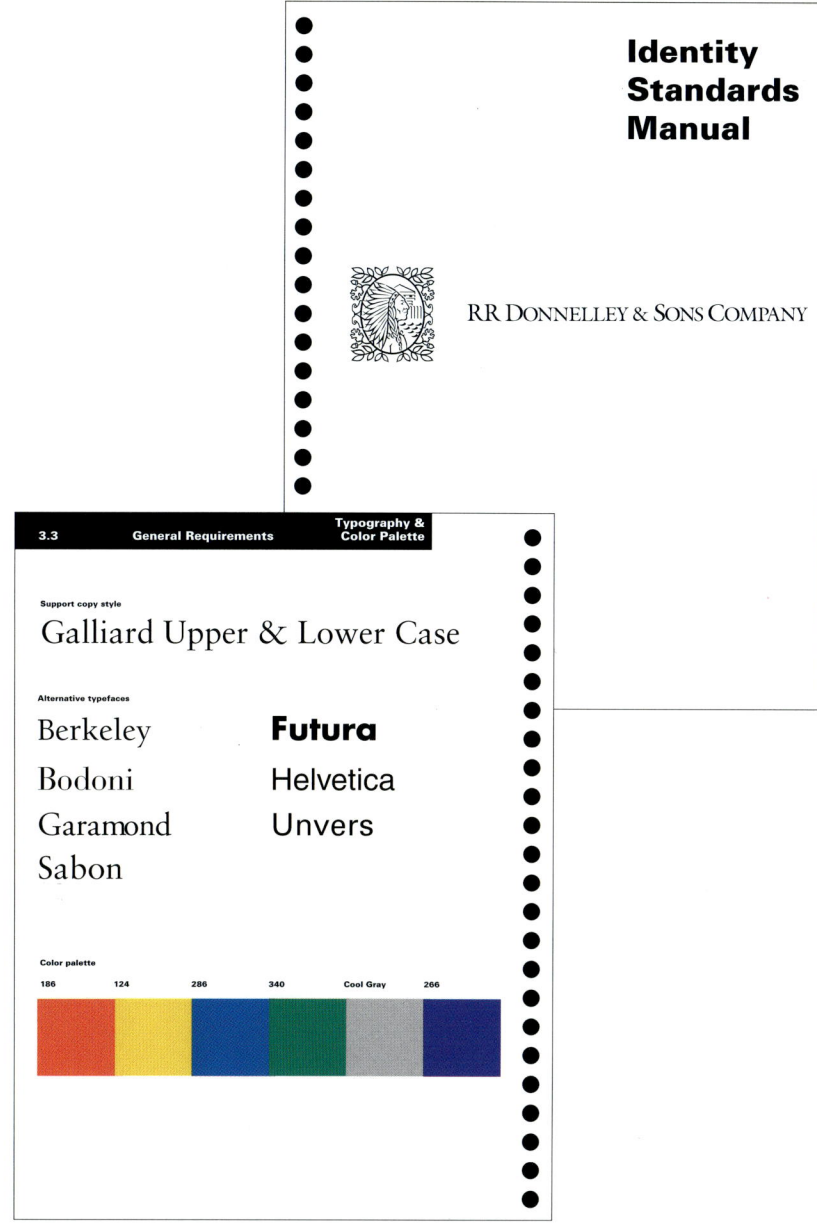

Homart Development Co., 1989, a corporate greeting card and holiday shopping bag. *Jobe's,* 1982, a plant food packaging, display and brand identity system encompassing nine products and 17 different packages. *Center for American Archeology* at Northwestern University, 1982, a mark and identity program evoking the spirit of the study of the life and culture of ancient peoples. *Motorola,* 1992, a "what-if" capability brochure using art as a metaphor for the quality routinely demanded at Motorola.

Kovach Design Co.

Consolidated Papers, Inc., 1993, a brochure for Reflections, Consolidated Papers' premier paper stock, demonstrates quality and expands the reader's imagination.

36

Michael Glass Design, Inc. 213 West Institute Place
Suite 612
Chicago, Illinois 60610
Telephone 312.787.5977
Fax 312.787.5974

Columbia College,
image brochure for corporate
fundraising, cover, Chicago,
1992.

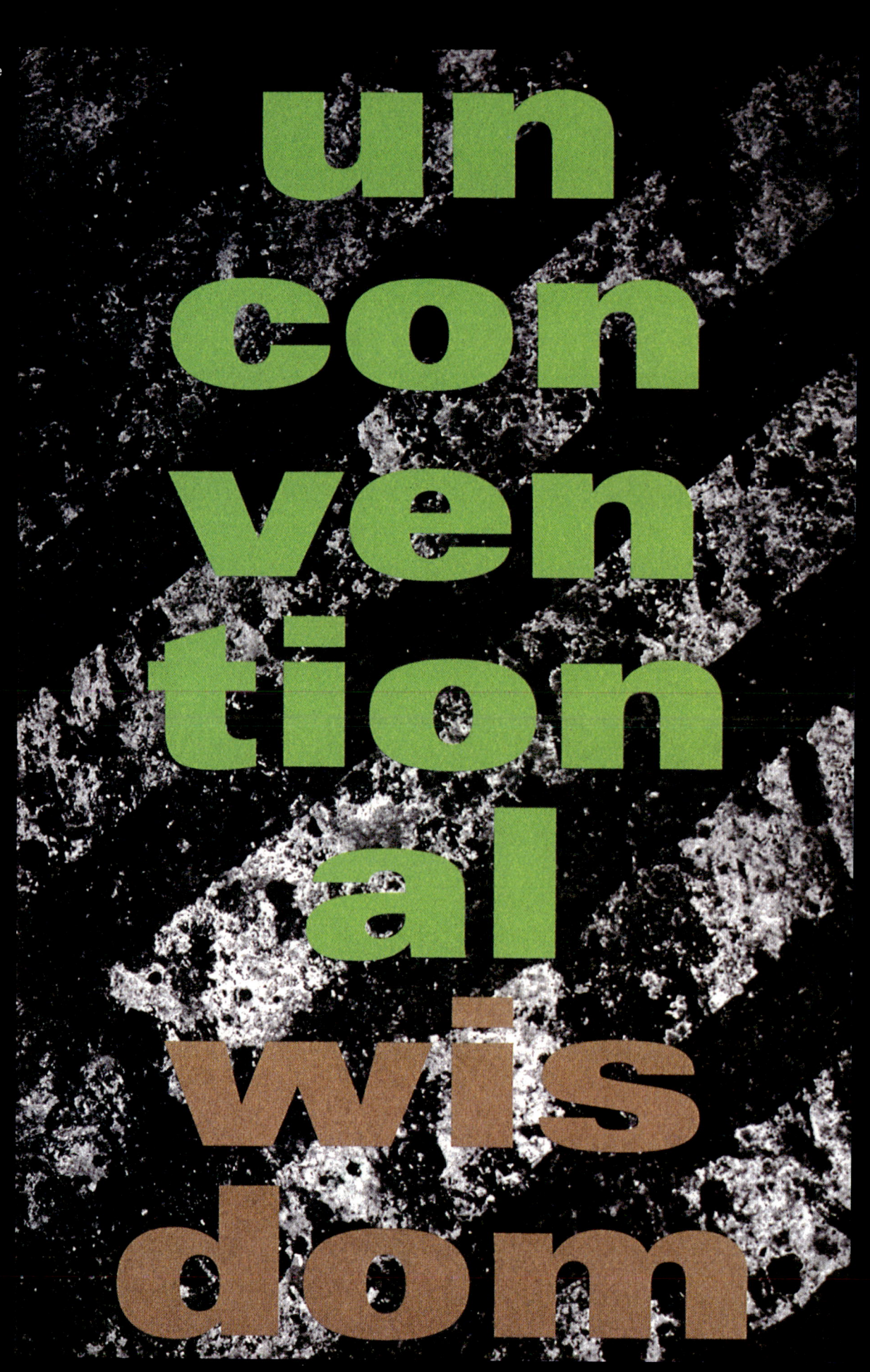

un
con
ven
tion
al
wis
dom

Michael Glass Design, Inc.

associations
between thoughts and meaning

affinities
sharing responsibility and
mutual respect

applications
using design to identify solutions

concerns
finding enlightened answers to
client needs and desires

connections
discovering opportunities to turn
liabilities into assets

relationships
forging bonds with diverse
corporate and cultural entities

relevance
creating a design environment in
which efforts and energies merge

Michael Glass, photograph
by François Robert, 1991.

38 · Michael Glass Design, Inc.

State of Illinois Building, directories, Chicago, 1988. *Top Right*

Chicago Cubs, interior signage program for Wrigley Field, Chicago, 1991. *Center Right*

Communicate, Inc., image and interior signage for corporate sales, Chicago, 1990. *Below Right*

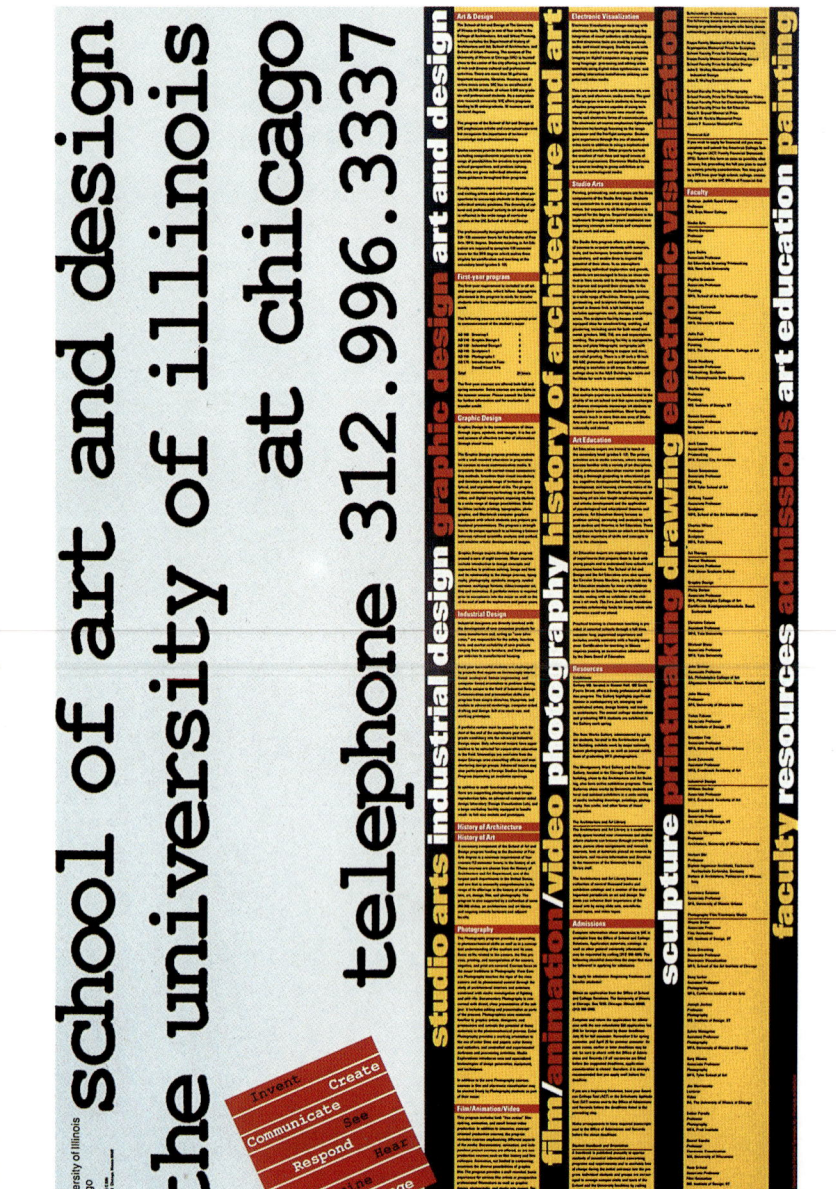

University of Illinois at Chicago, School of Art and Design, recruitment poster, 1991.

Oilily, store design and signage, Chicago, 1989.

Michael Glass Design, Inc.

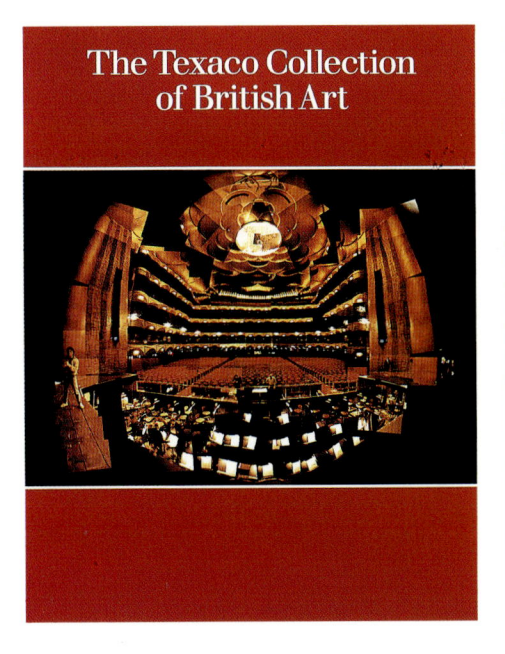

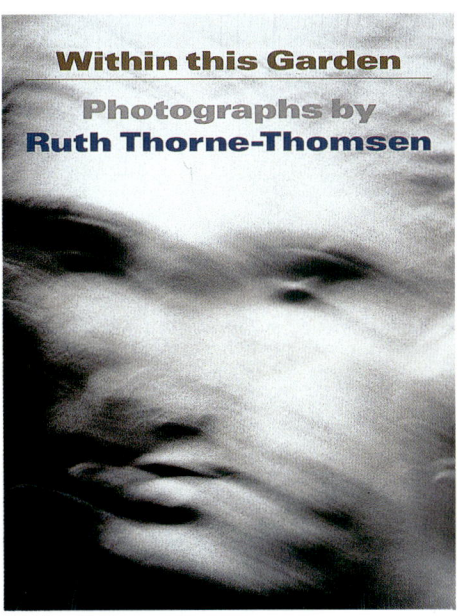

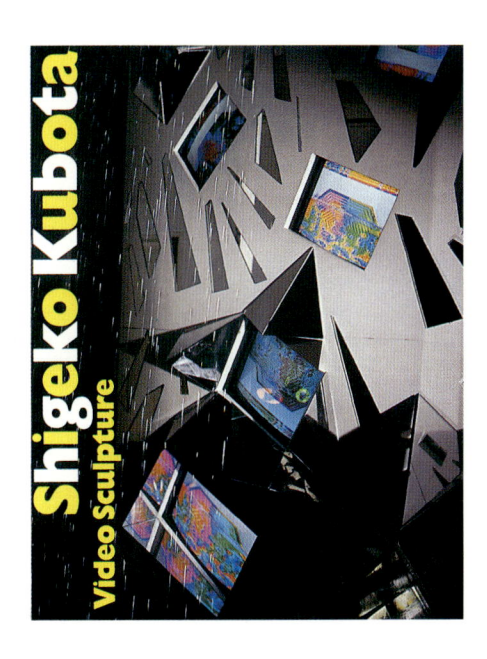

The Texaco Collection of British Art, corporate collection catalogue, London, 1993. *Top Left*

Within this Garden, Photographs by Ruth Thorne-Thomsen, exhibition catalogue, Museum of Contemporary Photography, Chicago, 1993. *Top Center*

Shigeko Kubota, Video Sculpture, exhibition catalogue, Museum of the Moving Image, New York, 1991. *Top Right*

Art Chicago International, exhibition catalogue, Chicago, 1993. *Bottom*

Michael Glass Design, Inc.

Identity programs, 1985–1992.

Marquette Venture Partners, venture capital, Chicago

Goodstuff and Rockwell, retail repurchasing, Chicago

The Environments Group, interior design, Chicago

The Rookery Building, Chicago

W.E. O'Neil Construction Company, Chicago

North Pier Chicago, office and retail, Chicago

Stericycle, medical waste recycling, Chicago

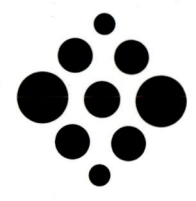

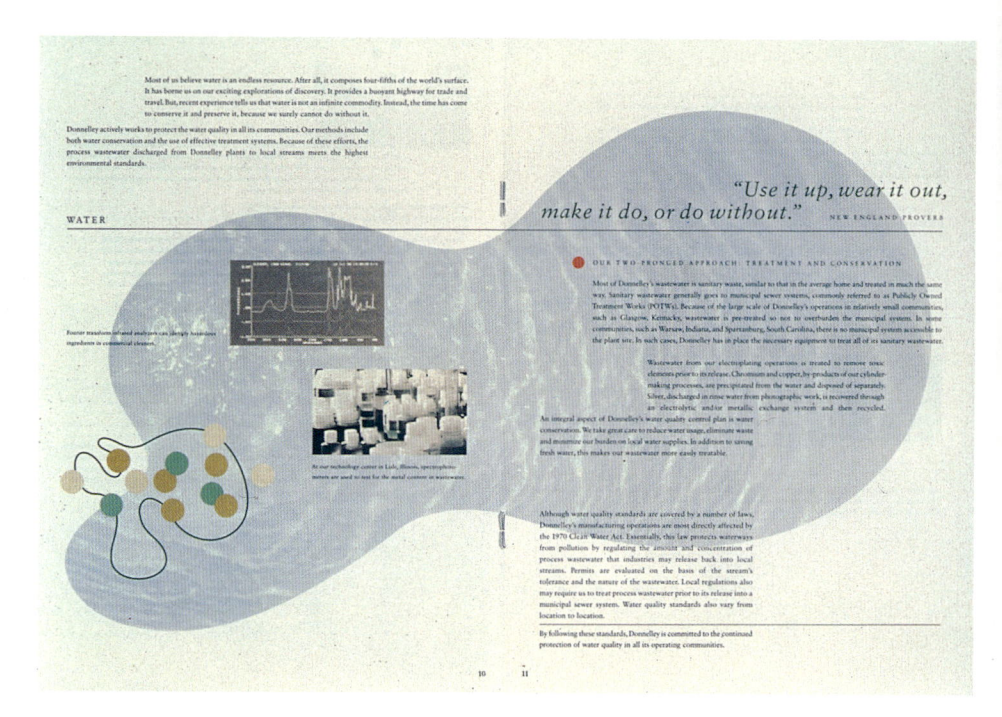

R.R. Donnelly, Printing Clean, environmental corporate responsibility brochure, Chicago, 1990. *Above*

Michael Glass Design, Inc., self-promotion, Chicago 27 Designers, 1991. *Below*

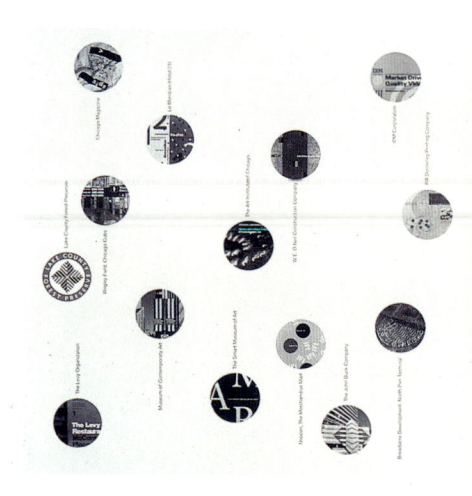

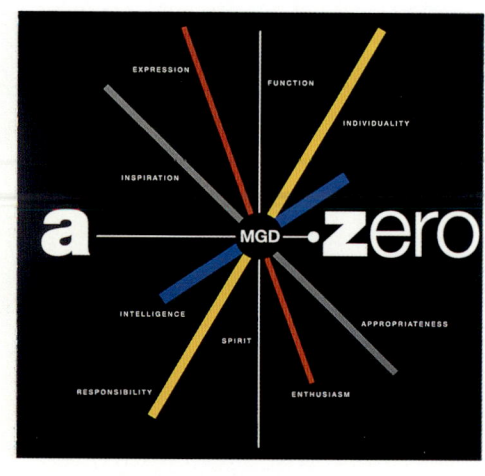

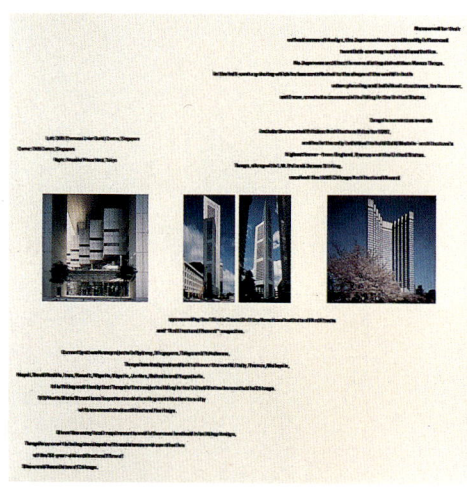

The John Buck Company, leasing brochure, American Medical Association, Chicago, 1985. *Above*

Michael Glass Design, Inc.

Neenah Paper Company, promotional brochure for annual reports on uncoated papers, Wisconsin, 1991.

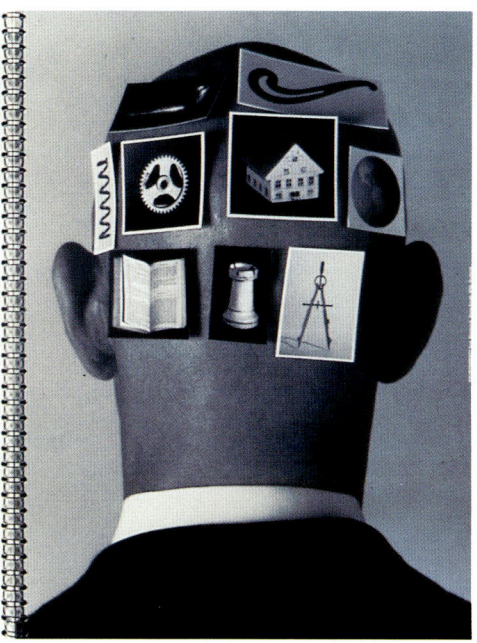

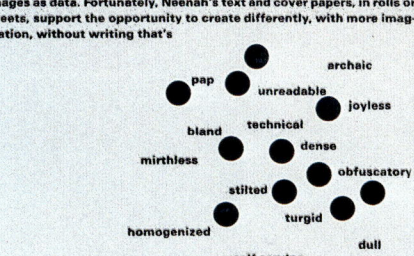

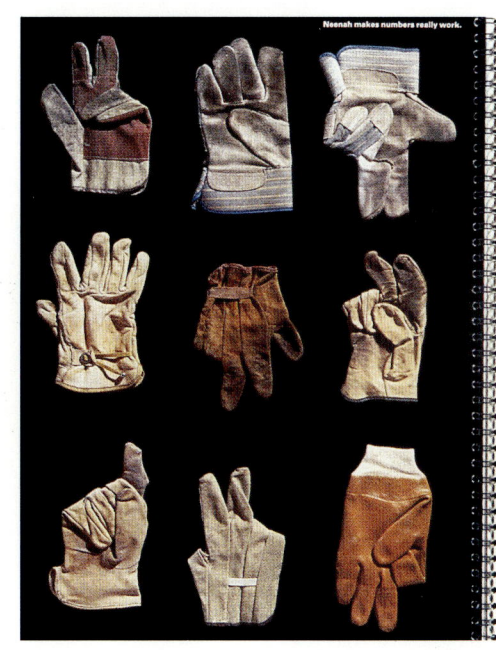

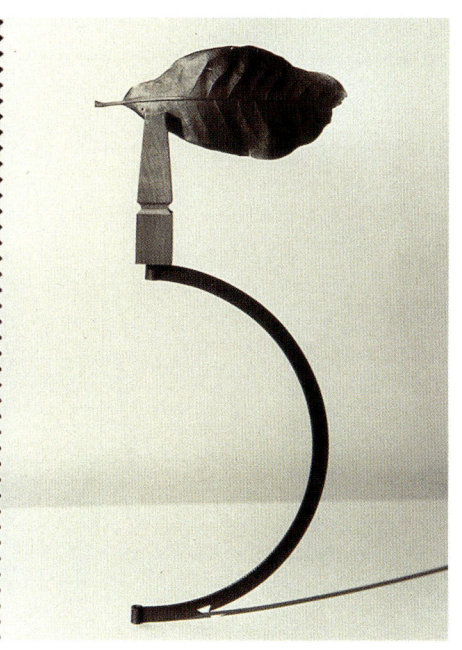

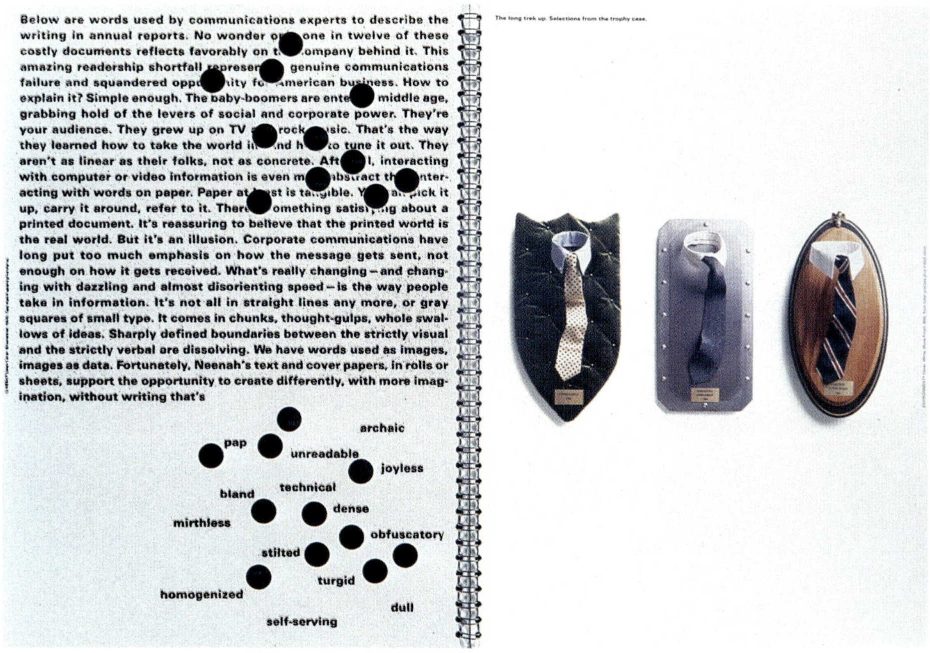

Michael Glass Design, Inc.

North Pier Chicago, environmental graphics, Chicago, 1985. *Top Left*

Arlington Park Race Track, silk design, Gretchen Bellinger, Chicago, 1988. *Center Left*

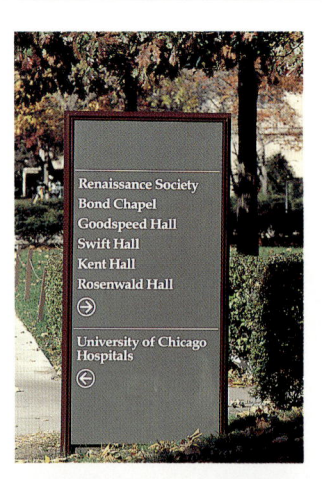

University of Chicago, environmental signage program, Chicago, 1991.

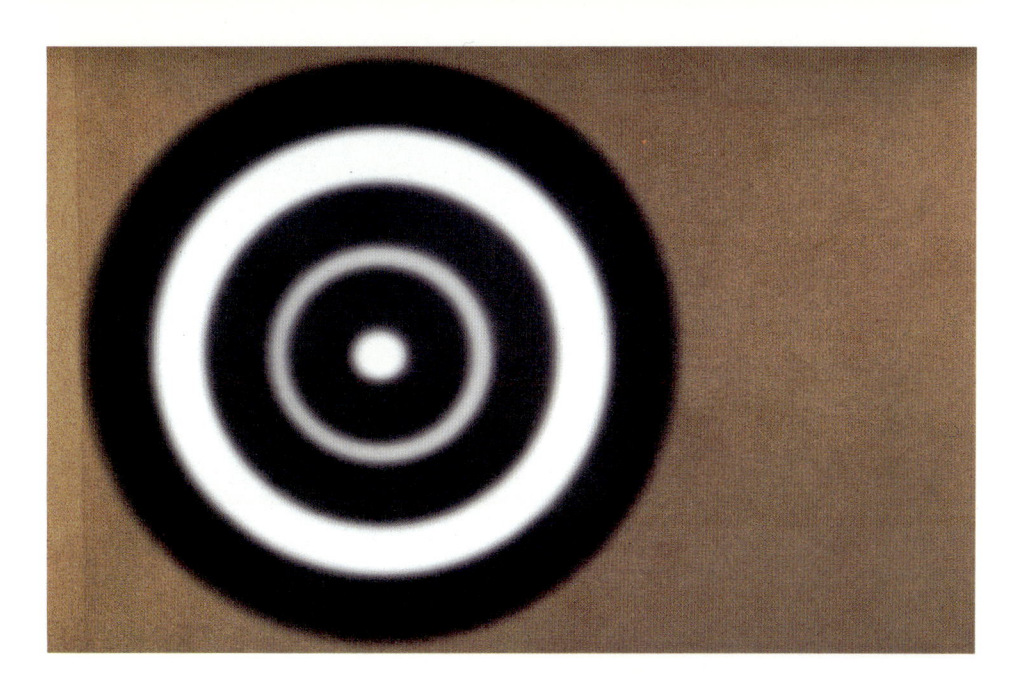

Columbia College, image brochure for corporate fundraising, Chicago, 1992.

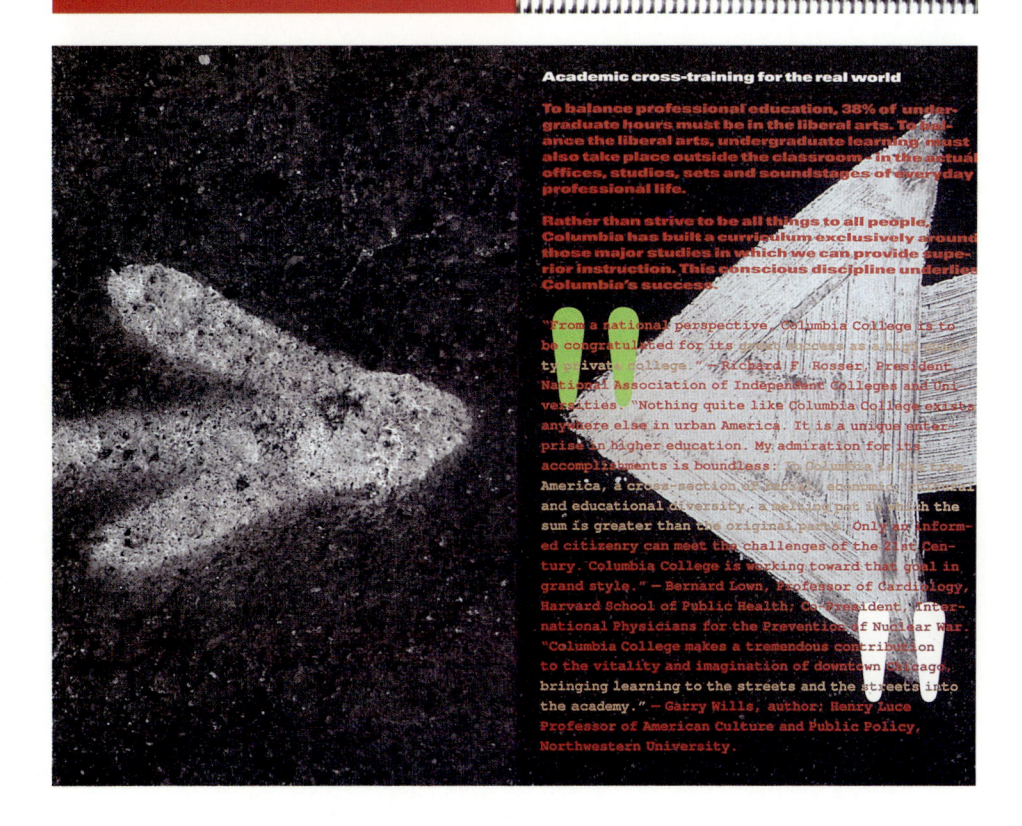

44

VSA Partners, Inc.

542 South Dearborn
Suite 202
Chicago, Illinois 60605
Telephone 312.427.6413
Fax 312.427.3246

*Illinois State Toll
Highway Authority*
Annual report for state agency
that builds, collects tolls and
maintains Illinois tollways.

will not be limited to print applications. We are preparing and positioning ourselves to apply our talents to other media to best achieve client objectives. We are proud of the level we have reached thus far in our work, and thankful to our clients for the opportunity to achieve it.

46

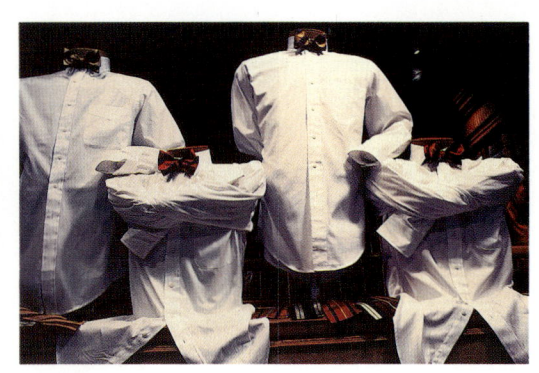

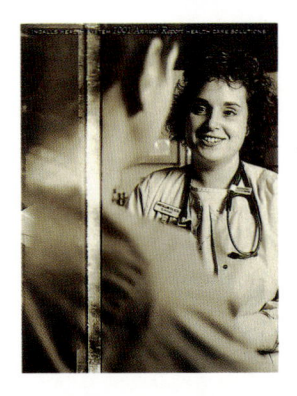

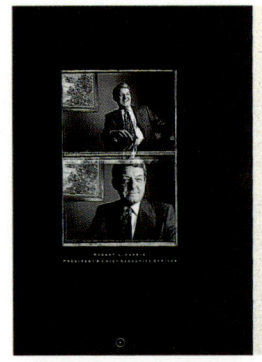

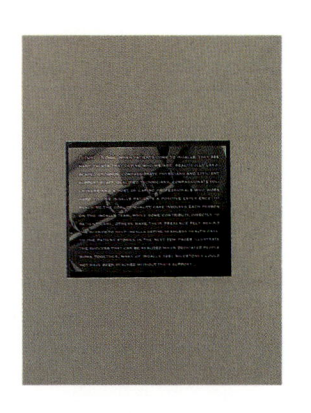

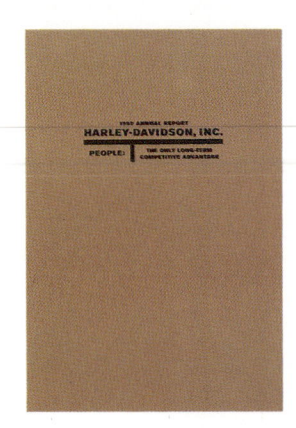

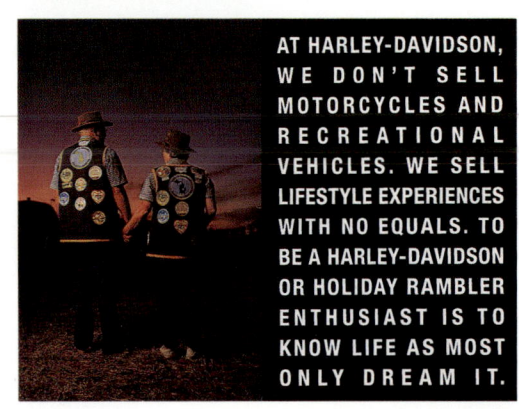

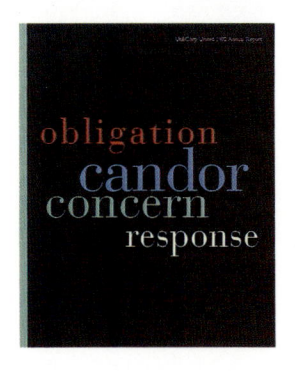

VSA Partners, Inc.

Annual Reports

LaSalle National Corporation
Report featuring key customers for a $10.3 billion multi-bank holding company.

Ingalls Health System
Illustrates seamless healthcare for south suburban based hospital and affiliated centers.

Harley-Davidson, Inc.
A lifestyle and manufacturing presentation of an American legend, Harley-Davidson, Inc.

UtiliCorp United Inc.
Annual report and investor materials designed for a $6 billion international public utility holding company based in Kansas City, Missouri.

Chicago Board of Trade
Internationally recognized annual report design produced for the world's largest futures and options trading organization.
Opposite Page

Growing competition, both domestic and abroad, is an increas-
important concern at the CBOT. In the last several years, the
industry has undergone dramatic changes. While the CBOT
had little competition for its products and services, today the
is faced with numerous challenges from competitors both
and international.
Before the global boom unleashed by the U.S. Treasury bond
the CBOT held more than 50 percent of the world's market-
Only a handful of exchanges existed outside the U.S., and
traded extremely small volumes of agricultural commodities.
there were 40 futures and options exchanges. These offered
on debt instruments of their respective governments, which
virtually carbon copies of the CBOT T-bond contracts. Today,
are more than 60 exchanges and our world marketshare has
In 1992, the Chicago Board of Trade received
from the Commodity Futures Trading Commission to trade Clean Air futures
contracts based on the U.S. Environmental Protection Agency's market
dioxide emission allowances. The CBOT became the recognized "Environ-
Exchange" last autumn when designated by the EPA as the administrator of
allowance auction.
CB90ST

Metalux PC/2
Comprehensive new product identity and launch for Cooper Lighting, the world's largest manufacturer of commercial lighting products.
Above Left

Gleason, McGuire & Schreffler Identity Program
Comprehensive firmwide identity program for a 25-member law firm.
Above Right

Playboy Condom Packaging
Complete European and Far East retail identity and packaging program for a full line of contraceptive products.
Left

VSA Partners, Inc.

DanceAspen
A brochure highlighting the events for the annual international dance festival.
Above Left

Peaberry Coffee
Name development and complete identity program for Colorado based coffee franchise.
Right

Pro bono

Each year VSA contributes about ten percent of its time towards organizations such as the Design Industries Foundation for AIDS. Our feeling is that as designers we have a responsibility to our society, environment and culture.

DIFFA Ball
Two invitations to DIFFA/Chicago's annual fundraising theme gala. This organization and event raises money for AIDS healthcare, service and outreach programs in the Chicago area.
Above Right

INTERNATIONAL FASHION
MADE IN AMERICA
HART SCHAFFNER & MARX
WOOL FOR Hart Schaffner & Marx BEGINS IN THE VAST PASTORAL PLAINS OF AUSTRALIA, WHERE SELECTIVE BREEDING PRODUCES SUPERFINE FLEECE.
WITH AN INIMITABLE INTERWEAVE
CULTIVATED TODAY, A HEMISPHERE AWAY,
IN THE PASTORAL HEARTLAND OF AUSTRALIA. CONTINENT
OF SHEEP. HERE, TEMPERATE CLIMATE, THE ACCLAIMED
AUSTRALIAN MERINO SHEEP, AND A HERITAGE OF
SKILLFUL BREEDING COMBINE TO PRODUCE WOOL OF
EXCEPTIONAL QUALITY, RICHNESS, TEXTURE AND
RESILIENCE. THE WORLD'S FINEST FLEECE. FROM THE
WORLD'S LARGEST PRODUCER, FINE AUSTRALIAN WOOL.

we recycle
use more than once
before you throw anything away ask yourself ... can it be reused?
discrimination
is against the law
each an individual every one special
this is a smoke free environment
smoking is harmful

VSA Partners, Inc.

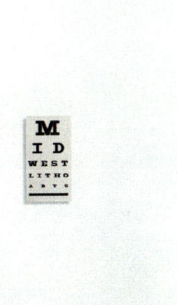

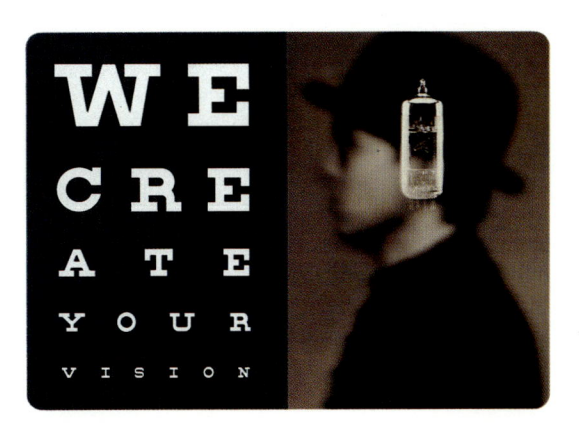

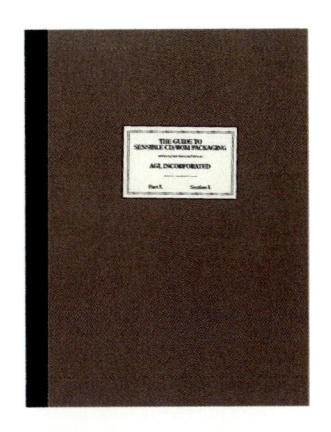

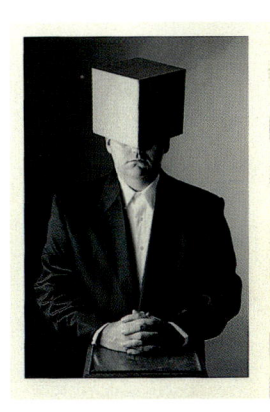

Hartmarx Corporation
A handmade, letterpress portfolio for Hart Schaffner and Marx fall collection.
Opposite Page, Top

Posted Communications L.P.
Posters that enable businesses to comply with a range of legal, health and policy issues. They provide information, awareness and motivation for employees, while enhancing the work environment.
Opposite Page, Bottom

Midwest Litho Inc.
Brochure and direct mail program for high quality pre-press color separator.

AGI, Incorporated
Capabilities overview, written and photographed in a "retro handbook" style, for a manufacturer of CD-ROM packaging.

Mohawk Paper Mills, Inc.
An invitation to the introduction of Mohawk's solution to the accessible, inclusive and spatially sound paper specifier.

Holleb & Coff
Firm description brochure for a 110-member law firm based in Chicago.

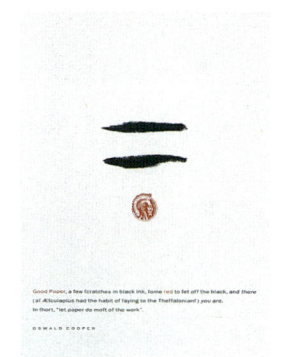

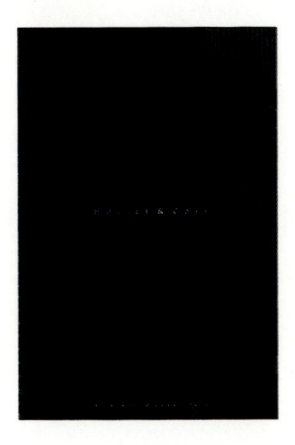

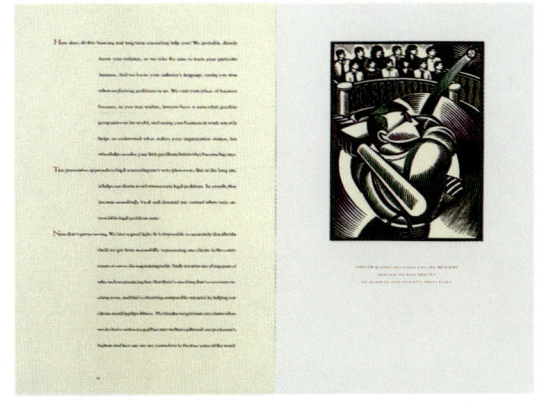

Telephone 312.649.5688
Telephone 312.645.1156
Fax 312.649.0376
Cellular 312.316.3564

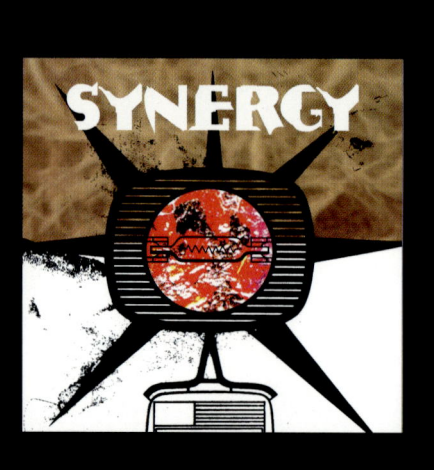

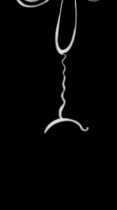

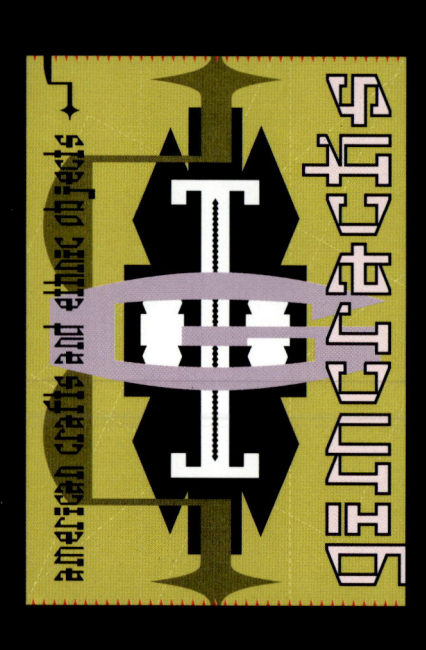

SEGVRA

TURN THE TARGET. FLIP THE CROWD.

Segura Inc.

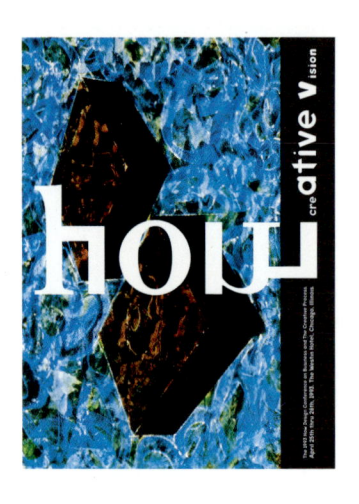

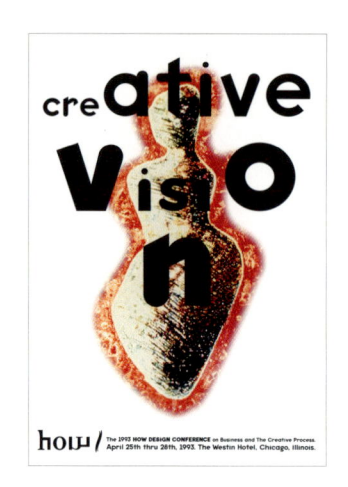

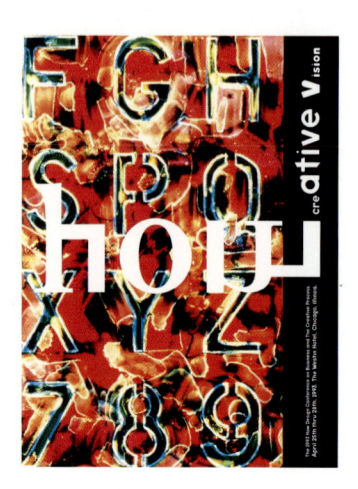

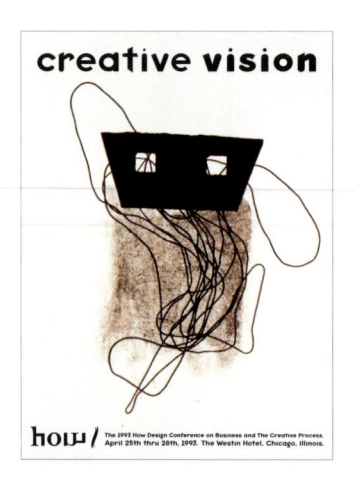

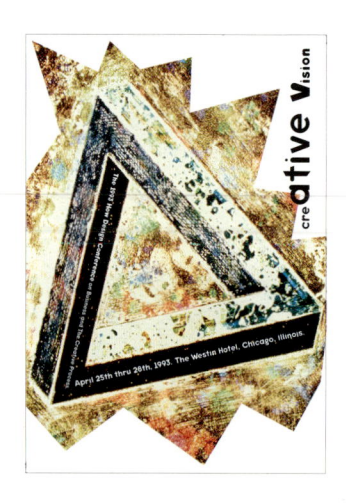

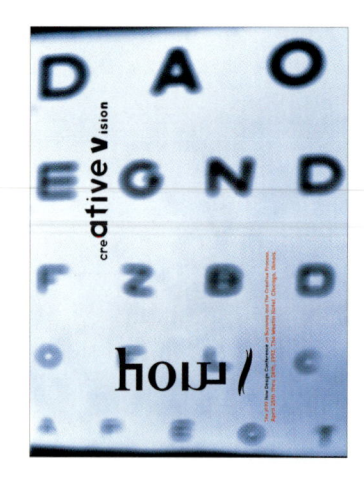

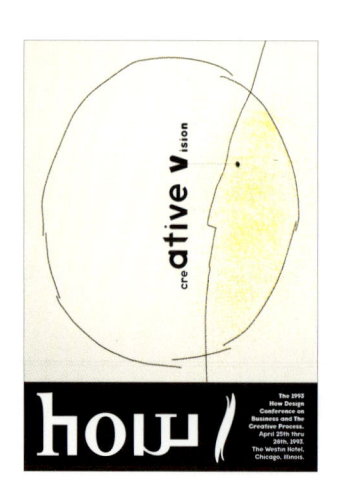

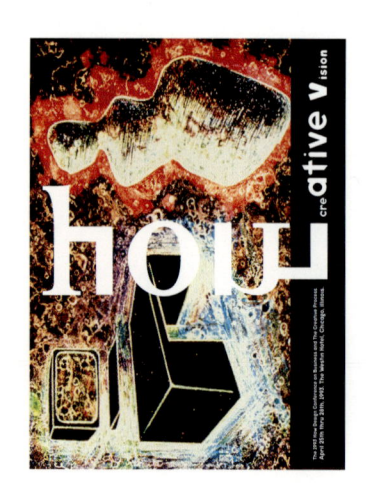

Illusion

Illusion

Illusion

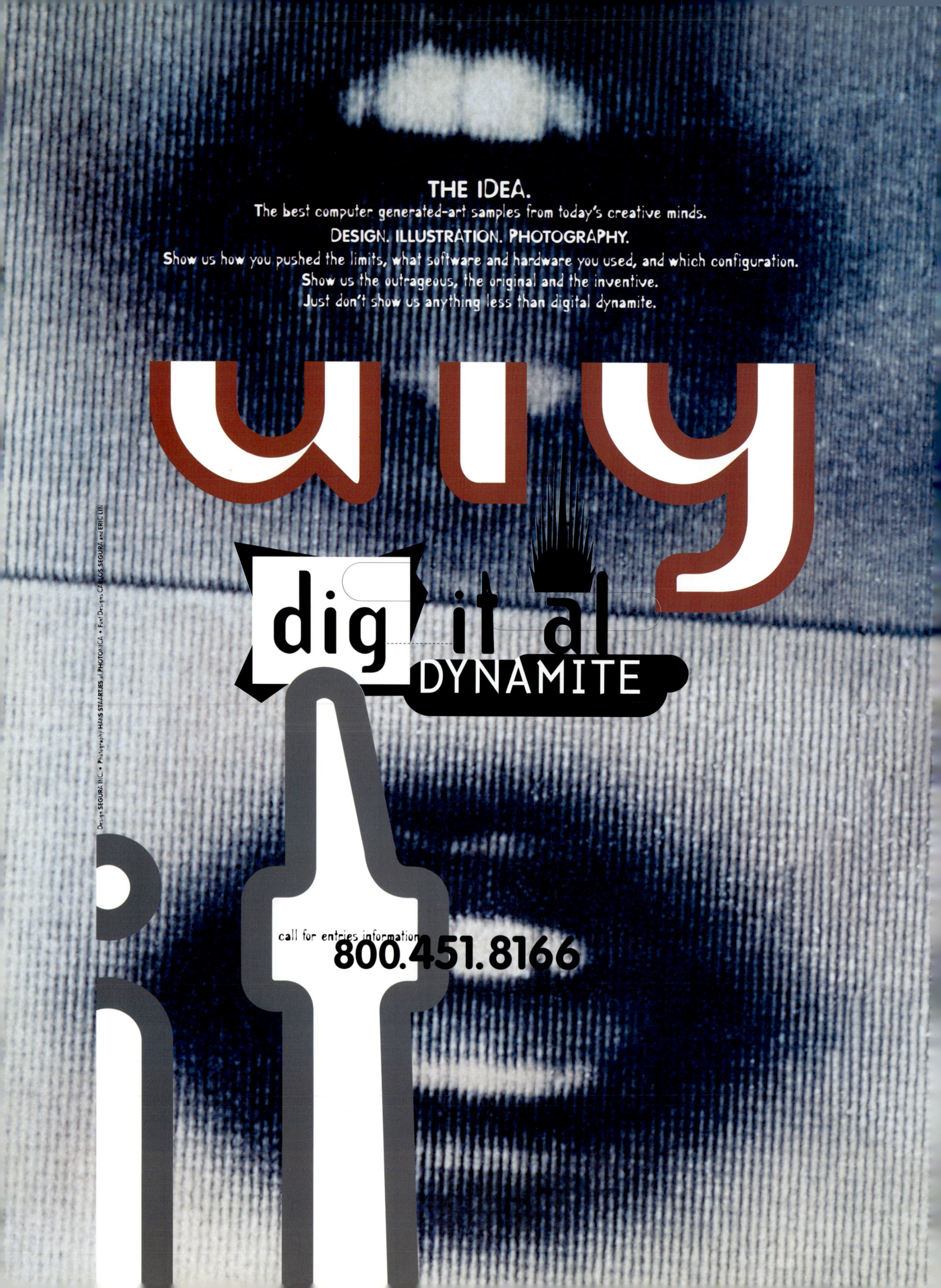

THE IDEA.
The best computer generated-art samples from today's creative minds.
DESIGN. ILLUSTRATION. PHOTOGRAPHY.
Show us how you pushed the limits, what software and hardware you used, and which configuration.
Show us the outrageous, the original and the inventive.
Just don't show us anything less than digital dynamite.

digital DYNAMITE

call for entries information
800.451.8166

Segura Inc. 57

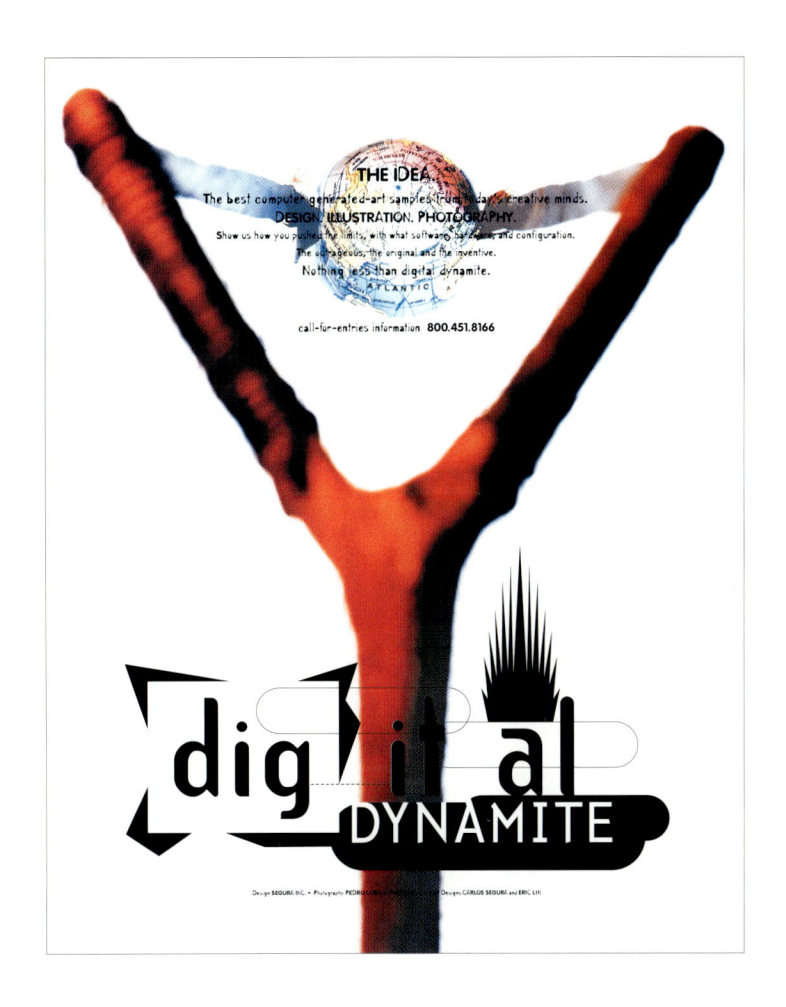

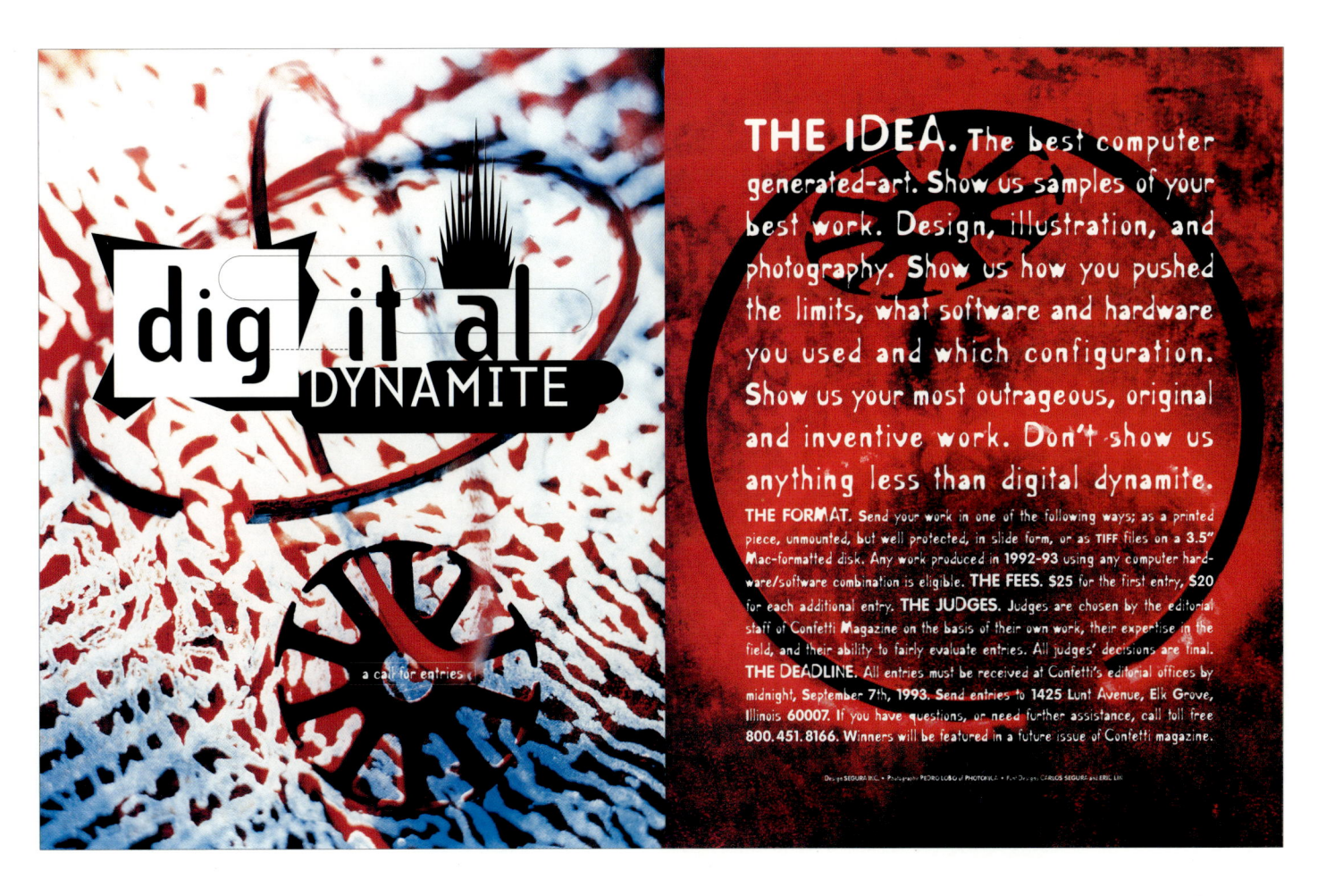

MUSKEGON

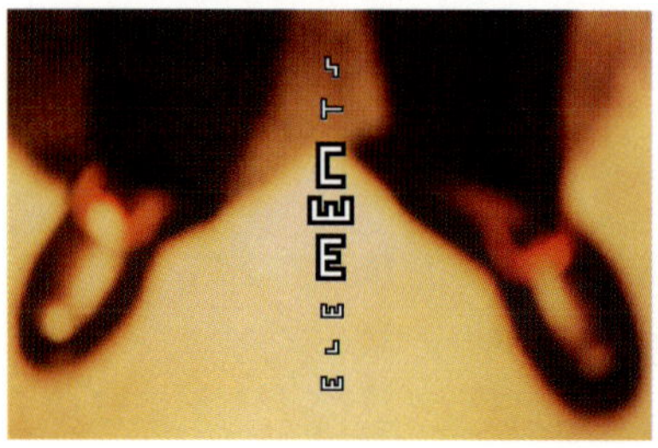

SALISBURY

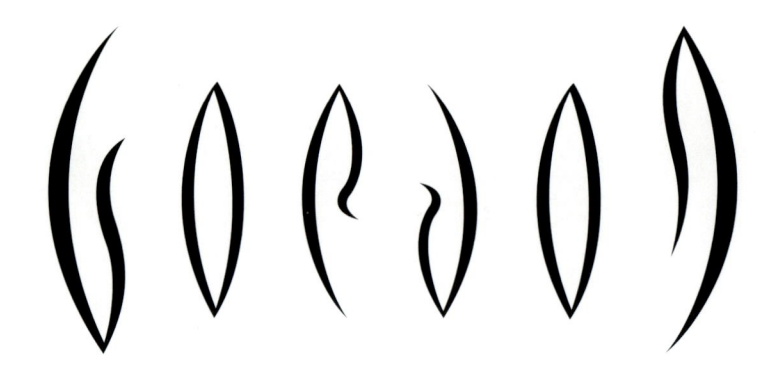

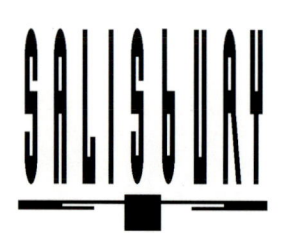

NEOCON/92

THE WORLD EXPOSITION ON WORKPLACE PLANNING AND DESIGN

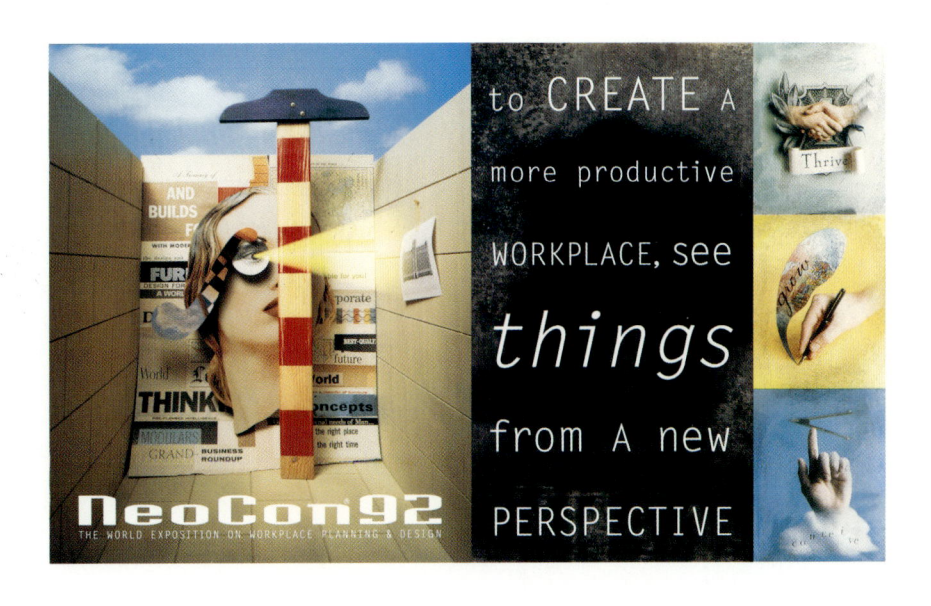

Environmental graphic design for USG Interiors Inc. architectural products showroom. *Top Row*

Identity program and environmental graphic design for Chicago Architecture Foundation Tour Center and Book Store. *Center Left*

Name development and total retail graphic/signage program for Omni Superstore, a division of Dominick's Foods, Chicago. *Center Right*

Yorktown Shopping Center identity and total signage program for Pehrson/Long Associates. Lombard, Illinois. *Bottom*

Nicholas Associates

Principal:
Nicholas Sinadinos

Date Founded:
1989

Size of Firm:
4 Employees

Selected Clients:
Ambassador Greetings
Cabot Cabot & Forbes
Chicago Architecture Foundation
Dominick's Finer Foods
Dragonette, Inc.
Frank Lloyd Wright Foundation
The Great Atlantic & Pacific Tea Company
Hallmark Cards Australia
Kinney Shoe Company
Krueger Design Group
Leo's Dancewear
Montgomery Ward
Salinas y Rocha/Mexico
USG Interiors Inc.
White Hen Pantry Stores

"Quality is the enduring ability to meet and exceed enlightened expectations." Nicholas Sinadinos, President and Design Director of Nicholas Associates believes that clients able to distinguish the added value of quality design are this graphic design office's strongest partners. The firm's designers create quality by basing their work in simple, meaningful ideas and concepts. These are made memorable and effective by creating innovative and appropriate visual ideas that have impact. With an appetite and an award-winning skill for managing diversity from annual reports and packaging to signage systems and identity programs, Nicholas Associates has brought to each of its distinctly different clients a design solution tailored to unique, individual business objectives. Nicholas Associates' clients understand the need to differentiate their businesses and believe that design can help accomplish this strategic goal.

Cabot Cabot & Forbes Asset Management services brochure. *Above*

Miner & East capabilities brochure highlighting construction and management services. *Top*

Conway Park marketing/leasing brochure for Cabot Cabot & Forbes Asset Management. *Center*

100th anniversary capabilities brochure for Chicago Metallic Corporation. *Bottom*

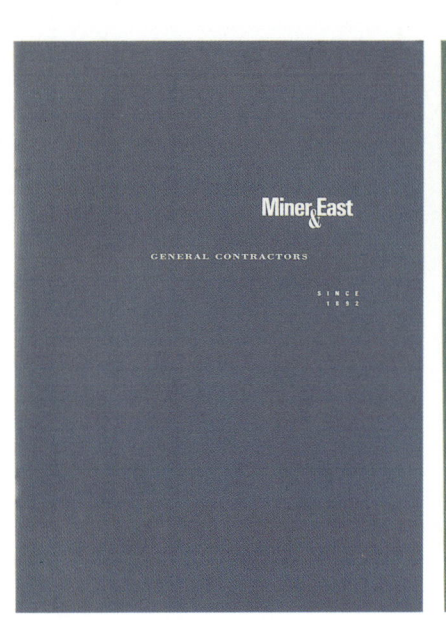

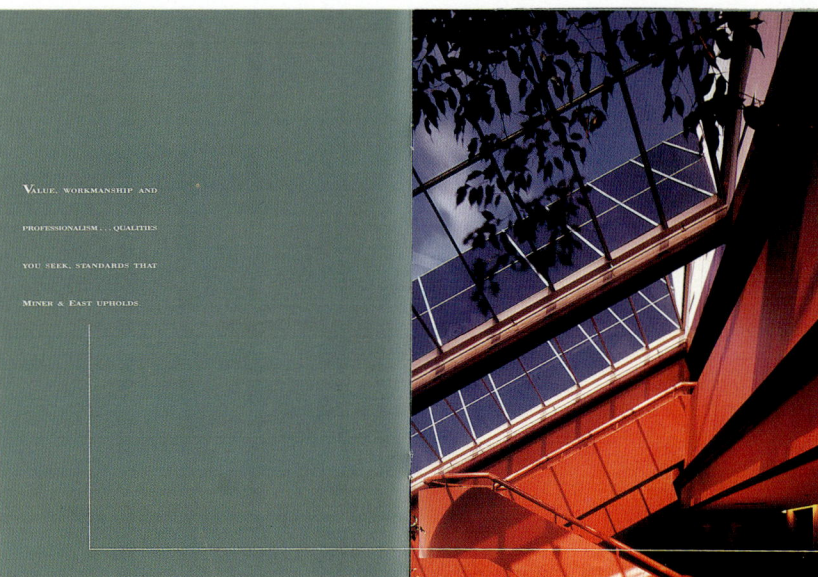

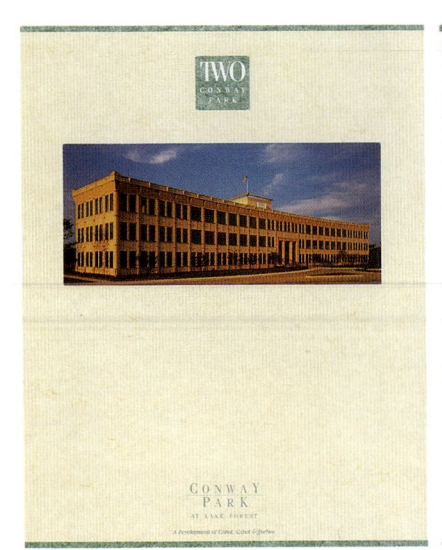

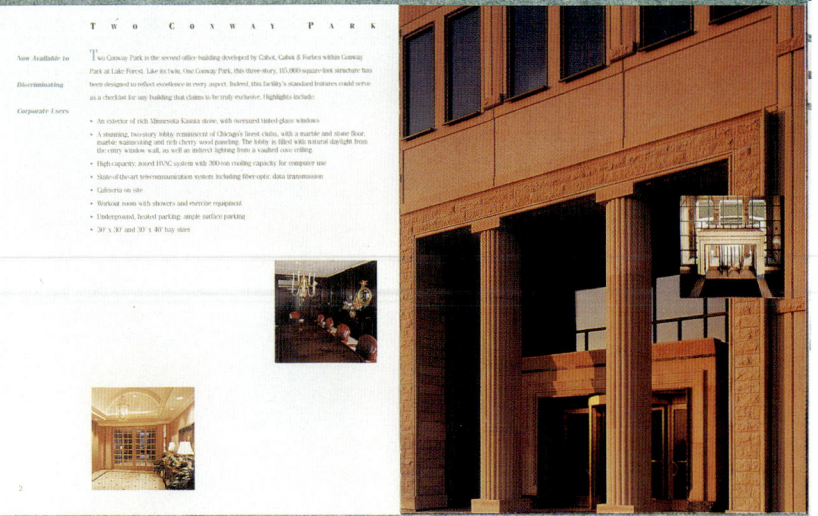

Nicholas Associates

Top to Bottom:
Promotional packaging design for Sigman Photography to house images produced in multi-media format and presented on diskette.

Total retail image design for Encantos de Antonieta, an intimate apparel division of Salinas y Rocha Department Stores/Mexico City.

Brand name development, label and packaging design for Aquas Sparkling Water.

Packaging design and brand identity for West Hydroponics, manufacturers of components for aquatic growing systems.

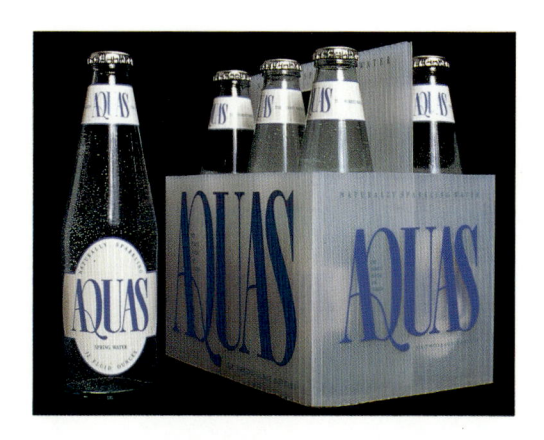

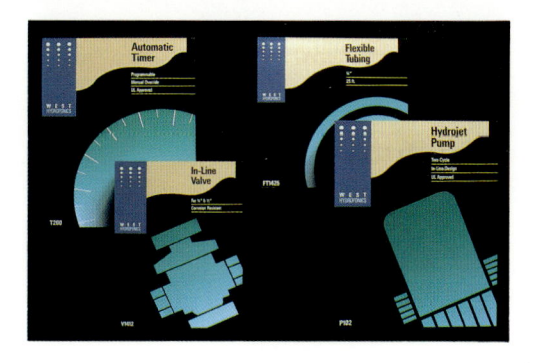

New product introduction catalog for Leo's Dancewear Incorporated. *Center*

National advertising campaign for Leo's Dancewear Incorporated. *Bottom*

Opposite Page, Left to Right: Brandmark for the Easy Spirit Shoe division of U.S. Shoe Corporation.

Retail identity program for HawkQuarters the Chicago Blackhawks hockey team official store.

Identity program for Eidos, Inc. management consultants, Chicago.

Mark for Discovery, a promotional event produced by USG Interiors Inc.

Retail identity program for Encantos de Antonieta intimate apparel specialty division of Salinas y Rocha Department Stores/Mexico.

Identity program for HandHeld Video a video production services company.

Retail identity program for Treats 'N More specialty candy & coffee stores.

Identity program for Quality Directions management consultants, Chicago.

Identity program for Krueger Design Group/ Los Angeles based retail interior design office.

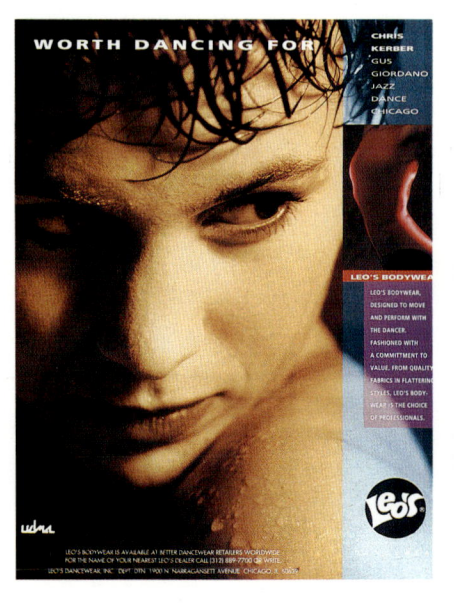

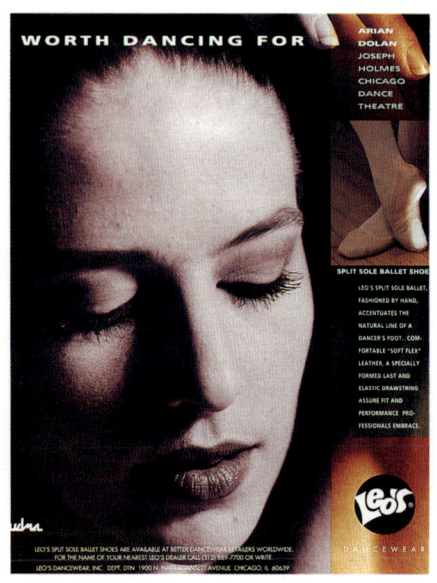

Nicholas Associates

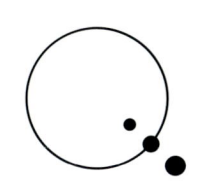

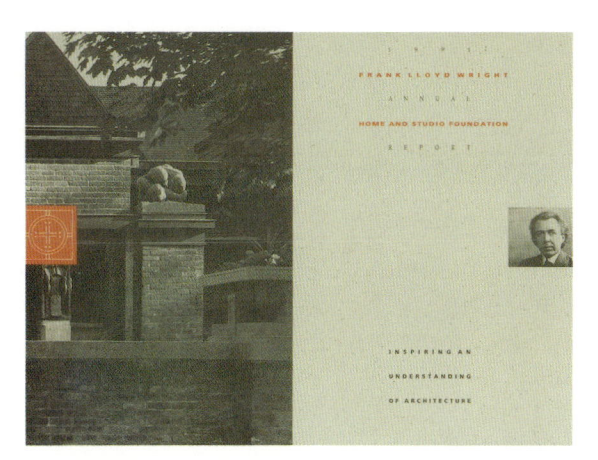

Annual report design for the Frank Lloyd Wright Home & Studio Foundation, 1991. *Top*

Apollo Tours marketing brochure series for travel to Greece. *Center*

Edwards Construction Company capabilities brochure. *Bottom*

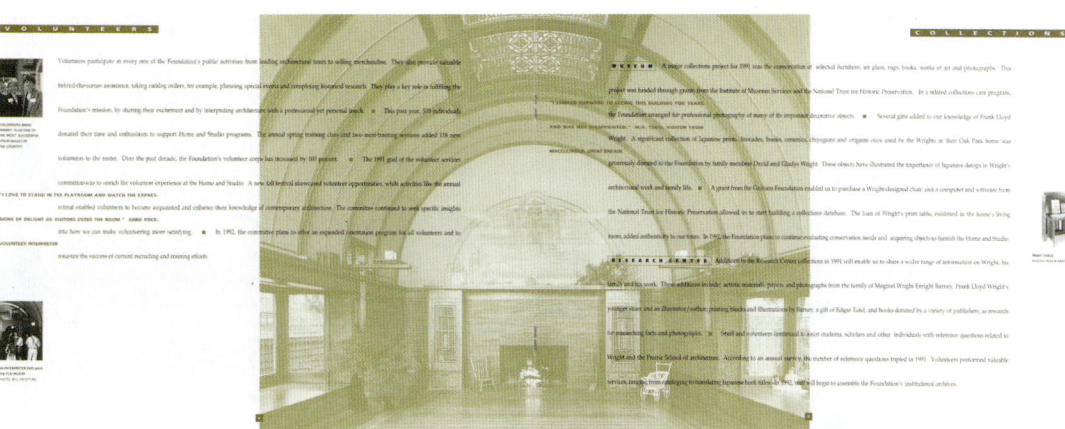

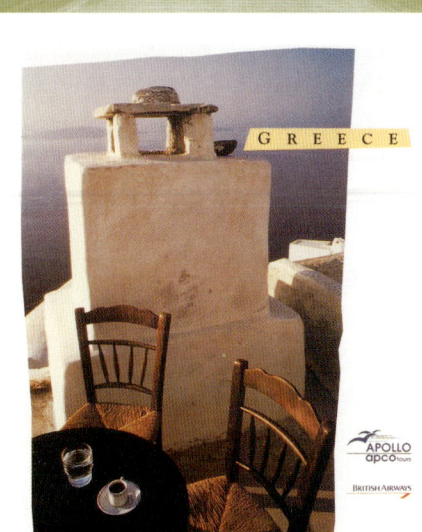

Nicholas Associates

Retail identity program for White Hen Pantry Convenience Stores.

SOURCE inc.
September 2, 1992
Mr. Robert C. Lewis
Manager, Marketing Materials & Presentations
American Management, Inc.
6 Kingston Rd.
Hartford, Connecticut 06484
Dear Bob
I look forward to talking to you.
Sincerely,
James G. Hansen
Chairman/CEO
Source Inc.
Design & Marketing
116 South Michigan Avenue
Chicago Illinois 60603-6009
weber
Scotts
WEST BEND
BLACK & DECKER
EKCO
AMERICA'S KITCHEN TRADITION
Performer
The West Bend Company
Weber-Stephens Products Co.
Master Lock Company
COMMUNICATE BENEFITS INSTANTLY
ADD MERCHANDISING POWER
BUILD BRAND LOYALTY
DEMAND ATTENTION
Packaging designed to sell
Master
GENESIS 5
FIREPLACE
ONE-TOUCH PLUS

Source/Inc.

Managing Perception to Create a New Reality

This year Source, Inc. celebrates its twenty-fifth year in the package design business. Proud of its achievements serving many of the nation's most distinguished brand names, Source chose to celebrate the occasion by honoring its long-term commitment to that magical marketing ingredient—creativity. The designs on the following pages cover a broad spectrum of industry categories from food to financial services— and each serves as an excellent example of the firm's determination to provide its clients with stimulating, emotionally charged designs that are both highly creative and strategically grounded. Even its own new "sky's-the-limit" identity serves as a reminder that the business of design is to manage perceptions and create exciting new realities. Source believes that in the face of increasingly intense competition it is the new and exciting, not the timid and predictable, that will engage and motivate the consumer.

James G. Hansen, Chairman, and William J. O'Connor, President

Power Brands, Inc. *Top*
Oscar Mayer Foods Corporation, *Bottom*
McCain Citrus Inc. *Opposite Page*

BŌKŪ
Anytime Cooler
KEY·LIMEADE
McCain
12 FL. OZ. (355ml)
BŌKŪ
Anytime Cooler
ORANGE ICED TEA
McCain
10 FL. OZ. (295ml)
BŌKŪ
Anytime Cooler
CHERRY LEMONADE
McCain
10 FL. OZ. (295ml)
BŌKŪ
Anytime Cooler
LEMON ICED TEA
McCain
12 FL. OZ. (355ml)
BŌKŪ
Anytime Cooler
CHERRY LEMONADE
McCain
12 FL. OZ. (355ml)

72 Source/Inc.

Weber-Stephen Products, *Top*
Weber-Stephen Products, *Bottom*
Gerber Products Company, *Opposite Page, Top*
J.M. Smucker Company, *Opposite Page, Bottom*

ETAPE 3
Légumes
Agneau
Gerber
NOUVEAU
ETAPE 1
Poire
Gerber
ETAPE 2
Jardinière de Légumes
Gerber

SMUCKER'S
Simply
FRUIT
Smucker's Simply Fruit Spreadable Fruit
All Fruit
Sweetened with
Concentrated
Fruit Juices
SMUCKER'S
Simply
FRUIT
BLACK
CHERRY
Spreadable
Fruit
NET WT.
10 OZ.(284g)
SMUCKER'S
Simply
FRUIT
PEACH
Spreadable
Fruit
SMUCKER'S
Simply
FRUIT
BLACKBERRY
Spreadable Fruit
SEEDLESS
NET WT.
10 OZ.(284g)

74 Source/Inc.

Citicorp Credit Services, *Top*
Citicorp Credit Services, *Bottom*
Dun & Bradstreet Information Services, *Opposite Page, Top*
Dun & Bradstreet Information Services, *Opposite Page, Bottom*

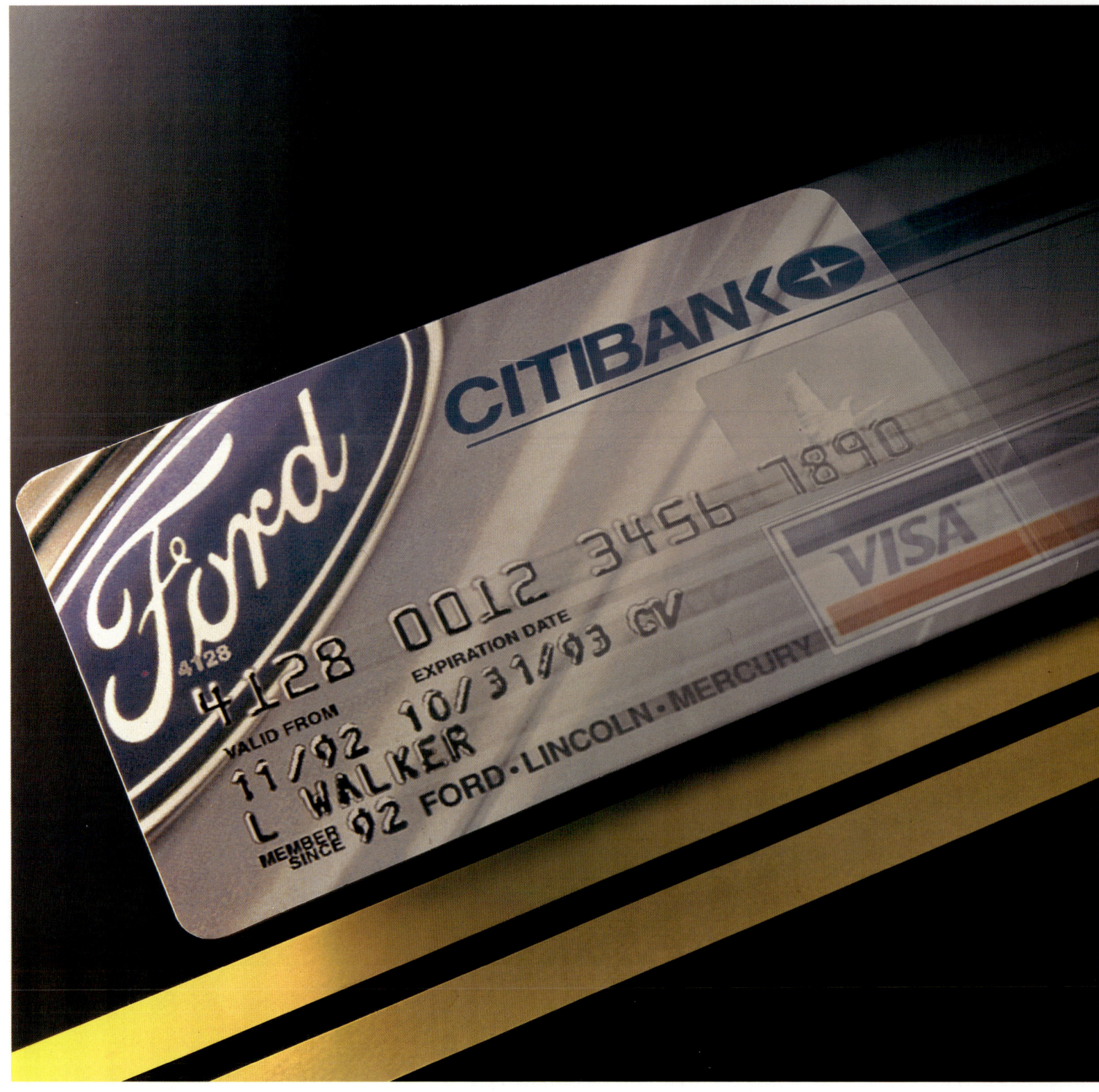

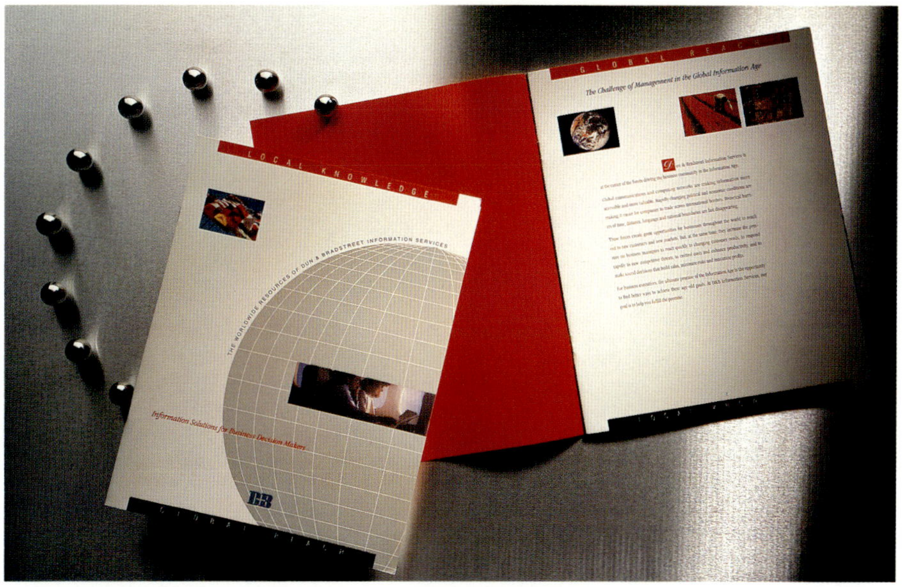
GLOBAL REACH
The Challenge of Management in the Global Information Age
LOCAL KNOWLEDGE
THE WORLDWIDE RESOURCES OF DUN & BRADSTREET INFORMATION SERVICES
Information Solutions for Business Decision Makers

1992 PRICE GUIDE
Information solutions for
profitable business decisions
Dun & Bradstreet Customer Service Center
1-800-234-3867

Some of the associates who have shared with me their enthusiasm, inspiration, energy and support:
Gail Aalund, Bruce Beck, Wendy Blatner, Mike Borchew, Amy Cahill, Pat Chester, Ron Coates, Kay Fulton, Bill Hafeman, Trisha Hammer, Les Holloway, Pat Potokar, Tom Kosak, Anne Levy, Bob Lipman, Bud Mabrey, Rebecca Michaels, Ellen Mardock, Charles Morris, Hank Robertz, Randi Robin, Shenaya Bhote Siegel, Rhonda Inouye Taira, Jack Weiss, Mary Kay Wolf.

Selected Clients: Acme Metals Incorporated, American Marketing Association, Asian Sources Publications, AT&T Information Systems, Blossom Industries, Cass Communications, Inc., CMC Consultants, Crain Communications Inc., The Executive Technique, Field Museum of Natural History, First Chicago, Fraser, Gannett Media Sales, Grumman/Butkus Associates, Harper Collins, Henry Crown & Company, Motorola University Press, Museum of Science and Industry, Northwestern University, Synnestvedt and Systat, Inc.

Design concept and formats for *Crain's Small Business,* for the Crain family of publications, including grids, logotype, department and feature layouts, new typeface selections for heads, captions, body text and initial caps. *Below*

Symbols for: *The Rapid City Journal, Waukegan Public Library* and *Champion Packaging Co. Opposite Page*

Annual source book from Cass Communications for media buyers. Photo Illustration, Mouli Marur. *Opposite Page*

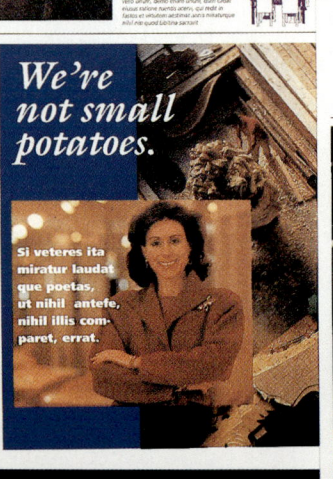

Principals:
Hayward R. Blake
Simone L. Blake

Date Founded:
1961

Hayward Blake & Company

For more than four decades, Hayward has worked to visualize the equivalent of the journalist's five W's, asking the questions of himself, his associates and his clients. He has sought to solve the assorted riddles of communication and to produce responses, results and rewards. Working in all appropriate media, materials and matrices, he has continued to develop his skill of observation and the ability to perform.

Currently, he is focusing his efforts onto the design of publishing projects, particularly books and magazines. Symbols, logotypes, photography, illustration and most importantly typography are all newly fueled by electronic impulses which burst forth with glee and an occasional gasp of magnetic exhilaration—or exasperation.

Overriding all of the above is the continuing joy of solving communication problems.

He loves this business!

Hayward Blake & Company

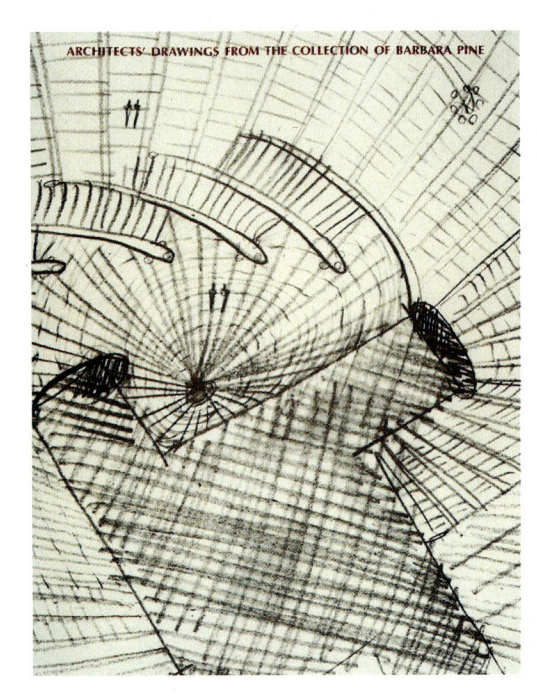

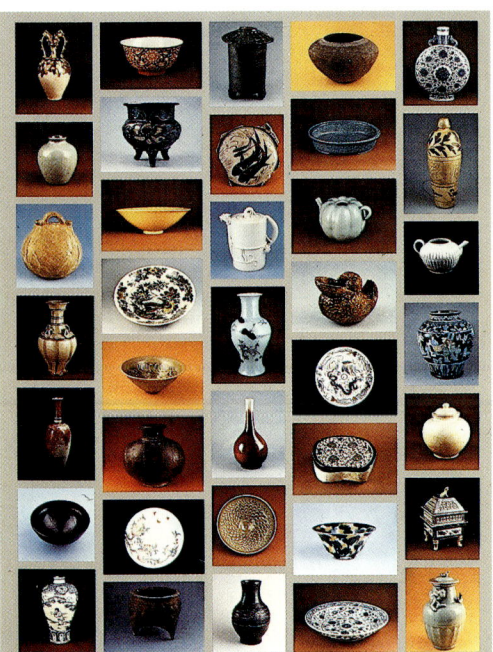

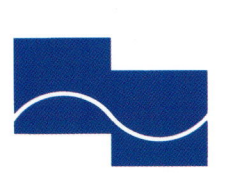

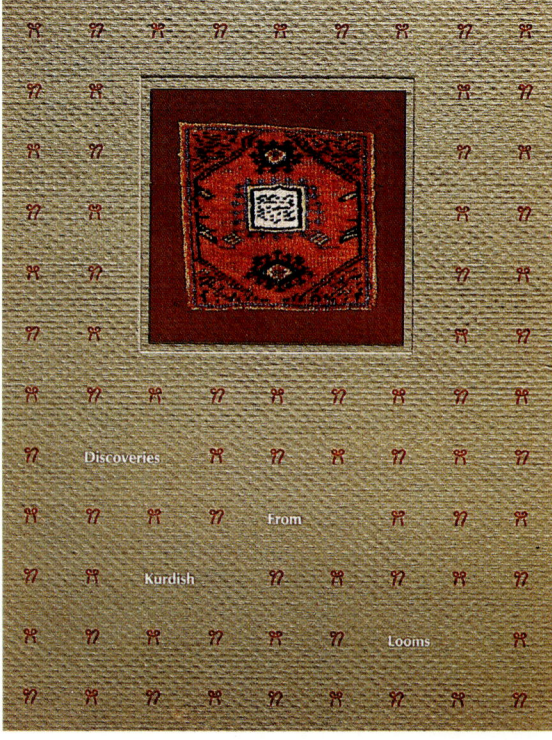

Five exhibition catalogs for the Mary and Leigh Block Gallery at Northwestern University: *Architects' Drawings from the Collection of Barbara Pine; Painting at Northwestern: Conger, Paschke, Valerio; Discoveries from Kurdish Looms; Exploring Society Photographically.* All catalogs were designed in a 9x12 size with a spine for shelf identity. *Opposite Page*

Symbols for: *The Goodman Theater Center, The Doctors and Dentists of Northbrook Court* and *Glasses Ltd*. *Both Pages*

In preparation for their Centennial, The Field Museum of Natural History commissioned a boxed set of nine books to celebrate the event and the opening and reinstallation of their major collections. The first three books produced were for the *Gems, Pacific* and *Egypt* exhibitions. *Above*

Recommended reading for all classes in the social history of dance. *From the Ballroom to Hell,* published by Northwestern University Press. *Right*

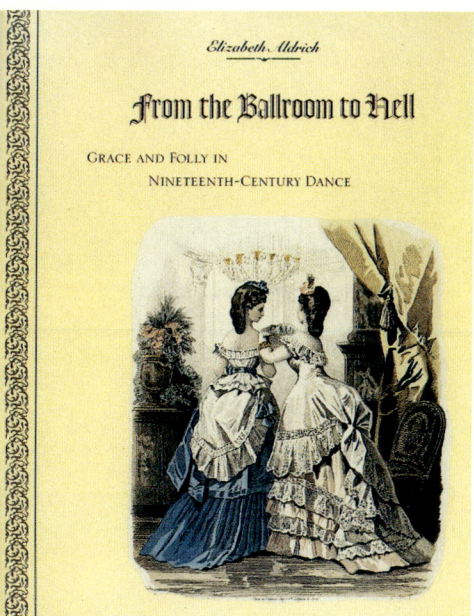

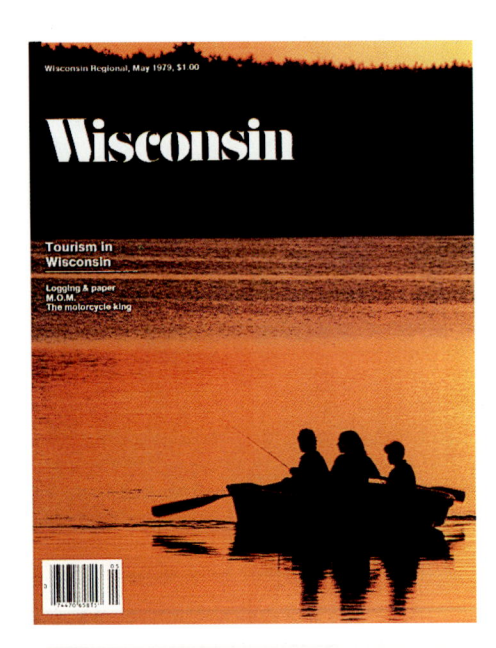

Design of monthly magazines: *Wisconsin,* Madison, WI; *Northshore,* Winnetka, IL; *Chicago Times,* Chicago, IL; *Online Access,* Chicago, IL; and *LFA/Review,* a quarterly publication for Lake Forest Academy, Lake Forest, IL. *This Page*

Design program including logotype, all typography, color system, layout grids, formats and a guidelines manual for *Computer Products, Timepieces,* and *Electronics* for The Asian Sources Group, Hong Kong. *Opposite Page, Top*

A new publishing program for the people of Motorola by Motorola University Press: *The Idea of Ideas,* Robert Galvin; *Your Creative Power,* Alex Osborn (abridged by Robert Galvin); *The Philosophy Memos,* Bill Weisz. Published in cloth and paper. *Opposite Page, Bottom*

Symbols and logotypes for: Wisconsin Magazine, Blossom Industries, Heco Envelope Company and Small Motors Inc. *Both Pages*

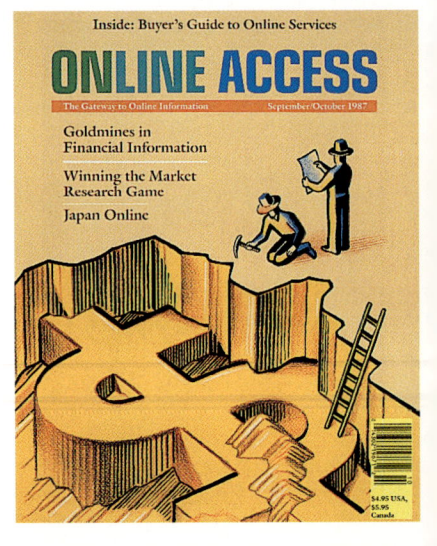

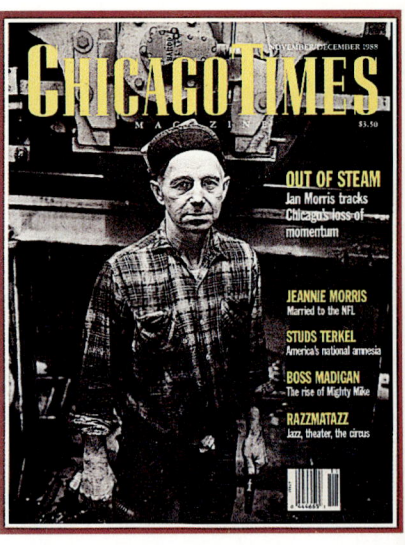

ASIAN SOURCES
TIMEPIECES
Serving volume buyers worldwide
March 1990
1989 Industry Review: Exports and Quality Rise
Simplicity the Key to Children's Watch Flip-tops
Thailand's and Malaysia's High-Tech Balancing Acts
Silver Oxide Batteries/Plastic Watch Caps
swatch QUARTZ
SWISS

ASIAN SOURCES
COMPUTER
PRODUCTS
Serving manufacturers and volume buyers worldwide
March 1990
Desktop Publishing's Sophisticated New Systems – from Mice to Scanners
CPU/DRAM Availability Sparks 386 Board Production
Shedding Light on the Gray Market
Cargo that's programmed to arrive in better shape.
Call Cathay Pacific
CATHAY PACIFIC CARGO
ARRIVES IN BETTER SHAPE

ASIAN SOURCES
ELECTRONICS
March 1990
Switched on electronics always arrive in better shape.
Call Cathay Pacific
CATHAY PACIFIC CARGO
ARRIVES IN BETTER SHAPE

THE IDEA OF IDEAS
"We can and should apply consciously, confidently, purposely and frequently, the simpler, satisfying, appropriate steps to create more and then better ideas."
THE PHILOSOPHY MEMOS:
Bill Weisz
Articles, Speeches & Quotations
Alex Osborn
Your Creative Power

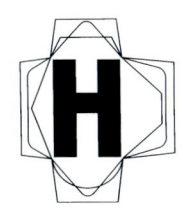

Hayward Blake & Company

Booklet and poster for *"The Code"*, a program to promote corporate personal values to the people and the clients of The Executive Technique. *Opposite Page, Top*

Original graphic statement for *Green Architecture,* a juried invitational exhibition titled *A Celebration of the Tree* for The American Center for Design, The Chicago Athenaeum and The Office of The Mayor. *Opposite Page, Bottom Left*

Chicago Education, a poster from the book produced by the 27 Chicago Designers to celebrate the sesquicentennial of the city of Chicago. *Opposite Page, Bottom Right*

Symbols for: *CMC Consultants Inc.; Grumman/Butkus Associates; CKR Real Estate Development; Walden Properties* and *Darnell Development Corporation. Both Pages*

Annual Report for Acme Metals Incorporated. Photographer, Archie Lieberman. *Right*

Identity program for Systat, Inc., a statistical software developer. The program includes: logotypes, manuals, disk labels, stationery, forms, marketing pieces, posters, brochures, displays and advertising. *Below*

A COLORING BOOK
WITH DRAWINGS BY
just add color
CONTEMPORARY ARTISTS

Concrete principal Jilly Simons insists on simplicity in design and in the way it is produced. Simons' philosophy reflects her belief that "limits stimulate." Concrete's design solutions, however, are anything but limited in their passion and imagination. Born in the concrete jungle of New York and raised in dissonant South Africa, Simons founded Concrete in 1987. Immediately her office began to build a solid body of work (and an impressive client portfolio) that has been published, honored, and exhibited extensively throughout the U.S. and internationally. Concrete's work, though conceptually complex, evolves seamlessly into pieces that are graphically unfussy and have a signature elegance of execution. The foundation of this work is communication, and that communication resonates.

Scott O'Brien

HOW DOES IT FEEL TO THINK?

tautological

Concrete

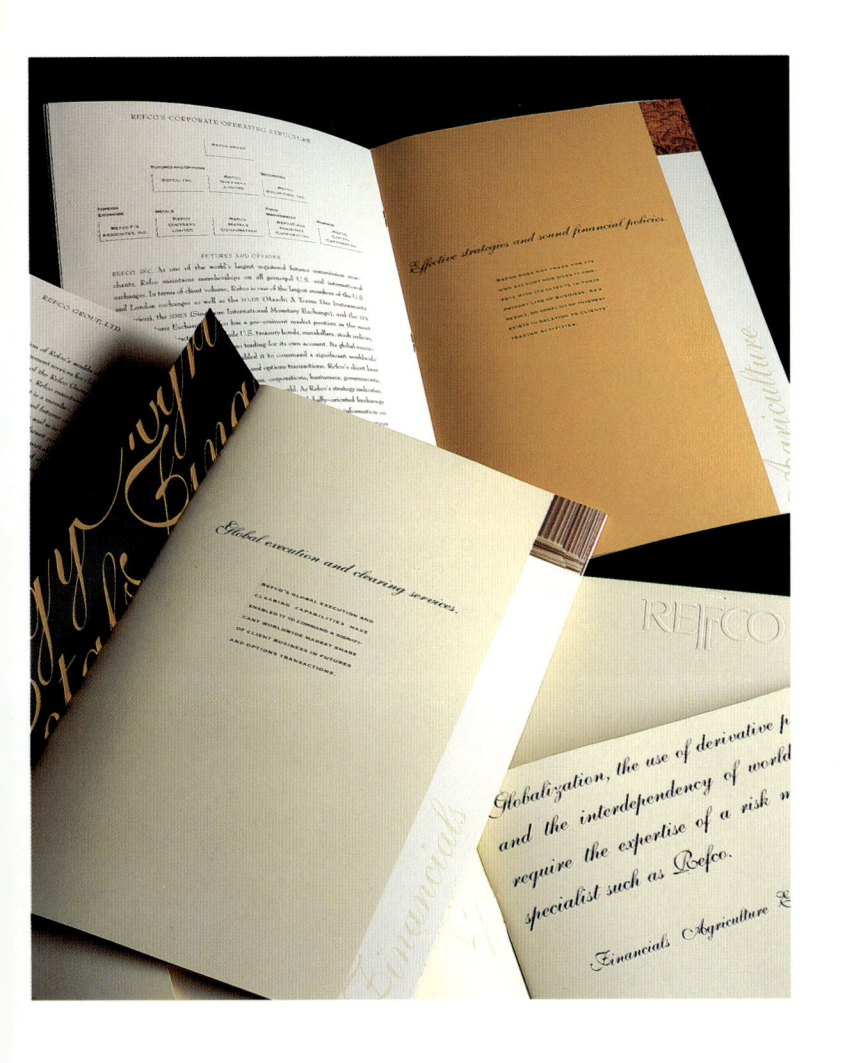

How Does It Feel to Think? published by Concrete. The piece challenges viewers to stretch logic taut and create visual associations of their own. *Opposite Page*

Capabilities brochure for Refco Group, one of the world's largest risk management firms. *Left*

Brochure for photographer Christopher Hawker, known for his unique Polaroid prints. *Right*

AHHA

ugly IS IN THE EYE OF THE BEHOLDER

PULL

THINGS ARE GOING TO GET UGLY.
UGLY

WARNING
Mohawk has determined that exposure to the enclo papers m produc

This paper promotion contains a
WARNING

Concrete

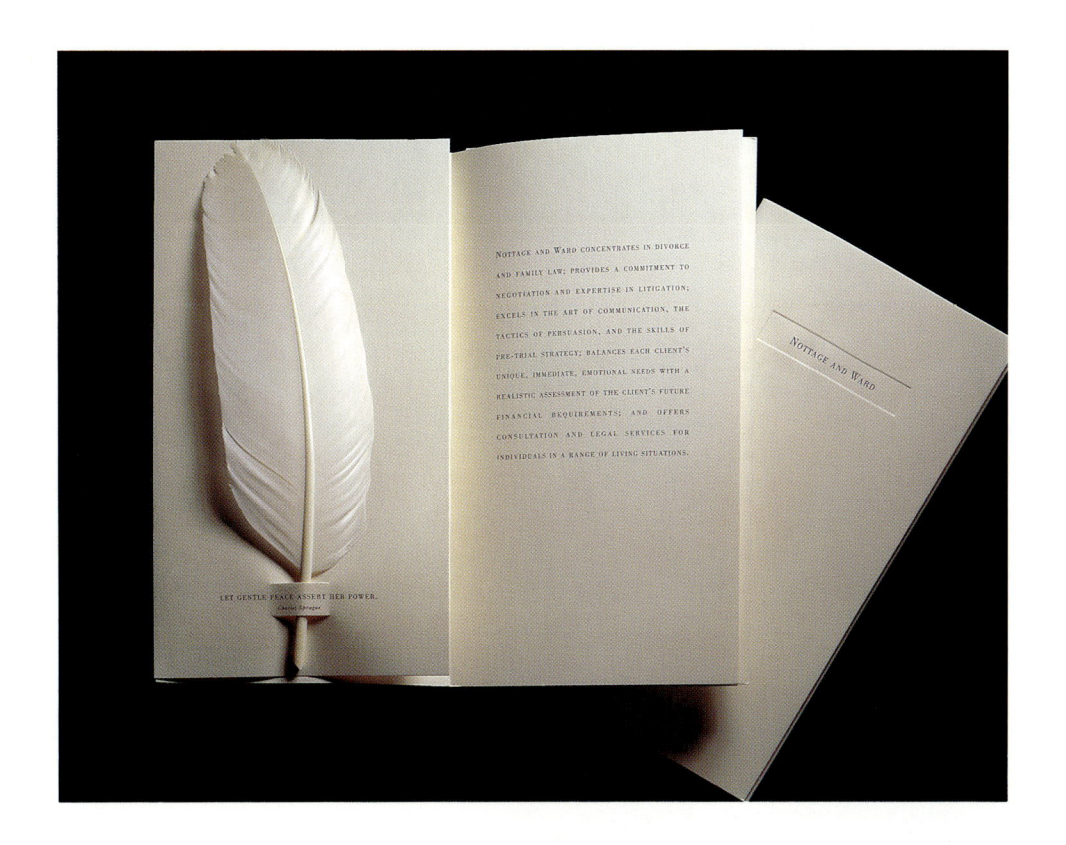

89

Things Are Going to Get Ugly paper promotion for Mohawk Paper Mills. An ironic interplay demonstrates the beauty and practicality of the papers. Writer: Deborah Barron. Photos: François Robert. *Opposite Page*

Marketing piece for Nottage and Ward, a legal practice, communicates the firm's sensitivity to the individual needs of its clients. Writer: Deborah Barron. *Top*

Invitation to a Bossa Nova benefit for The Renaissance Society, a contemporary arts organization. Photo: Daniel Arsenault. *Bottom*

RESERVE 7
FEDERAL RESERVE BANK OF CHICAGO
ANNUIT
> half empty <
RESERVE 7
FEDERAL RESERVE BANK OF CHICAGO
SECOND QUARTER 1993
< half full >
%
7
FEDERAL RESERVE BANK OF CHICAGO
FOURTH QUARTER 1992
bill
note
RESERVE 7
FEDERAL RESERVE BANK OF CHICAGO
THIRD QUARTER 1992

Concrete

Covers from *Reserve/7*,
a quarterly publication for
the Federal Reserve Bank
of Chicago. Photos: Alan
Shortall, Daniel Arsenault.
Opposite Page

Spreads from *Reserve/7*.
Photos: Alan Shortall, Kevin
Anderson. *Top*

Various identities. *Bottom*

Chicago history tells us there is a rich design legacy here. A distinctive, creative, unique community of people who actually came from Basel, Germany to work and study. The Bauhaus shaped culture, art, style, trends, fashion, furniture, film; every area of life. It enabled the creative spirit of an entire country, if not the global community, to embrace and fluorish with it for decades. After that period, during the 1970s and early 1980s, design in Chicago was all but dead on the national memory banks.

But what is happening now in Chicago? At first blush, the same thing as everywhere else in this country. Anything goes. More is more. Experimentation over content. We are over-loaded with imagery while ideas continue to elude us. Style, not substance, permeates our culture.

The grid that helped a generation of designers solve tough problems has been abandoned. Technology now competes for its rightful place in design future.

Although I seem to forget, or want to forget, most of what has been done in the last two decades, I see not only a resurgence, but a true movement in Chicago to shore up the old ideology with a fresh viewpoint and make this city a dominant player in the next stages of design's maturity. Yes, at second look, under a veiled cover is a ground-swell of new firms, young, talented, fearless creative people, testing the historic boundaries and pushing the discipline. The baby boomers are saying hello to Generation X, inhaling the MTV roadmap, assimilating technology as it becomes mainstream and brandishing their own unique perspective on design with a vengeance. It's refreshing, and I see it fluorishing in the same spirit we find when studying the masters of a bygone era.

We are not just competing for a place in design future. It has gone beyond just that, just as Chicago theater, art, advertising, architecture and financial markets are now respected on both coasts.

When I was fifteen, my old Uncle Chris used to relentlessly pound into my stubborn head every day, "You must leave the mark of your time. That's why you are here." I didn't understand him then. Little did I know that I would spend the rest of my life blindly devoted to that idea. And how absolutely incredible that so many young, enthusiastic people in our community are striving for that same idea, consciously or otherwise.

Those efforts are elevating Chicago in the eyes of an international audience to a place in the nanosecond-paced future of our industry. A city that wants to compete and wants to be the best, follows no one and has the collective heart to do

Windy City Communications 350 West Hubbard Street
Chicago, Illinois 60610
Telephone 312.464.0390
Fax 312.464.0396

American Academy of
Pediatrics annual reports.
Right and Below

St. Francis Hospital of
Evanston mission statement
brochure. Photographer:
Ron Seymour. *Bottom*

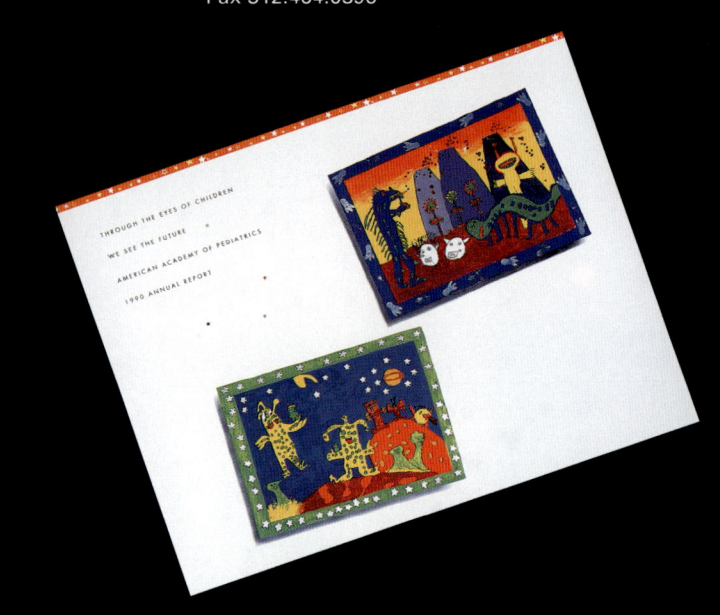

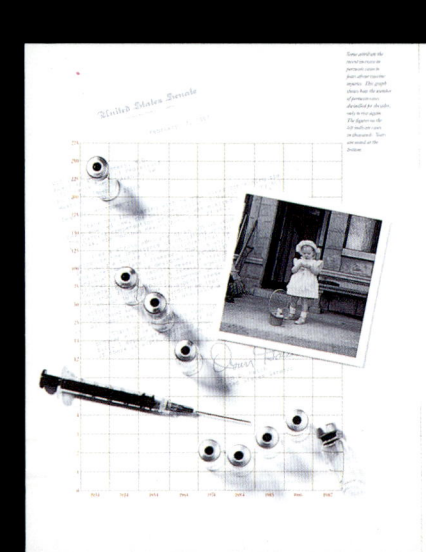

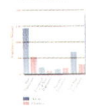

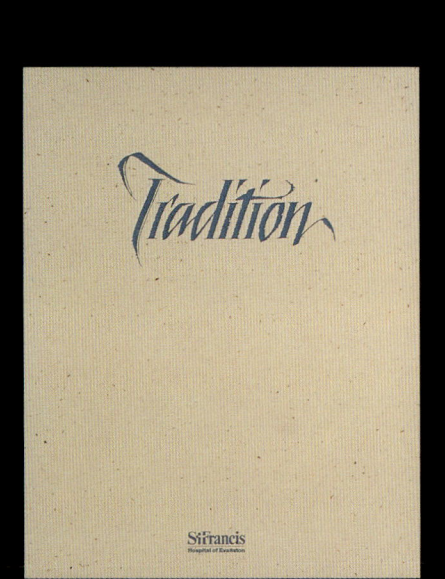

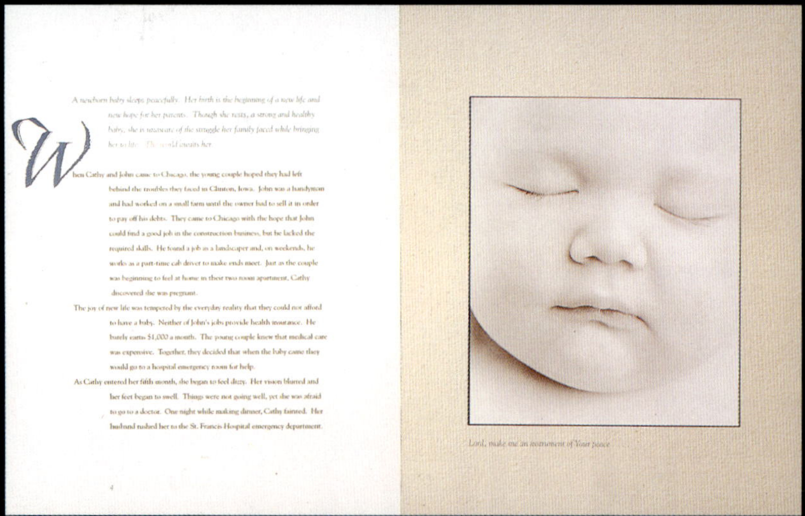

With roots firmly planted in graphic design, Windy City Communications seldom shys away from a business communications challenge. The diverse creative talents and innate curiosity of its people continue to redefine the firm to its clients in corporate communications, marketing, advertising, human resources and training. Deciphering the need is as gratifying as devising the solution. So the company asks as many questions as it answers, often crafting strategies that require more than just copy and design, or ink and paper. Windy City Communications approaches every project with the same ground rules: Consider the possibilities. Create the message, not just the picture. Be elegant, yet practical. And above all, deliver a product that gets the job done!

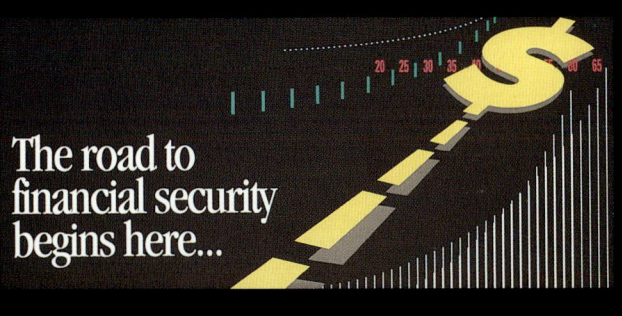

Direct mail brochures promoting Bell & Howell employee retirement plan. *Above*

Name, graphic identity and marketing materials for *Renuity*, a renewable annuity offered by Kemper Investors Life Insurance Company. *Right*

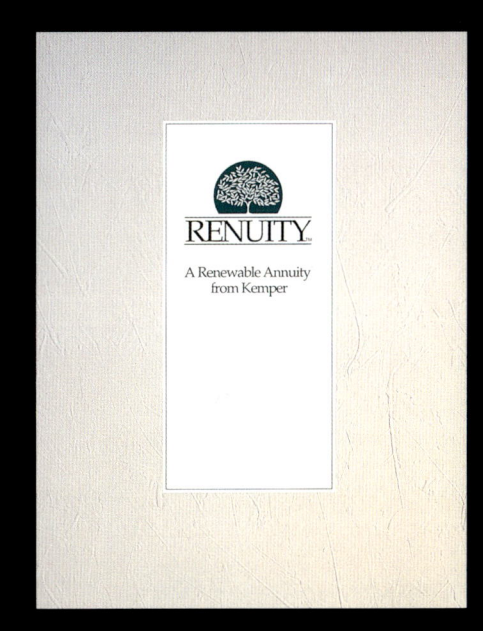

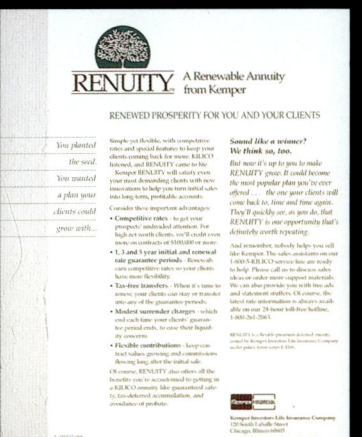

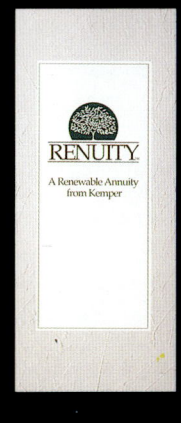

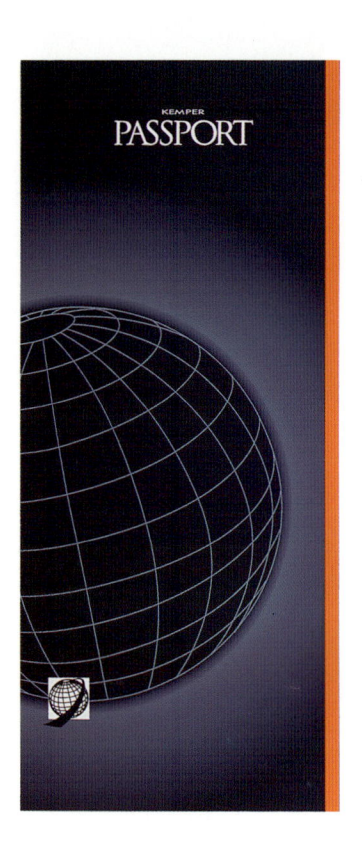

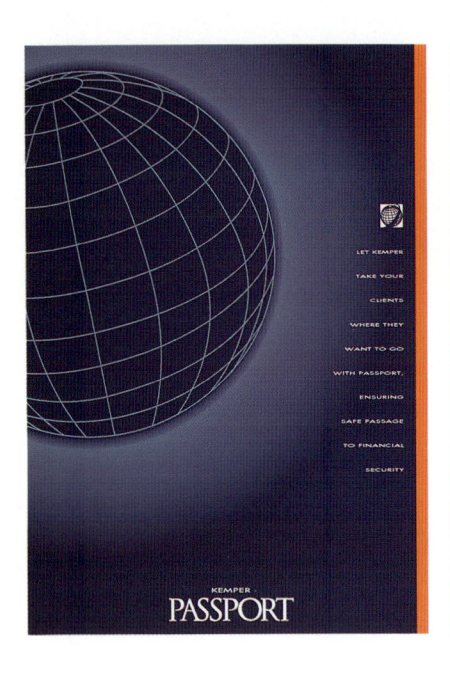

96   Windy City Communications

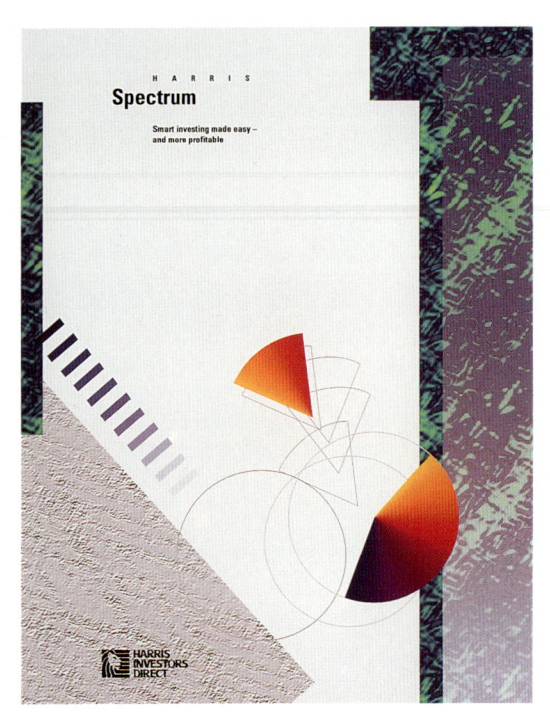

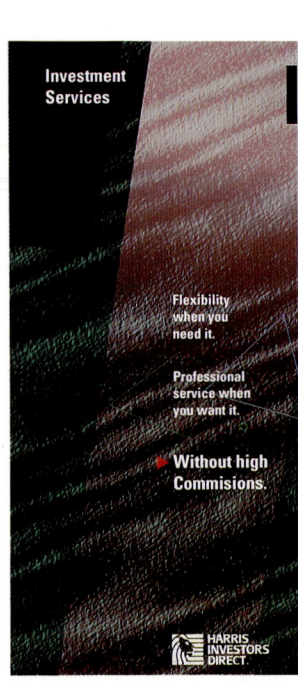

Name, graphic identity and proposed collateral for investment product. *Top*

Consumer sales materials for brokerage services. *Center*

Identity for the National Roofing Contractors Association annual meeting and exhibition in Orlando. *Bottom Left*

Conference identity for International Sanitary Supply Association annual meeting and exposition in New Orleans. *Bottom Right*

Design and copywriting for Haworth employee benefits enrollment guide. *Right*

Poster designs for recruiting high school students into high tech training programs. *Center*

Identity for school reform program sponsored by Leadership for Quality Education. *Bottom Left*

Identity for the National Roofing Contractors Association annual meeting and exhibition in San Diego. *Bottom Center*

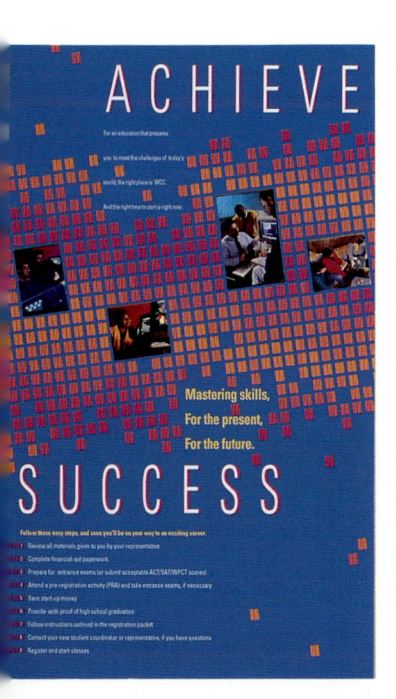

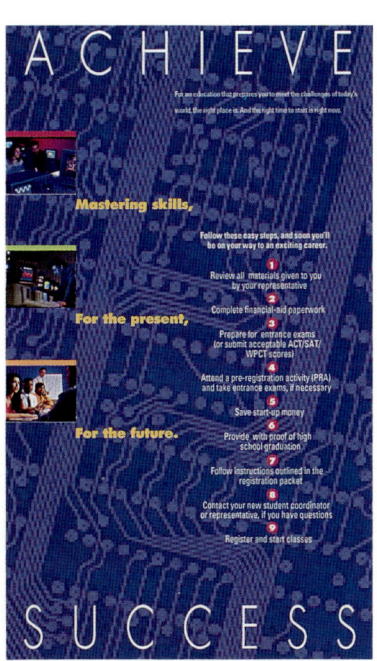

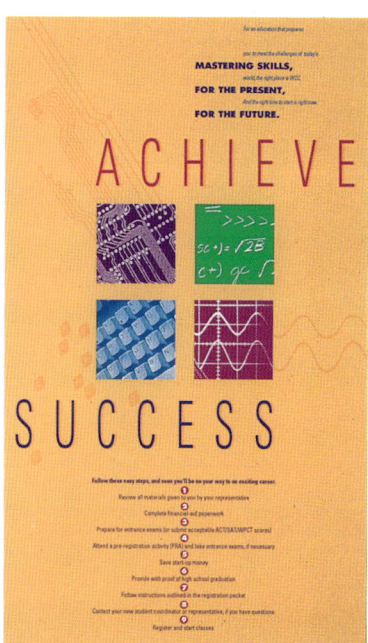

Windy City Communications

Commemorative graphic celebrating the twenty-fifth anniversary of Palmer Tube Mills Limited. *Top*

1991 Annual report for Palmer Tube Mills, Ltd. Photography: Robert Tolchin. *Center*

Spread from 1990 annual report for Palmer Tube Mills Limited. Illustration: Kenton Nelson. *Bottom*

Windy City Communications 99

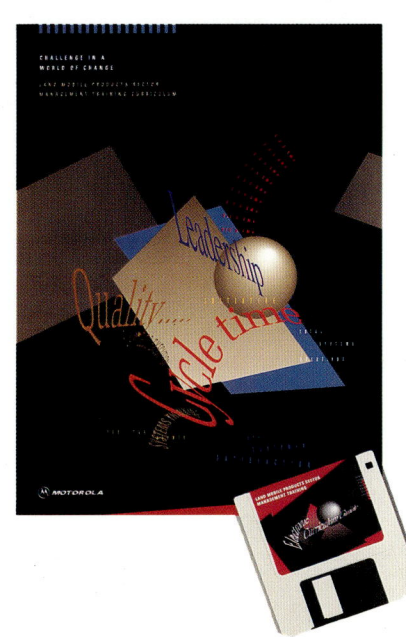

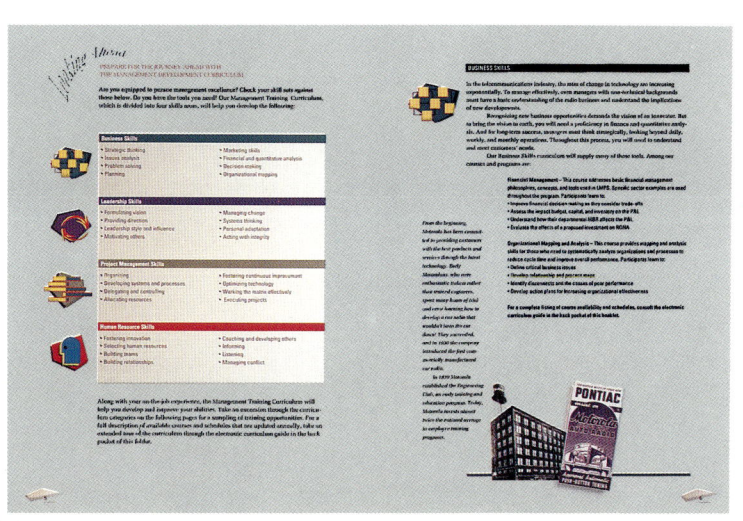

Motorola management training prospectus and hypermedia based training curriculum guide. *Above*

Design and copywriting of promotional brochure for Motorola hardware and software maintenance service. *Below*

Poster for Motorola CoveragePLUS specialized mobile radio system. *Right*

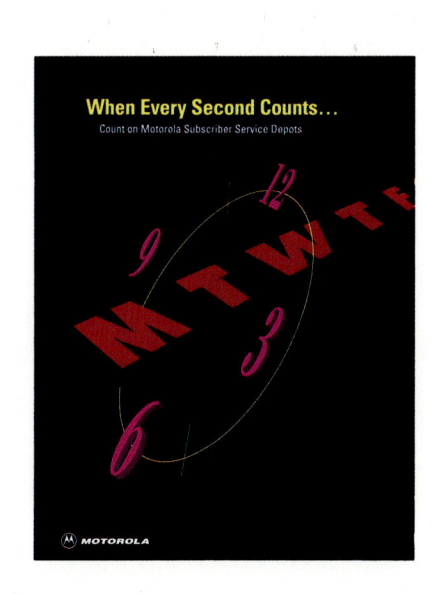

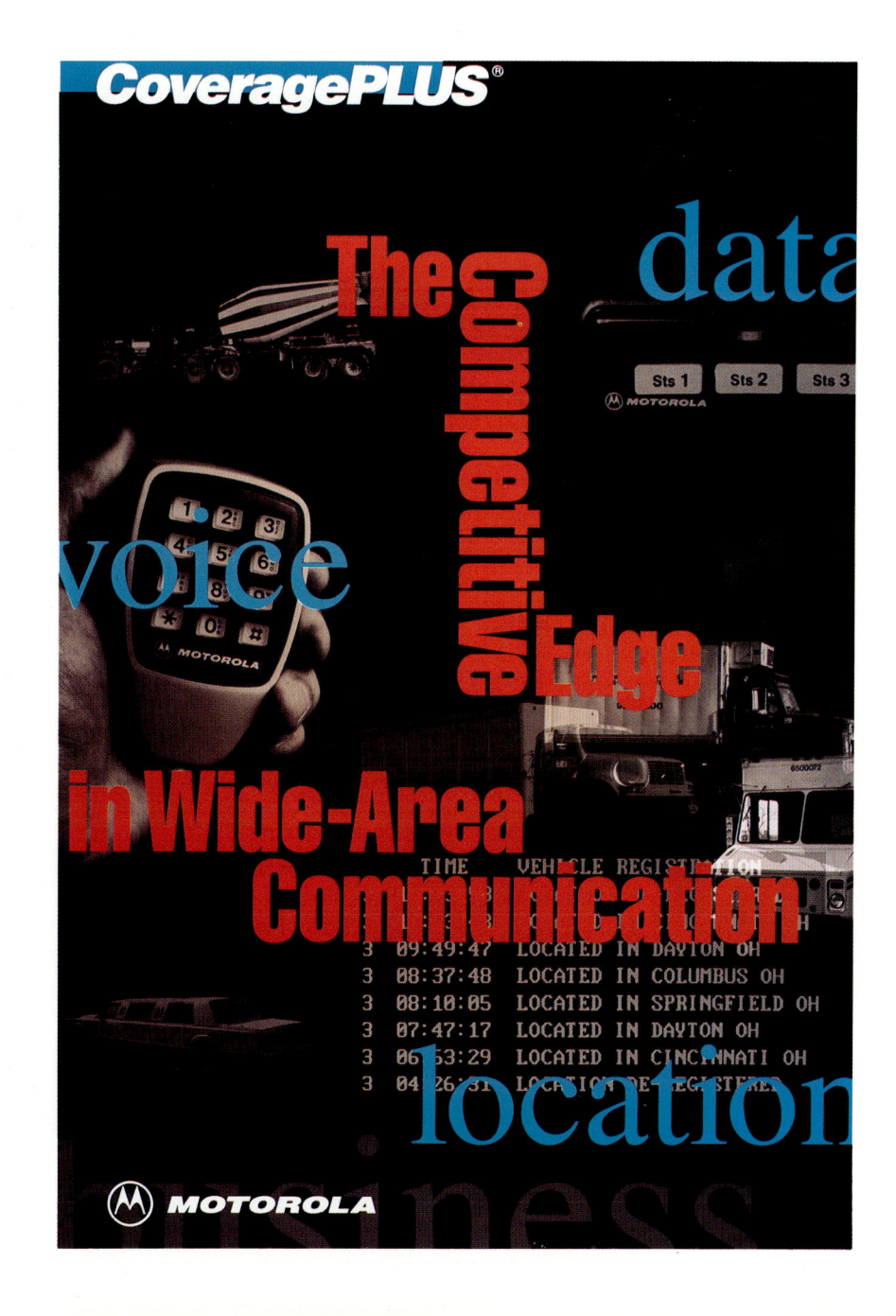

Poster for Dickens Street Summer Fest. Illustrator: Barbara Inzinga. *Right*

Hyatt Hotels and Resorts recruitment brochures. *Below*

Identity for Illinois State Toll Highway Authority. *Bottom Left*

Identity for Investors Direct, Inc., a subsidiary of Harris Bankcorp, Inc. *Bottom Center*

Identity for Quadrangle Ventures, a university owned joint venture holding company. *Bottom Right*

Windy City Communications

Hyatt International Hotels training prospectus and recruitment brochure. Photography: Kevin Anderson. *Top Left*

Hyatt International Hotels training prospectus and recruitment brochure. Illustration: Bill Miller. *Center Left*

Poster promoting mental health lecture series for Riveredge Hospital. Illustration: Ken Call. *Center Right*

Identity for Unified Data Products Corporation, a New Jersey based business forms manufacturer. *Bottom Left*

Identity for The Printery, a quality conscious quick-print service. *Bottom Center*

Name and identity for Heartland Park Topeka, a motorsports complex in Topeka, Kansas. *Bottom Right*

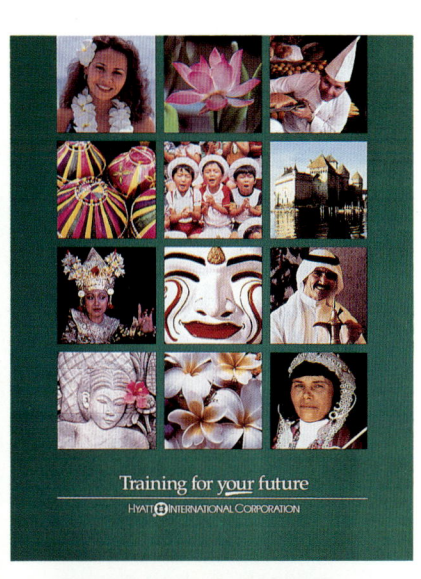

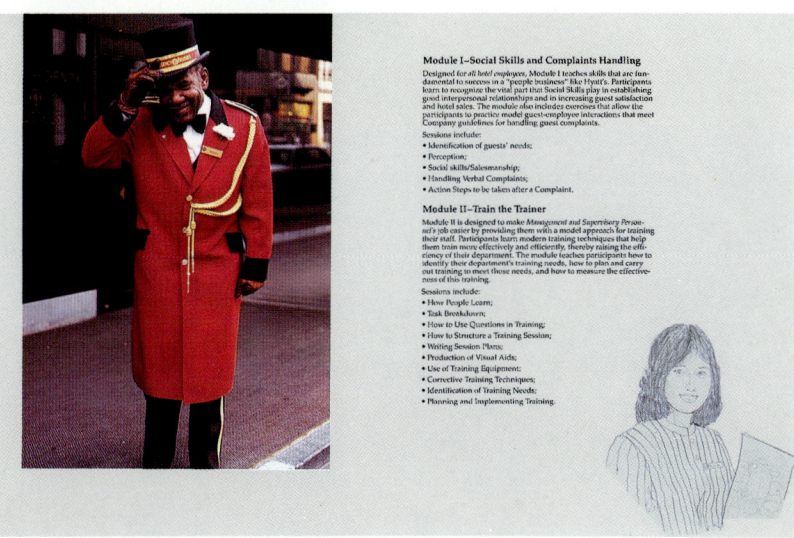

102 **Crosby Associates Inc.** 676 St. Clair
Chicago, Illinois 60611
Telephone 312.951.2800

Crosby Associates Inc.

Crosby Associates' philosophy is anchored in simplicity and directness with a goal of clarifying and amplifying the client's message. Since 1979, the firm has served the varied needs of more than a hundred clients, from multinational corporations to individual entrepreneurs, from education institutions to makers of branded goods. Projects range in scope from annual reports, sharply focused marketing pieces and naming schemes, to comprehensive visual identification programs and communications plans.

Visual communications designed by Crosby Associates are built on a foundation of client objectives and are guided by the belief that every element of a program should communicate a coherent organizational personality, and should contribute to the client's marketing goals. The firm's approach to communications problem-solving is a straightforward one. The process begins with a concentrated analysis of a client's communication needs – what a client is trying to achieve and why. Next, clear goals are established. Then visual development begins, followed by evaluation, implementation and quality management of the final product.

Projects on the following pages demonstrate Crosby Associates' ability to create and manage compelling and effective communications programs.

Crosby Associates Inc.

In developing identification programs for organizations of all types and sizes, Crosby Associates' commitment is to solutions that are appropriate, direct, fresh, and clear, without affectation or gimmickry. Each program is designed to perform in its own unique way, based on the communications goals of the client.

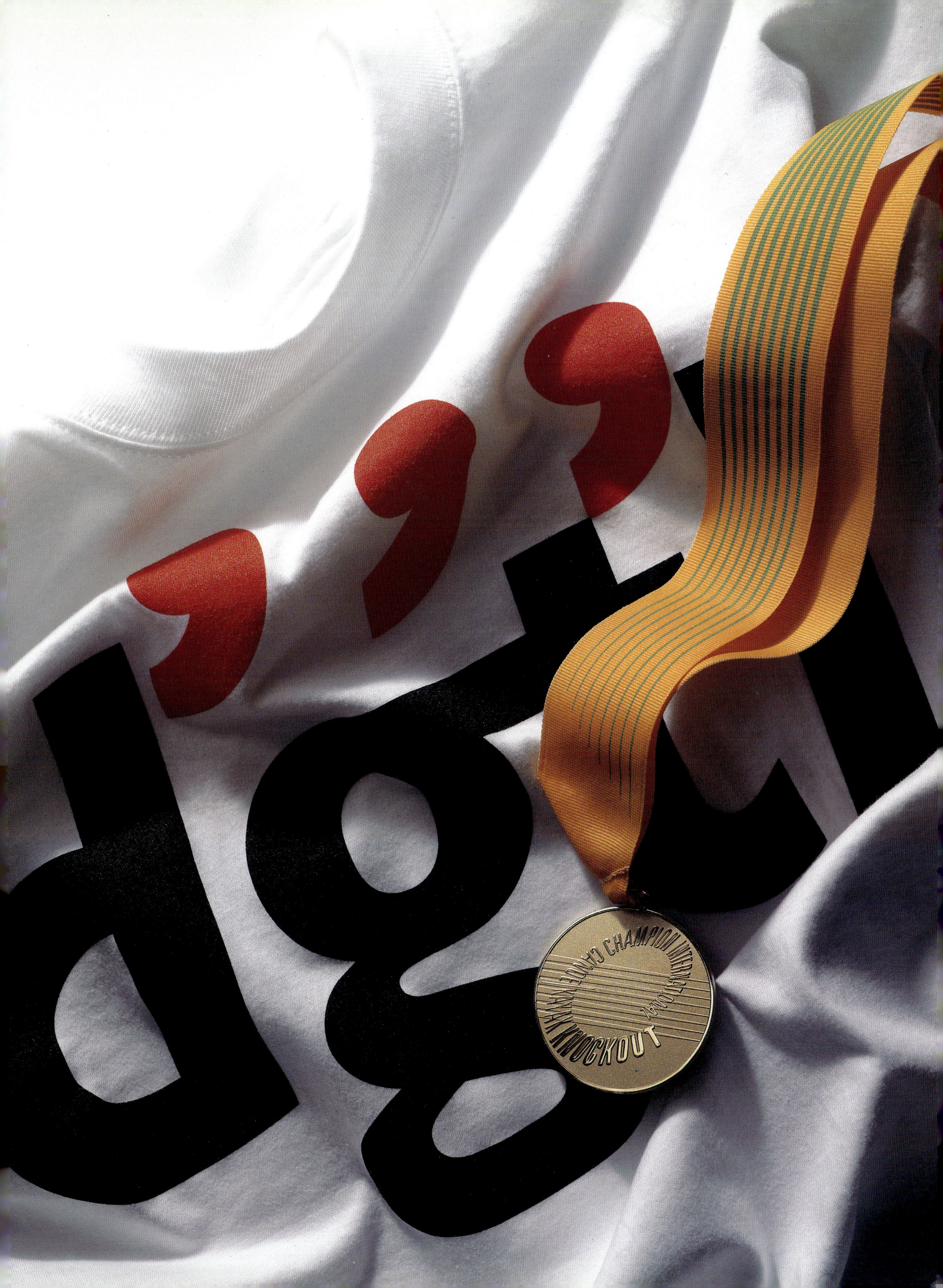

Crosby Associates Inc.

The annual report is a key communication of any publicly-held corporation. It not only acts as the vehicle to deliver the corporation's important messages, but often acts as the catalyst for defining those messages.

Crosby Associates assists in determining the client's message, and in developing visual solutions for delivering that message, while also conveying the personality of the client in both the form and content of the report.

Edison J. Brownlee, President, E.J. Brownlee Transportation

Crosby Associates Inc.

A series of sensuously appealing postcards were developed as a promotion for photographer Dave Jordano. The quality and beauty of the images ensured that the postcards would be put to use, and that the images would be sent on, creating a leapfrog effect that would maximize exposure.

For the Champion Carnival line of papers, five separate product swatchbooks were consolidated into a single, simple "sourcebook". Strong visual elements were created to identify the product and other communications associated with it. This solution not only reduced cost and inventory but made it easier for the customer to recognize, understand, and purchase the product.

Colors.

A unique conceptual approach boldly positions USG Interiors' new custom products service to architects and designers. *Top*

Gallery opening invitation series uses typography to create a unique visual and verbal identity. *Bottom*

Principal:
Mark Oldach

Date Founded:
1989

Size of Firm:
4 Employees

Mark Oldach Design

A mark is the essence of all visual language. On paper. On walls. On computers. It is the designer's job to add meaning and clarification to these marks. To add image, proportion, contrast and color. To transform marks into concept and emotion.

At Mark Oldach Design, creativity is a process, not a formula. A process that involves client, writer and designer as equal partners. To meet the client's objectives in a unique way. To integrate word and image, verbal and visual, type and symbol. A process that results in memorable communications.

Mark Oldach Design creates communication that is varied and broad. Reach for their work and you'll embrace books, posters and postcards. You'll touch marketing programs and communications systems. You'll experience image, identity and packaging. All unique. All demanding thought. And all evoking response.

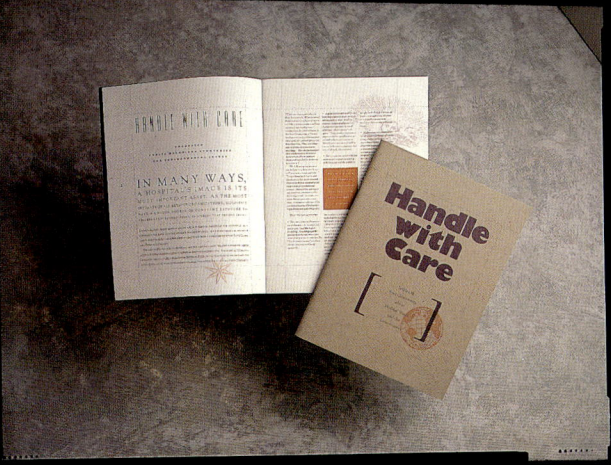

Left to Right: Designers Mark Meyer, Don Emery, and principal, Mark Oldach.

Communication programs developed for the American Hospital Association to assist hospitals position themselves as a community resource, *Top*, mobililize for a health care initiative, *Center*, and implement a community environmental awareness program. *Bottom*

Mark Oldach Design

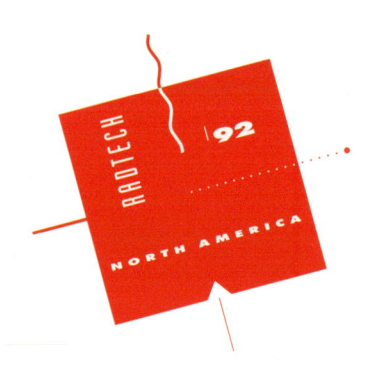

Bi-annual meeting identity for association that represents radiation-curing technologies. Identity is applied to promotional and informational campaign. *Above Left*

Packaging and information design for program communicating incentive benefits to company management. *Top Right*

Poster for dance troupe benefit. Poster is tiled and rotated in multiples when displayed. *Bottom Right*

Mark Oldach Design

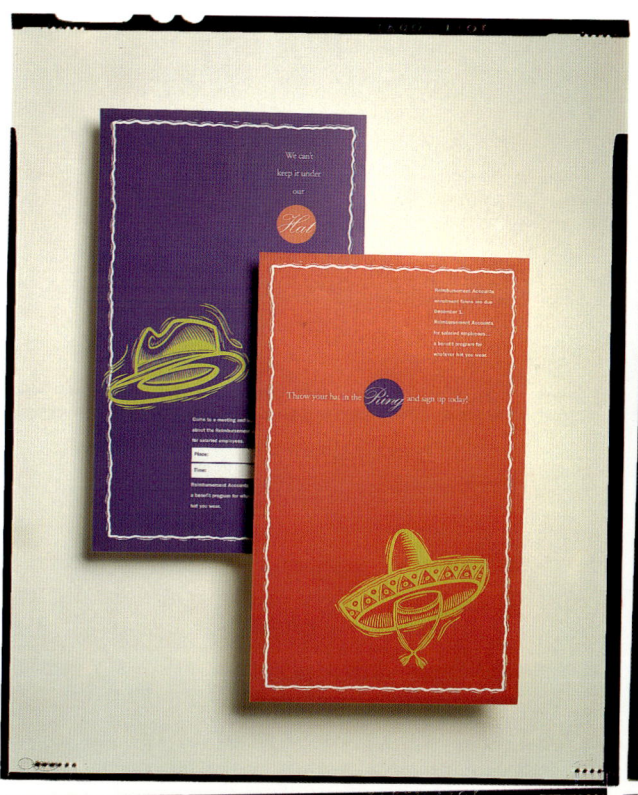

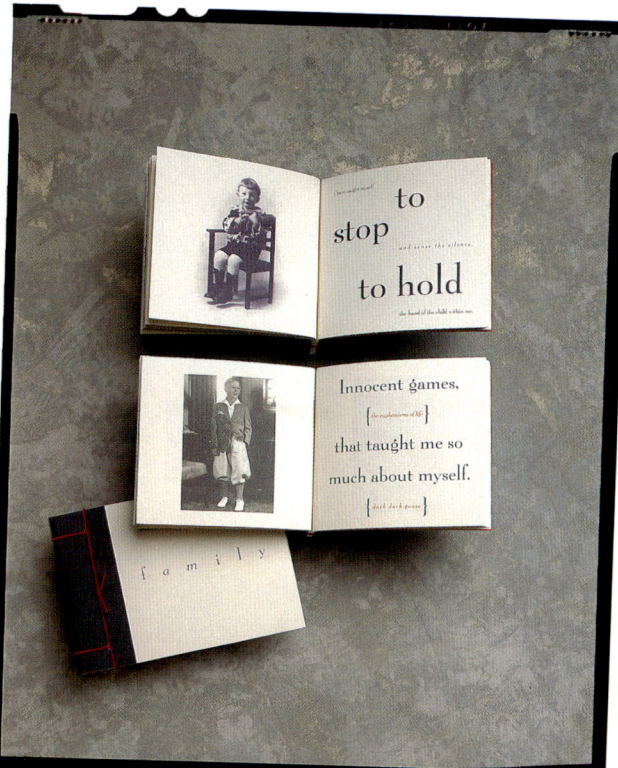

Identity program for CodeMaster, a healthcare administration software developer. Software tracks diagnostic and procedural coding for healthcare facilities. *Above*

Communications system informing Peabody employees of a new flexible benefits program that appeals to individual needs and lifestyles. *Far Left*

The designer's own family sets the tone for a universal message on family in this holiday self-promotion. *Left*

Spin wheels use whimsical imagery to encourage children to read in this reading enhancement program. *Bottom Left*

Letters of the alphabet are visually interpreted by illustrators in this project benefiting the American Center for Design. *Bottom Right*

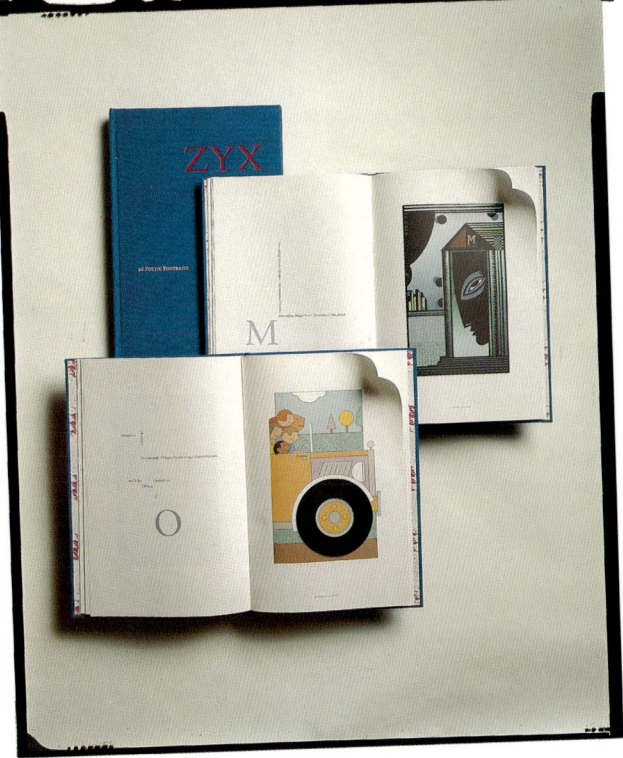

Mark Oldach Design

Annual meeting identity for National Safety Council based on the theme of Discovery. *Top Left*

Postcard series continually reinforces positioning of this printer using humor, design and focused communication. *Top Right*

Designer's self-promotion invites clients to share in the holiday spirit with paper chains they can assemble themselves. *Left*

Hands serve as metaphor for magic in this meeting promotion for the American Organization of Nurse Executives. *Bottom Left*

Mark Oldach Design

"m^r!ene:m@rks."

Copywriter's identity program using diacritical, punctuation, and proofreading marks.
Top Right

Each piece in promotional program cleverly and uniquely emphasizes this client's positioning as a creative 1, 2 & 3-color printer. *Right and Far Right*

Brochure for broadcast series relies on still and video imagery combined with creative typography to appeal to a young international audience.
Bottom Left

Communications program for Eli Lilly uses dream-like imagery to help educate employees on how to make wise investments.
Bottom Right

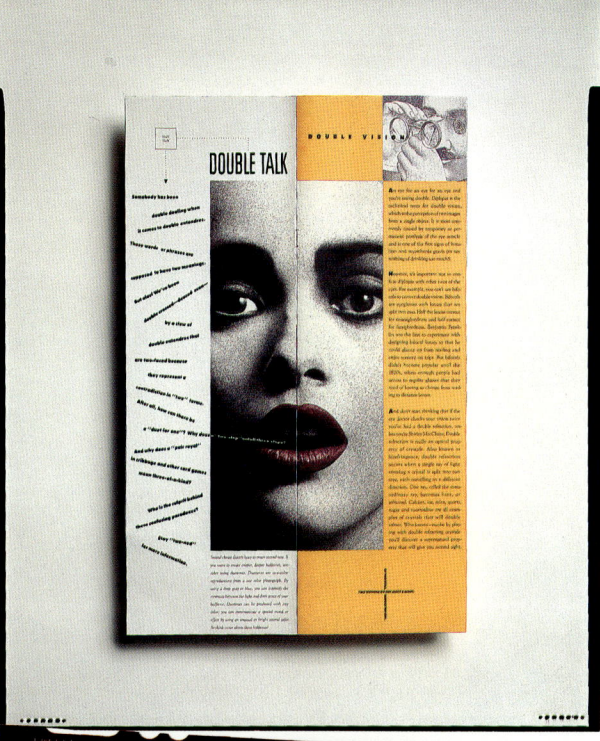

116 Mark Oldach Design

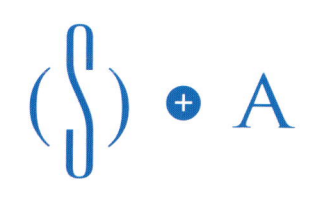

Identity program for Sourelis & Associates, an independent design business consultant, administrator and bookkeeper. *Above*

Translating future technology into applied thinking is simplified through design in this piece for Andersen Consulting. *Top Right*

Creative visuals and dynamic copy challenge the senses and heighten name awareness for this 4-color printer. *Center Right*

Designer's holiday greetings combine the firm's identity with a playful interaction of words and iconography. *Bottom Right*

Mark Oldach Design

Merging photography with whimsical imagery provides creative framework for Kindergarten Reading Program for ScottForesman.

Each Teacher's Guide is developed around a unique theme. *Below*

Packaging for sample kit
Top Right
Teacher's Guides
Center Right
Classroom manipulatives
Bottom Right

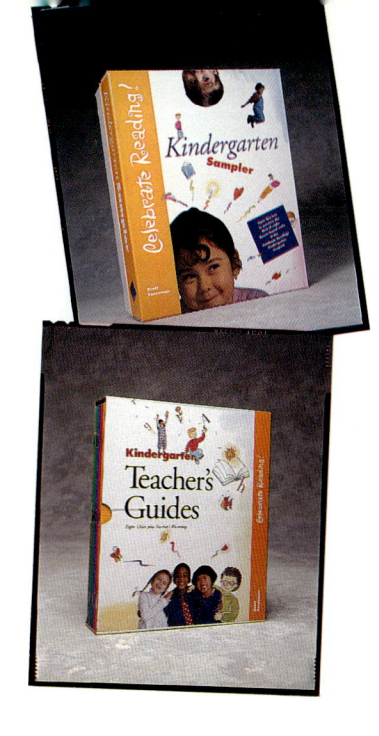

Pressley Jacobs Design Inc.
Chicago, Illinois 60606
Telephone 312.263.7485
Fax 312.263.5419

Portrait Photography:
Paul Elledge, Blair Jensen.
Studio Photography:
Dave Jordano, Werner Straube.

*Clockwise from Upper Left,
Opposite Page:*
Wendy Pressley-Jacobs
Barbara A. Bruch
Craig Ward
Kimberly Kryszak
William Lee Johnson
Amy Warner McCarter
Susan E. McQuiddy
Mark Myers

Pressley Jacobs Design Inc.

Principal:
Wendy Pressley-Jacobs

Date Founded:
1985

Size of Firm:
8 Employees

Selected Clients:
Continental Bank
Encyclopaedia Britannica
EHS Health Care
SC Johnson Wax
Mark Controls Corporation
The National Association
   of Realtors
Northwestern Memorial
   Hospital
Northwestern University
   Medical School
Platinum Technology Inc.
Spiegel, Inc.
Tribune Company
Vector Securities
   International, Inc.
Whitman Corporation
The Wyatt Company

Successful design work speaks for itself. It speaks with strength. It shouts. It whispers. It sings. It cries. It moves people. The work presented in these pages is testimony to the quality of the working relationship we build with our clients in the creative process. Relationships built on trust and respect, and infused with energy.

NEW YEAR'S RESOLUTIONS

90 WEEKS OF GREAT EXPECTATIONS

ONE Read more great novels TWO Smile more often THREE Eat more comfort A friend FOUR Eat more green leafy vegetables FIVE Have chocolate only once a day SIX Go to bed earlier, Get up earlier SEVEN Exercise daily EIGHT Use smaller type NINE Drink more water TEN Volunteer ELEVEN Floss everyday TWELVE Forgive someone THIRTEEN Stop procrastinating FOURTEEN Say hello to a street person FIFTEEN Smell the roses SIXTEEN Hang up your clothes daily SEVENTEEN Write a letter to an old friend EIGHTEEN Stop running yellow lights NINETEEN Don't let the water run while you're brushing your teeth TWENTY Work less, play more TWENTY-ONE Walk the dog TWENTY-TWO Practice safe sex TWENTY-THREE Eat less, sleep more TWENTY-FOUR Practice perspective TWENTY-FIVE Keep stop saying "like, ya know" TWENTY-SIX Stop smoking TWENTY-SEVEN Take public transportation TWENTY-EIGHT Remember your anniversary TWENTY-NINE Don't run with scissors THIRTY Read a child a bedtime story THIRTY-ONE Stop believing everything you hear THIRTY-TWO Listen better, talk less THIRTY-THREE Balance the checkbook THIRTY-FOUR Start bake bread THIRTY-FIVE Be the turn the TV off THIRTY-SIX designated driver THIRTY-SEVEN Recycle your garbage THIRTY-EIGHT Train the baby THIRTY-NINE Clippings, your positive attitude FORTY Take control of stress FORTY-ONE Plant a lawn FORTY-TWO Use the say thank-you FORTY-THREE VCR FORTY-FOUR Be the teach your parents to use the vegetable garden FORTY-FIVE Play more hockey FORTY-SIX Stop hitting the snooze button FORTY-SEVEN Design the holiday card sooner next year FORTY-EIGHT Plan for your retirement FORTY-NINE Wear your glasses FIFTY Buy street-wise FIFTY-ONE Kick a habit FIFTY-TWO Forgive yourself

Pressley Jacobs Design Inc.

121

New Year's card from our office to all of our friends, clients and suppliers. Fifty-two resolutions, one for each week of the year, in the form of a bookmark. Letterpress. *Opposite Page*

Whitman Corporation annual report with a focus on management. Rolling Meadows, Illinois, Photography: Mark Joseph. *Top Right*

Platinum Technology annual report. A gutsy approach uniquely reflective of this energetic, young company. Oakbrook Terrace, Illinois, Photography: various stock, Illustration: Cameron Clement. *Right*

Pressley Jacobs Design Inc.

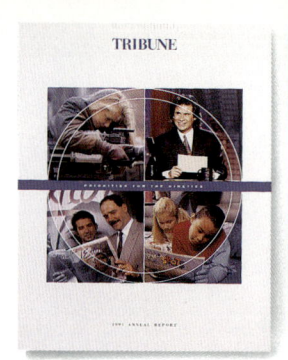

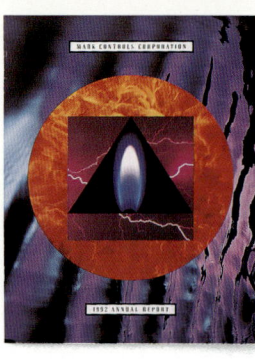

Tribune Company annual report with a focus on four strategic priorities to guide this information and entertainment company in the nineties. Chicago, Illinois. Photography: various Tribune Company staff photographers. *Top Left*

Mark Controls Corporation annual report depicting the range of the company's valve and control products, and the elements of production they control: liquids, high temperatures, electricity and natural gas. Skokie, Illinois. Studio Photography: Jim Imbrogno and stock. Location Photography: James Schnepf. *Top Right*

Employee annual report for SC Johnson Wax. A compassionate and open discussion about the business and the importance of each employee to the company. Text includes four languages. Racine, Wisconsin. Photographer: Tom Berthiaume. *Left*

A monthly publication for SC Johnson Wax. The publication provides a forum for "dialogue" about current business issues between North American employees and the company. Racine, Wisconsin. Photographer: Kevin Anderson. *Right*

123

A quarterly publication for The Wyatt Company that provides fresh perspectives on current management issues. A variety of photographers and illustrators are commissioned for each issue. Chicago, Illinois. Depicted: Photography: Paul Elledge, Greg Gillis, Glen Gyssler. Illustration: Jack Davis, Joel Peter Johnson, Wilson McLean, Lori Osiecki. *Upper Left*

Capabilities brochure targeted to referring physicians for the Department of Pediatrics EHS Christ Hospital and Medical Center, Oak Lawn, Illinois. Part of a comprehensive series of collateral for the department. Photographer: Eric Herzog. *Left*

Pressley Jacobs Design Inc.

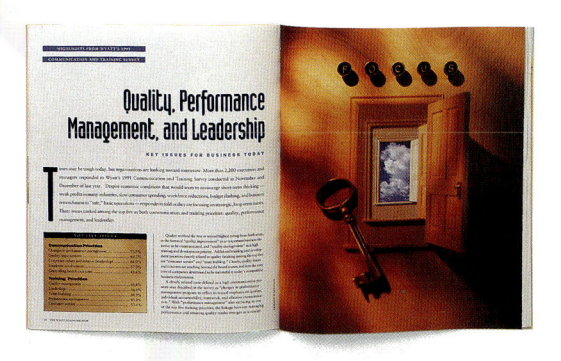

Right, Top to Bottom
Identity programs and marks for:

Vector Securities International, a securities analyst firm specializing in biotech and life sciences industries.

HOPE, an employee assistance program for EHS Health Care.

Heart Preservers, a consumer awareness program for cardiology services at EHS Christ Hospital and Medical Center.

Rape Victim Advocates, a not-for-profit organization that supports the victim of sexual assault.

Cardiac Services department of EHS Good Samaritan Hospital.

Real Estate Today, masthead for the official magazine of the National Association of Realtors, with a circulation in excess of 750,000.

126   H. Greene & Company   230 West Huron Street
Chicago, Illinois 60610
Telephone 312.642.0088
Fax 312.642.0028

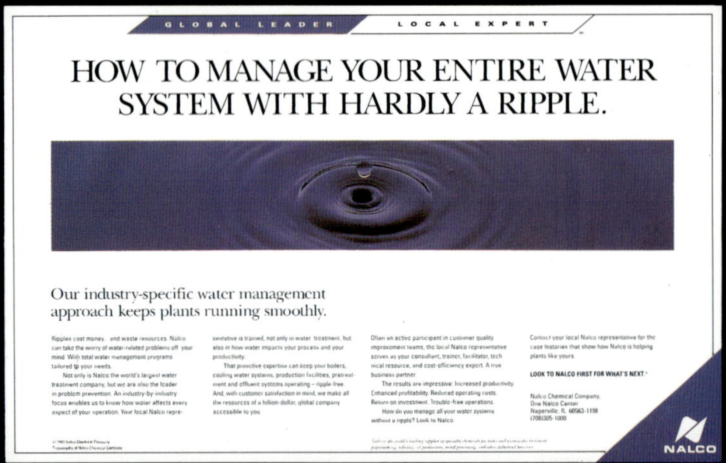

Communications program for Nalco Chemical, Basic Industries Group. Program consists of a comprehensive collateral kit, including folder and capabilities brochures for each division, and corporate and product print advertising.

Principal:
Howard Greene

Selected Clients:
Abbott Laboratories
Apple Computer
Corporetum
Comdisco
Dimension Works
Florsheim Shoe Co.
Grant Thornton
Information Resources Inc.
Kemper Financial Services
LaSalle National Bank
McCord Travel Mgmt.
Motorola Nortel
Nalco Chemical
NCR
Ogilvy & Mather
Wesley-Jessen

H. Greene & Company

Left, Front to Back:
Laura Gernon
Howard Greene
Toni Burdick
Nils Bunde

Right, Front to Back:
Tara Kassoff Gold
Joe Bond
Carol Timberlake
Dave Shipley

At H. Greene & Company, we don't consider ourselves so much a design firm as an idea firm.

We thrive on transforming sound thinking and ideas into great contemporary design through a hands-on, personal approach. Our philosophy has no room for creativity-by-committee. It is simply to allow talented and experienced people to actually do what they do best: create impactful design, collateral and advertising.

Our clients, ranging from Fortune 100 corporations to smaller and even start-up companies, generally have one thing in common: a need for multi-faceted campaigns in which the whole is greater than the sum of its parts. Leveraging our years of high-level experience working with national and international organizations, we are able to meet these needs through our unique, programs-oriented perspective.

Our strengths are first, in creating memorable concepts and bold design based on insightful strategic thinking. And second, in being able to integrate these elements into comprehensive communications programs which consistently deliver tangible, measurable results.

Program for Dimension Works, designer and builder of trade show exhibits, emphasizing a strong foundation in the basics. Campaign includes capabilities brochure, exhibit presentation piece, folder, invitations, print advertising.

128

Logo and poster for Chicago Children's Museum. *Right and Below*

Corporate collateral program for LaSalle National Bank. *Bottom Left*

Corporate identity and paper management program for Bayer, Bess, Vanderwarker advertising. *Bottom Right*

Identity, collateral and POP program for Motorola Triton II marine radios. *Top*

Program for Motorola-Nortel Communications, joint venture of Motorola and Northern Telecom providing wireless communication services for the entire western hemisphere. Materials include a comprehensive collateral kit with various folders and desktop-published presentation and report formats, paper management program, introductory 8-page advertising insert/brochure. *Bottom*

H. Greene & Company

129

The Apple Trade-Up
5 DAYS ONLY: MAY 13 - 17

More power to ya.

Need more computing power? Trade in your old computer and peripherals. Most brands and models accepted. Add some dollars of your own. And get an advanced new Macintosh system. With more speed. Color. Expandability. And all the power you need to stay ahead.

**VISIT THE CAMPUS COMPUTER STORES TODAY!
OR CALL 702-6086 FOR DETAILS!**

The power to be your best™

College campus trade-in program for Apple Computer. Materials include poster, t-shirt and brochures. *Top, Left and Right*

Apple Executive Forum. Kit includes binder, seminar materials and invitations. *Center*

Cover and spread of annual report for Meridian computer leasing corporation. *Bottom*

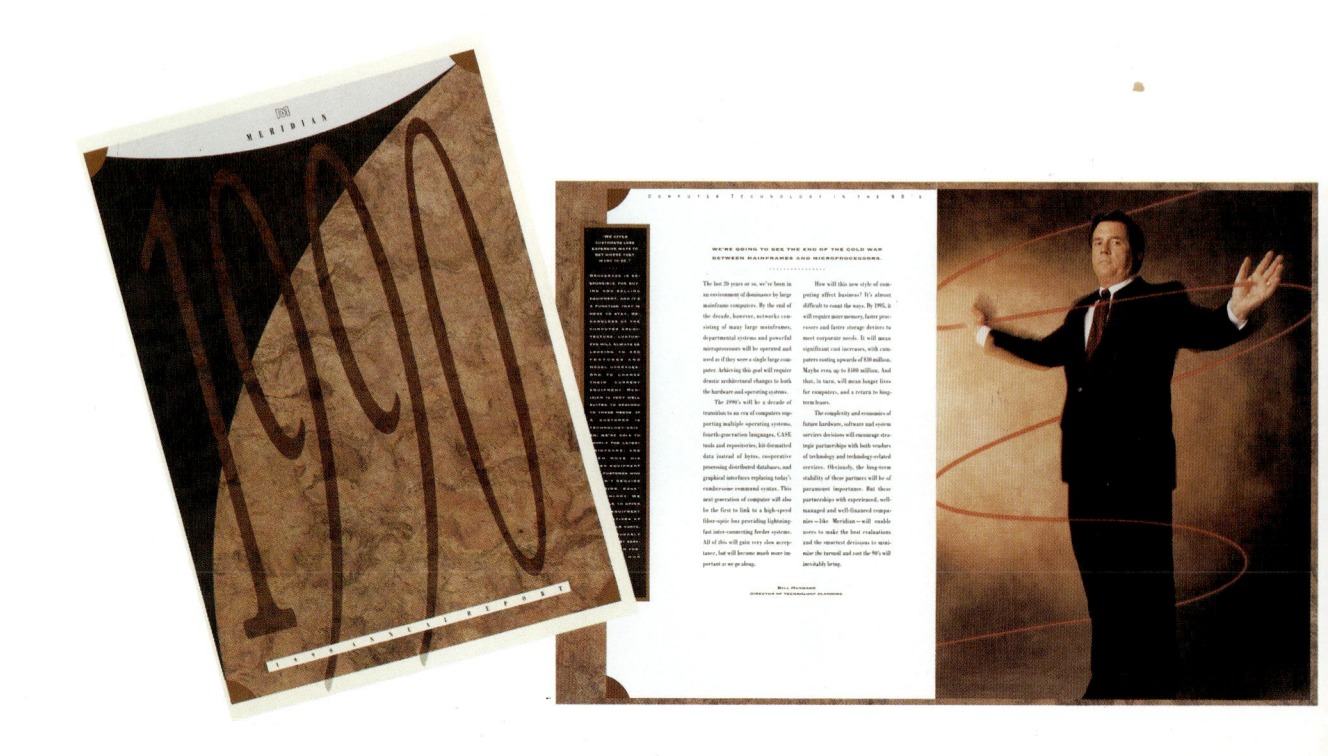

H. Greene & Company   131

Examples of collateral, packaging and point-of-purchase materials for Wesley-Jessen, maker of DuraSoft Colors, Complements and FreshLook opaque contact lenses.

POP easel introducing Complements Violet lenses.
Left

POP poster featuring various DuraSoft Colors lenses, using spokesperson Brooke Shields.
Below Left

Special promotion packaging for FreshLook contact lenses.
Below Right

Collateral program for Abbott Laboratories, including slipcase, binders, video case and corporate brochure. *Center Left*

Product brochures for Information Resources, retail grocery space management database and software systems. *Center Right*

Identity and collateral program for McCord Corporate Travel Management. *Bottom*

Program for CLASS, Comdisco's Integrated High-Tech Asset Management Software system. Materials include identity; full collateral program; software user manuals and packaging; mouse pad, sales force materials including video and sales presentation kit with slides and overheads, end user video, newsletter and direct mail. *Top Center, Opposite Page, Top Left and Opposite Page, Bottom*

Corporate communications for Comdisco: newsletter, corporate advertising. *Opposite Page, Top Right*

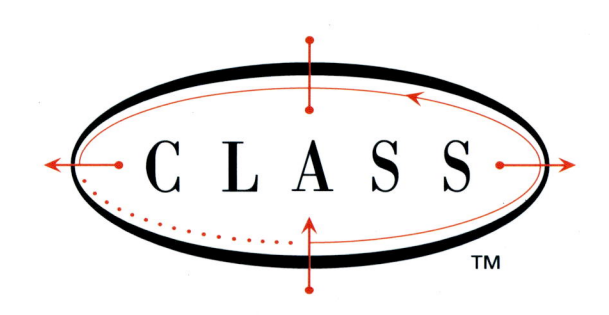

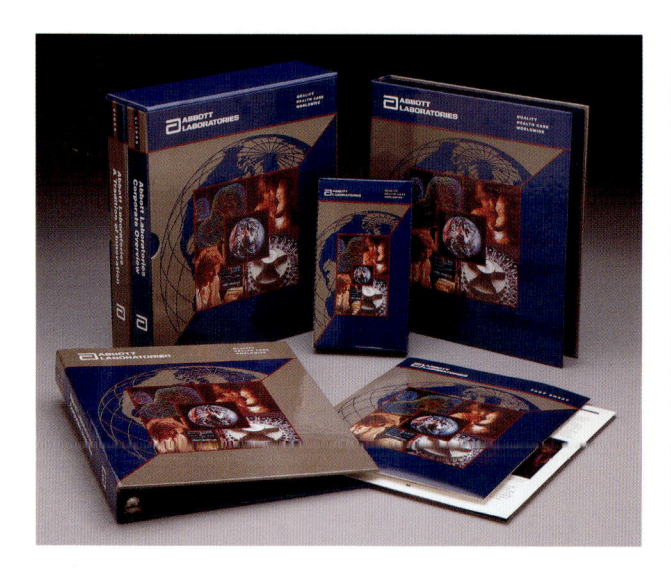

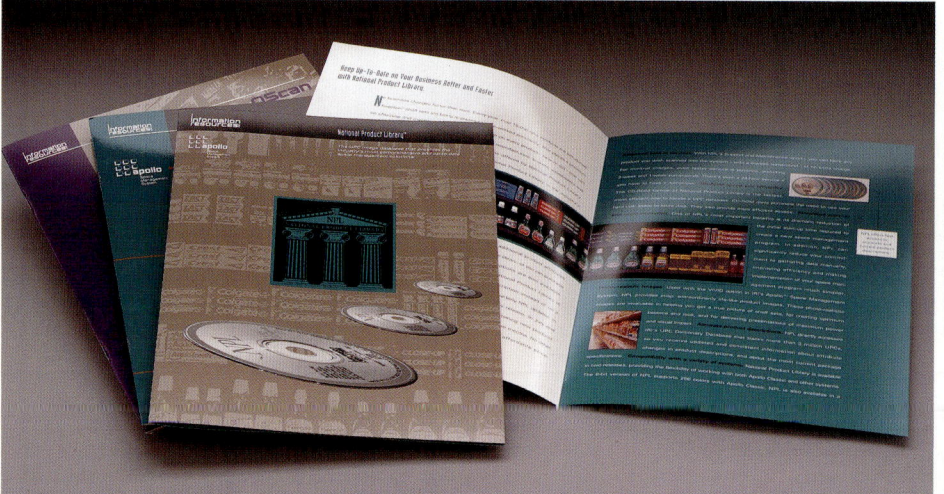

COMDISCO
ACCESS
HOW TO TAKE A SNAPSHOT OF YOUR ENTIRE HIGH-TECH EQUIPMENT PORTFOLIO ANY TIME YOU WANT TO.
CLASS
COMDISCO INTEGRATED ASSET MANAGEMENT SOLUTIONS

VOLUME V • ISSUE 1
COMDISCO
exchange
LEASE
HOW TO NEGOTIATE A FLEXIBLE LEASE AGREEMENT
Negotiating the best terms and conditions in your high-tech master lease agreements has always been important. But today, with rising costs, shrinking budgets, and intense competition among leasing companies vying for your business, it is more critical than ever.
The typical lease term for a big-ticket item is anywhere from 24 to 60 months. It is highly probable that during that time the equipment will undergo some type of alteration to better meet your changing needs and take advantage of the declining price/performance curve. In fact at Comdisco, 77% of the equipment we have out on lease is upgraded or replaced within 24 months, 95% within 36 months.
Because of this, it's important that you consider more than just the initial lease rate when selecting a leasing company. The true
Continued on page 8

"There is a way to measure the quality of your technology decisions."
"Don't reduce your technology costs in such a way that they can't continue to be reduced. The last thing you want is to save budget dollars today at the expense of mortgaging your future.
"With the right strategy, it's possible to continually reduce your costs. Is your current strategy letting you do that? To find out, use the market as a yardstick. Compare what's been happening to your expenses over the last few years with market trends. Then look at what's likely to happen in the future. That'll tell you the answer real fast.
"Every good technology strategy is built on a sound financial footing. That takes market knowledge and creativity. And that's where Comdisco excels.
"If you're not sure whether your strategy measures up to the realities of today, talk to us. We'll show you some smart ways to solve your problems, and we'll save you money. That's Comdisco's job, and nobody does it better."
Comdisco is one of the world's largest and most experienced independent high-tech asset consultants. Our strength is people like Russ West... people who know your problems and how to solve them. Let us show you how to measure—and improve—the quality of your technology decisions.
COMDISCO
HIGH-TECH ASSET MANAGEMENT SOLUTIONS

CLASS
IMPLEMENTATION GUIDE
MARKETING GUIDE
THE NEXT 11 MINUTES AND 10 SECONDS CAN SAVE YOU COUNTLESS HOURS OF TIME AND EFFORT.
Integrated Asset Management Solutions
FROM COMDISCO
CLASS For Windows
CLASS

Announcement for the annual conference of Grantmakers in the Arts. *Top Left*

Graphics for iced drink cans present a cool picture in the refrigerator case or on the retail shelf. *Top Right*

A silhouette of the product in one of its available colors adorn each side of this display package. The top utilizes the silhouettes as a check-off chart for the color of the product. *Center*

Playful names and wraparound photography create a point-of-purchase display when packages are placed side by side in the proper order–shows all the colors and possible configurations of the lamps. *Bottom*

Symbol for lighting company, Lightning Bug Ltd. *Below*

Porter/Matjasich & Associates

Principals:
Allen Porter
Carol Matjasich

Date Founded:
1981

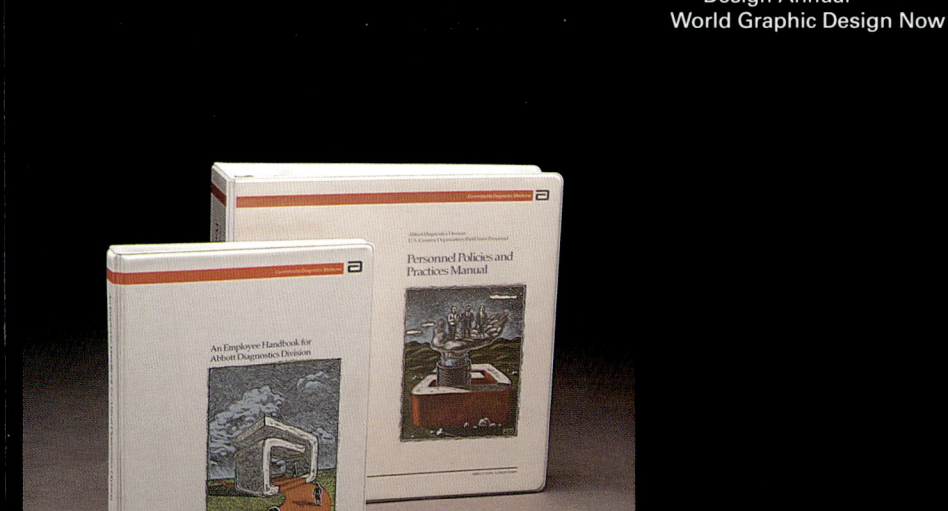

Selected Clients:
Abbott Diagnostics
AT&T
Vanco Electronics
Carver Wood Products
MRC Polymers
Arachnid
Saxon Paint
 & Home Care Centers
Lightning Bug Ltd.
Immtech International
Scott Foresman
Whitaker Carpenter Paper

Publications/Awards:
American Corporate Identity
Communication Arts
Creativity
Graphis Packaging
HOW Magazine
IDEA
Label Designs 3
Packaging Design
Package Designers Council
Print Casebooks
Print Regional
 Design Annual
World Graphic Design Now

When P/M&A opened its doors in 1981, Allen Porter and Carol Matjasich brought with them multi-disciplined design backgrounds and client involvement from many industries. Their work reflects a comprehensive approach to a client's communication needs as an integral part of strategic business planning.

"Whether their product sits on a retail shelf or is hidden deep within an industrial machine – whether they render a service or contribute to the cultural life of society, every organization must establish a clear perception of itself or others will do it for them."

Though the company is best known for its award-winning packaging, it functions as a single source for many of its clients, providing planning, design, writing, implementation and coordination for corporate identity, exhibits, print communications, and environmental design.

Symbol for copywriter and editor Victoria Frigo.
Top Left

Employee handbook and personnel guide with colorful illustrations and easy-to-read text for Abbott Diagnostics Division.
Center

Left to Right:
Robert Rausch
Carol Matjasich
Allen Porter

Porter/Matjasich & Associates

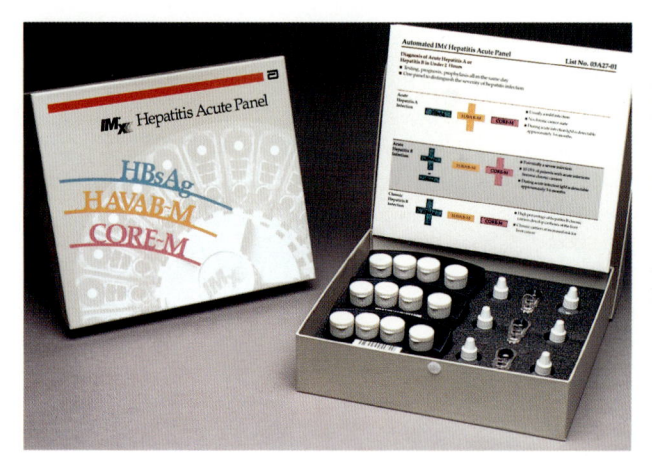

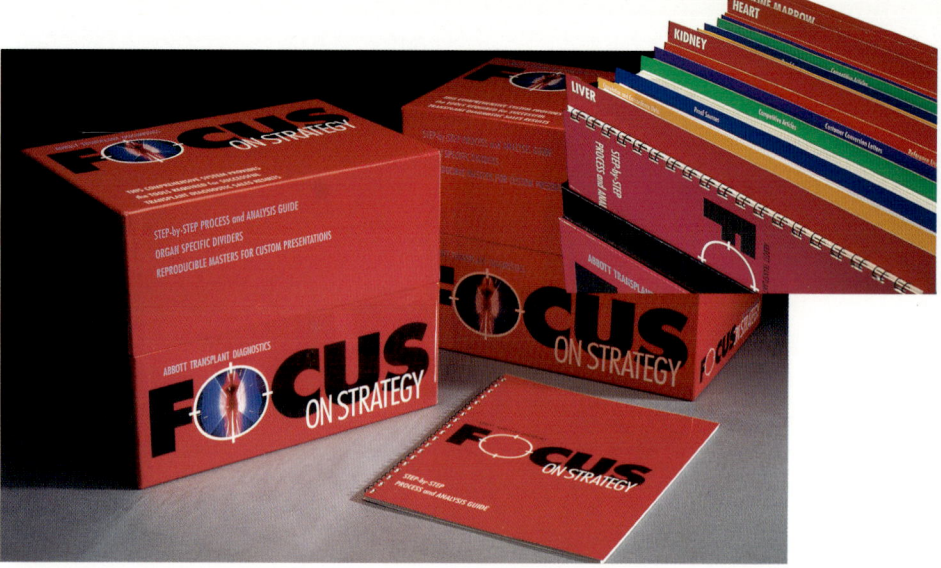

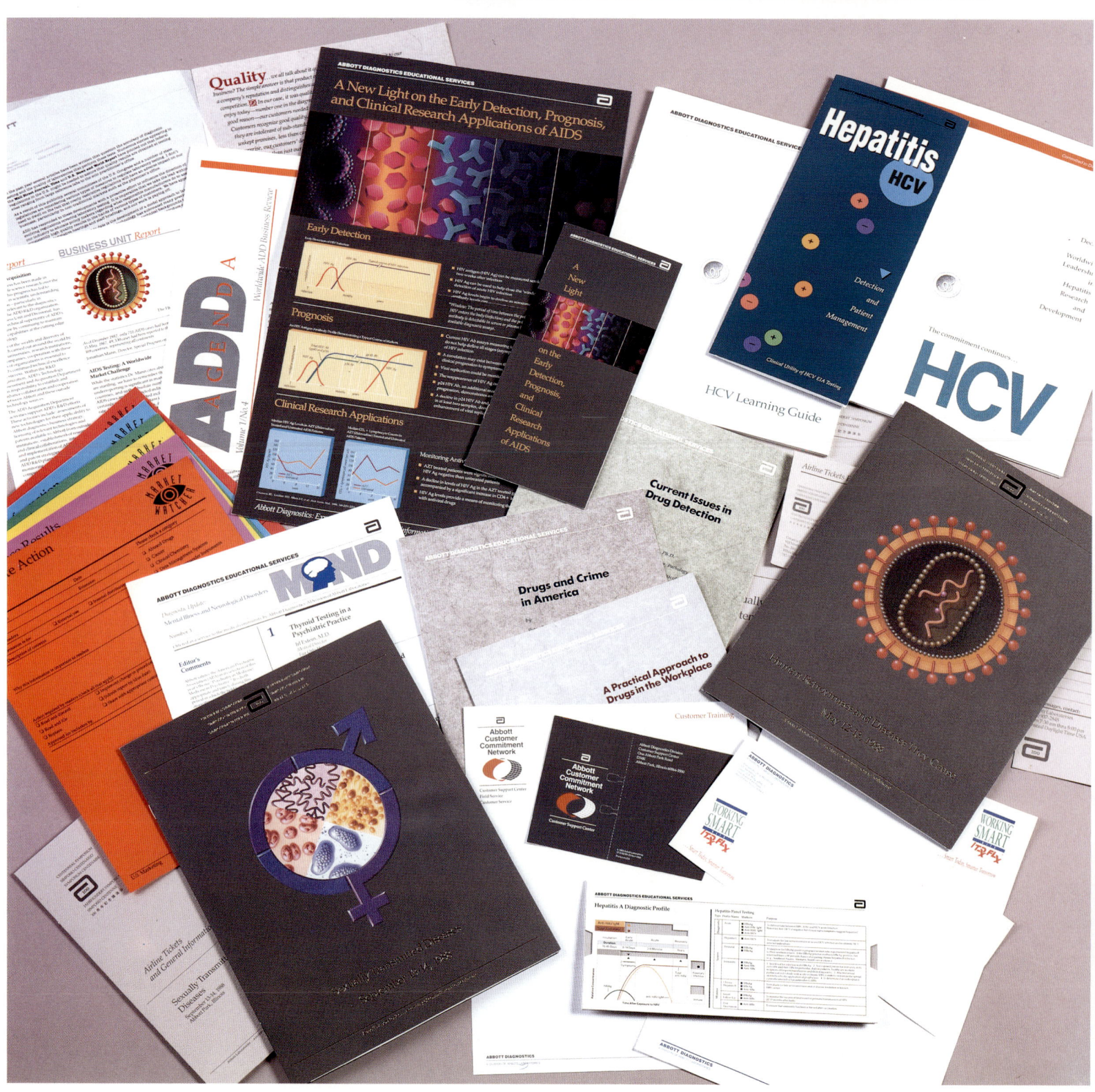

Easel-top package supports a fold-out sales presentation to promote hepatitis panel testing on Abbott's IMx assay instrument.
Opposite Page, Top Left

A reference/resource file system used by Abbott's sales representatives for presenting Cyclosporine organ transplant protocol.
Opposite Page, Top Right

An array of projects for Abbott Laboratories Diagnostics Division include: institutional/educational material, publications, and employee communications.
Opposite Page, Bottom

The PMC painting contractor line label features a design reminiscent of Saxon's original contractor business and of the period in which the company was founded – a marked contrast to their DIY retail label designs. *Left*

Symbol for Abbott's Thyroid Business Unit.
Top Right

Symbol for Abbott's internal communications program for US Marketing.
Center Right

Symbol for Abbott's Volwiler Society Awards Dinner.
Bottom Right

Examples from the paint label system designed for Saxon Paint & Home Care Centers. A color-code system unifies the type of paint across brand lines.
Bottom

Porter/Matjasich
& Associates

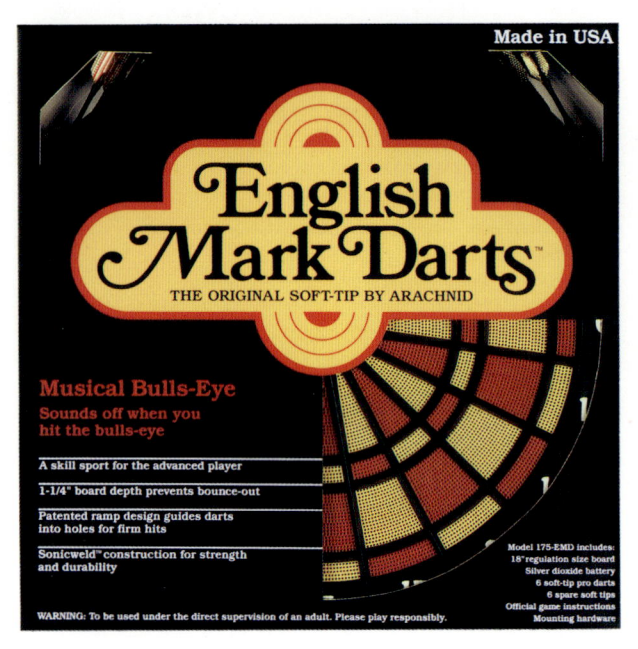

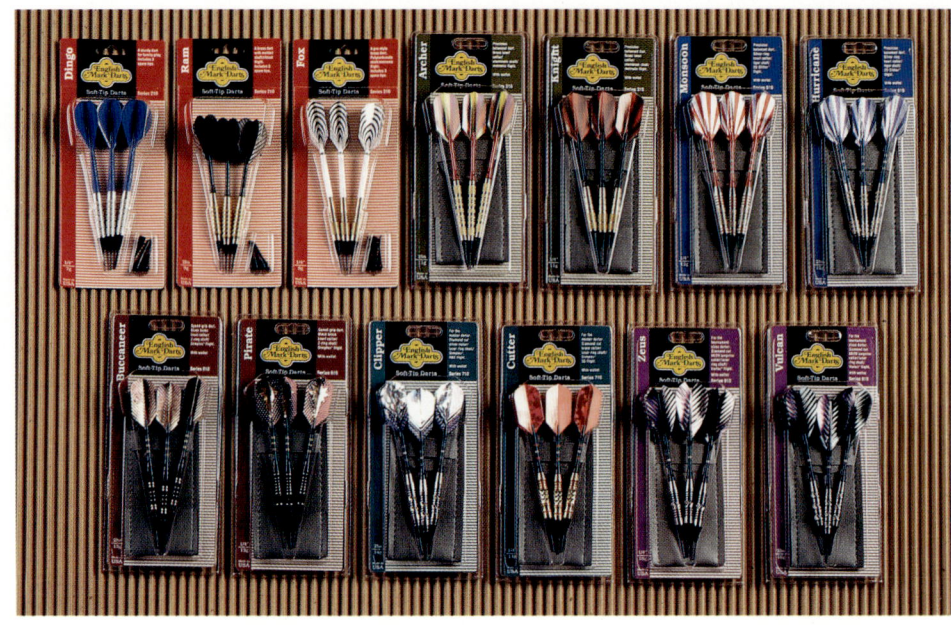

VENTO₂

A new logo brings consistency and brand recognition to this line of mass market soft-tip darts, and dart boards. *Top*

Symbol for a manufacturer of oxygen enrichment systems. *Center*

PaperVision, a marketing tool for a midwest paper distributor directed to designers and corporate specifiers of printing papers. The color-coded modules of the system contain sample swatchbooks of different types of paper. *Bottom Right*

With the market demand for recycled paper, a module for those products was added to the original PaperVision system. *Bottom Left*

Package for Shark Darts highlights the interactive feature of the game – allows the customer to test the musical bulls eye without removing the product. *Opposite Page, Top Left*

The story of AT&T's new midwest headquarters and the history of the company's presence in the area are featured in this booklet presented to employees and visitors to the building. *Opposite Page, Top Right*

139

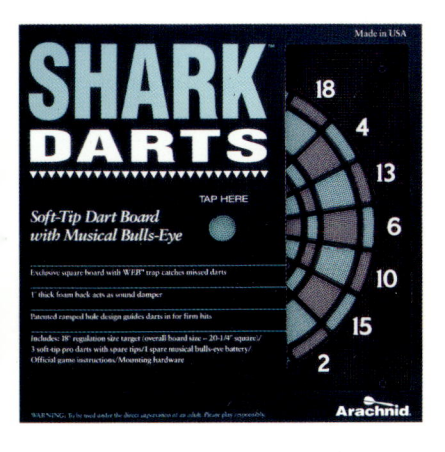

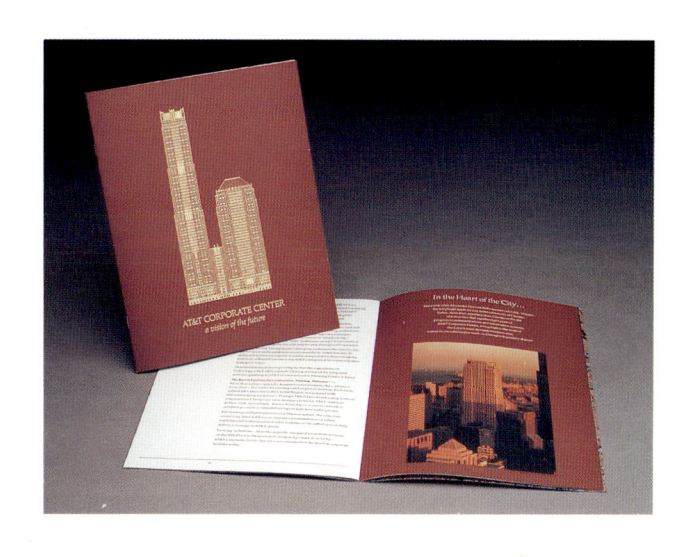

Porter/Matjasich
& Associates

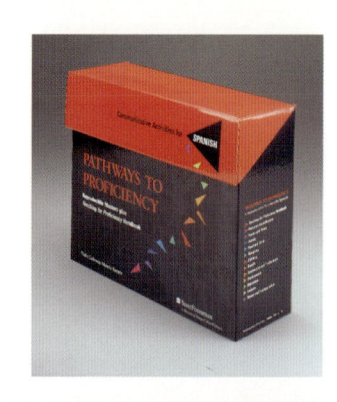

Package design for Scott Foresman's "Pathways to Proficiency" Spanish Language Program.
Opposite Page, Top

Corporate identity program for a plastic recycler uses a global image to symbolize the function and scope of the company. The use of a single color throughout the identity system provides economy, consistency, and increased recognition.
Opposite Page, Bottom

Carded packaging for electronic accessories creates a strong corporate identification throughout the entire line of product areas including audio, video, and telephone.
Top Right

A new identity, catalog design, and point of purchase display helped revitalize this 100 year-old manufacturer of wooden office desk accessories.
Center and Bottom

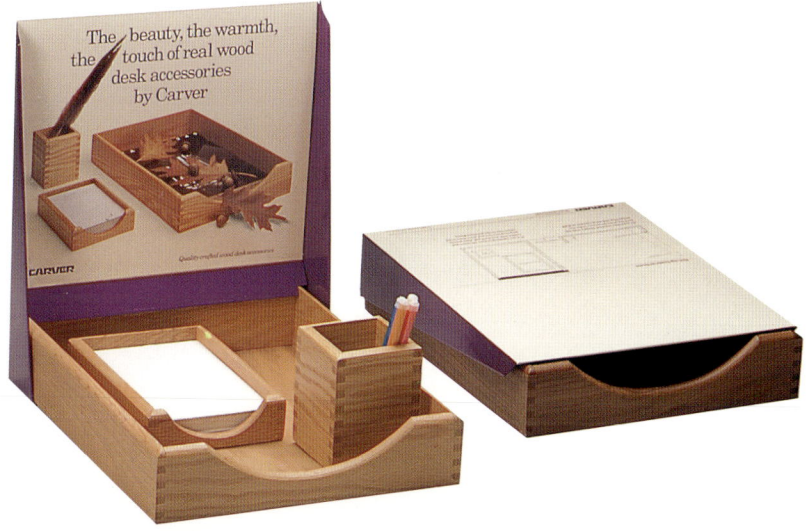

Cagney + McDowell, Inc. 711 South Dearborn
Suite 204
Chicago, Illinois 60605
Telephone 312.461.0707

Cagney + McDowell, Inc.

+ . . .
Design is the collaboration of many. The combination of individual insights, talents and perspectives.

At Cagney + McDowell, we solve problems. We listen to our clients and work with them, side by side, to orchestrate content and images that actively communicate ideas and information. In today's complex and crowded business environment, we help our clients make the right impression.

144

Quarterly magazine publication for EHS Health Care, a major provider of health and wellness services in the Chicago area.

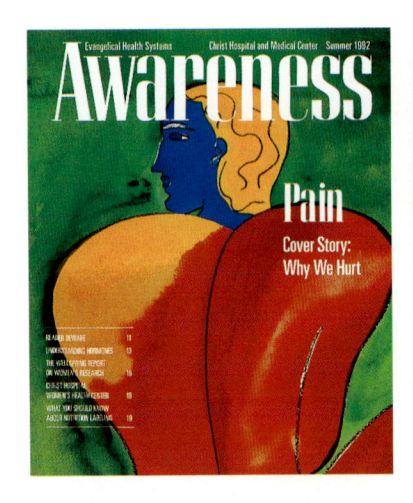

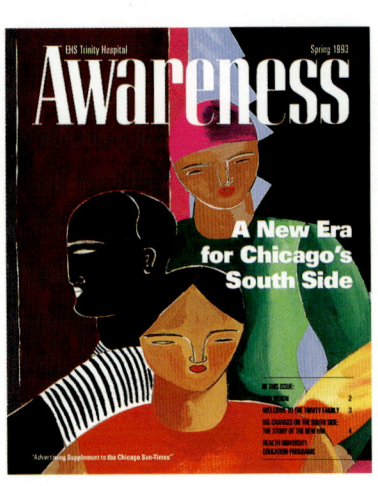

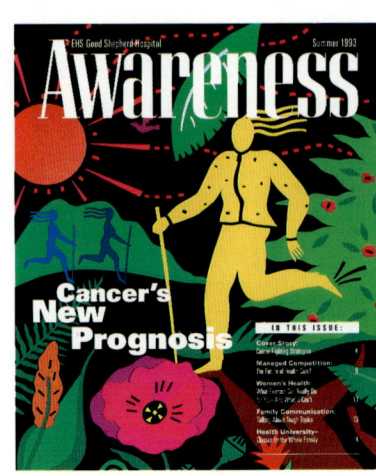

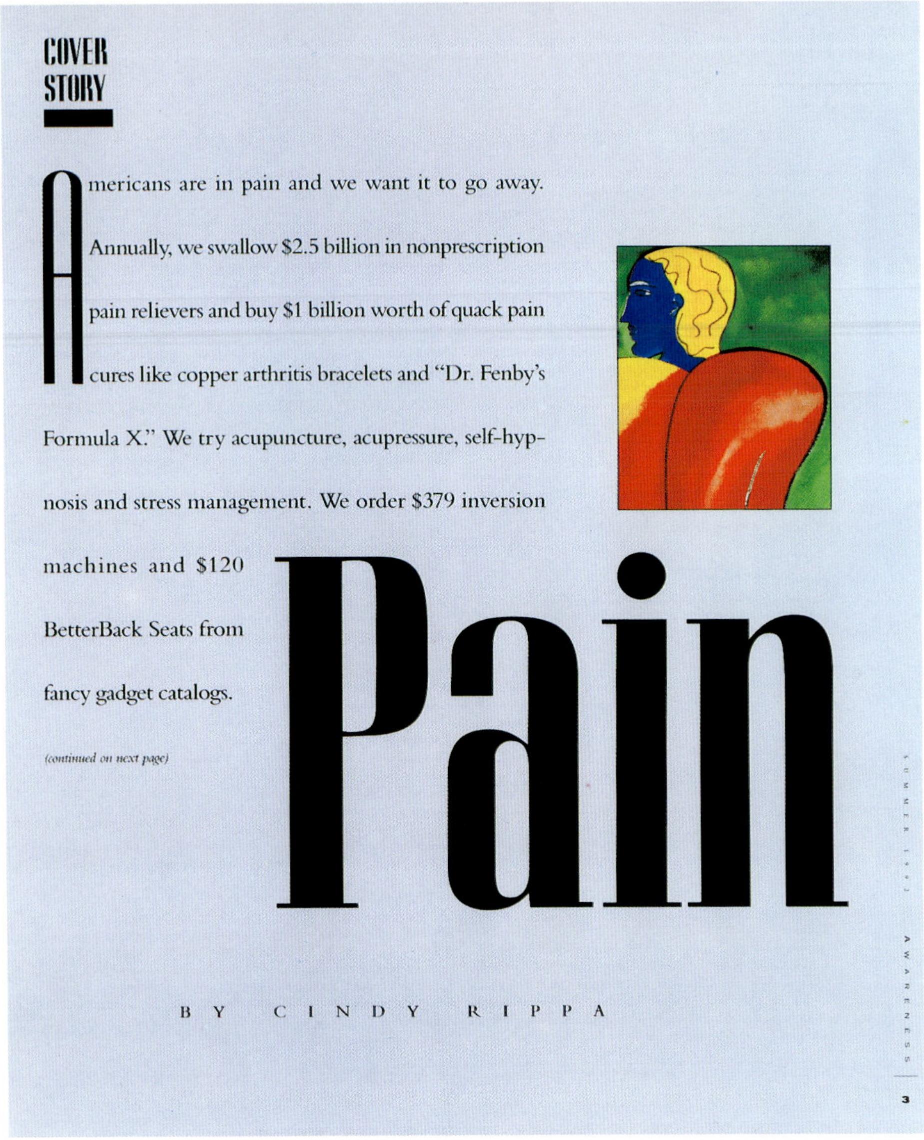

COVER STORY

Americans are in pain and we want it to go away. Annually, we swallow $2.5 billion in nonprescription pain relievers and buy $1 billion worth of quack pain cures like copper arthritis bracelets and "Dr. Fenby's Formula X." We try acupuncture, acupressure, self-hypnosis and stress management. We order $379 inversion machines and $120 BetterBack Seats from fancy gadget catalogs.

(continued on next page)

Pain

BY CINDY RIPPA

Performance report for Bell Sports Corp., the leading manufacturer and marketer of bicycle helmets in the United States.

Cagney + McDowell, Inc.

146 Recruiting brochure and poster for Kraft General Foods, the largest food company in America.

Identity for the Artifact Center at the Spertus Museum of Cultural Heritage. *Top left*

Annual report for Unitrin, Inc., an insurance services company. *Bottom left*

Annual report for Walgreen Co., the leader of the U.S. chain drugstore industry. *Top right*

Fact book for Morton International Inc., a manufacturer and marketer of specialty chemicals, airbags and salt. *Bottom right*

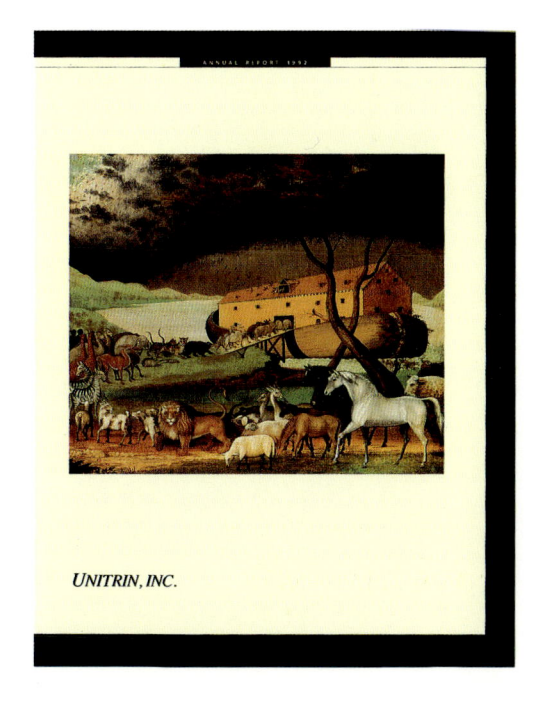

Cagney + McDowell, Inc.

148

Capabilities brochure for Ward Howell International, an executive search consulting firm. *Top*

Logotype for Ganton Technologies Inc., a design engineer and manufacturer of precision tooling and die-casting. *Bottom left*

Annual report for the Arthur Andersen Worldwide Organization, a professional services consulting firm. *Bottom center*

Annual report for USG Corporation, a developer, manufacturer and marketer of building products. *Bottom right*

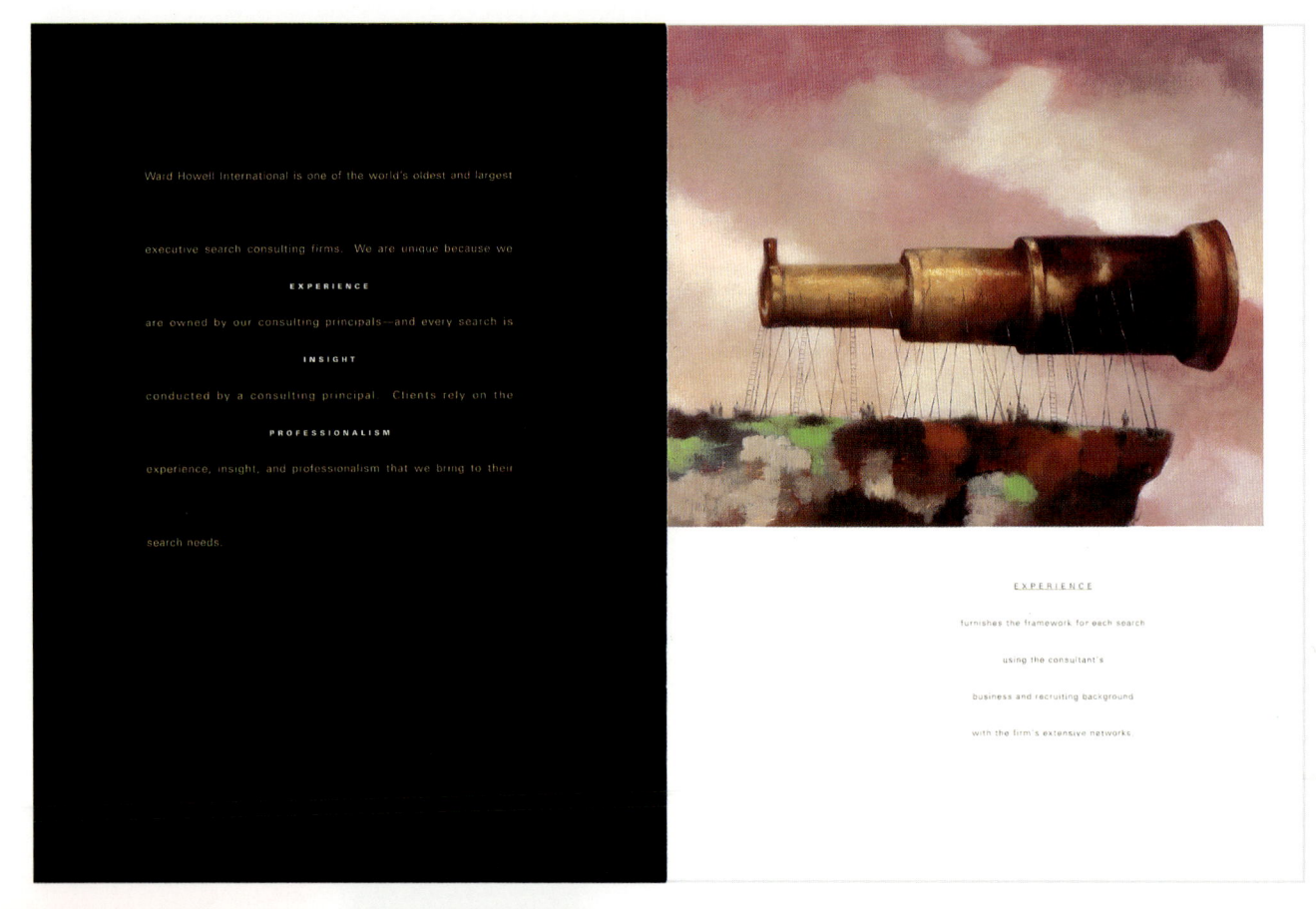

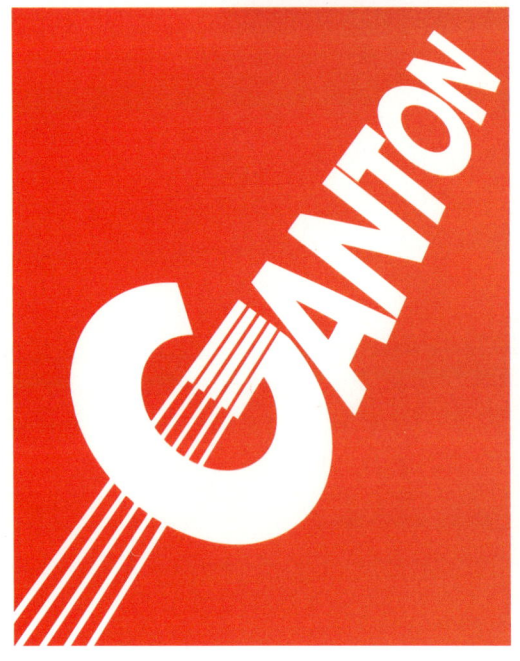

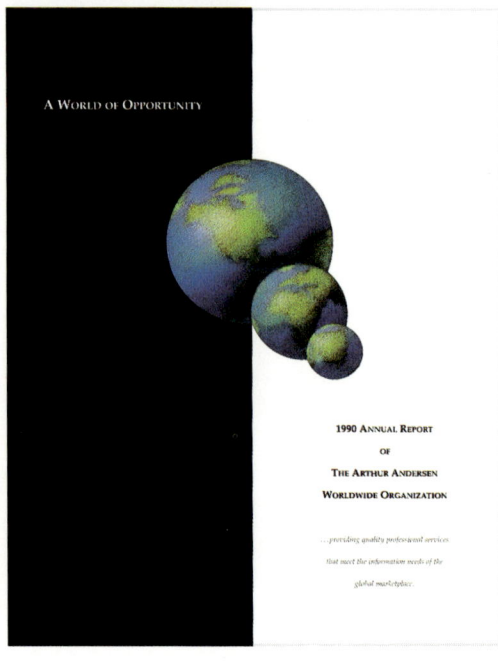

Identity for Midtown Center, an inner city educational program and foundation. *Top left*

Identity for ALIGN, a manufacturer and distributor of architectural precision tools. *Top right*

Cagney + McDowell, Inc.

Annual report for EHS Health Care. *Bottom*

REACH FOR EXCELLENCE

A L
I
G N

Joseph Smith

Joseph Smith was referred to Paul W. Crawford, M.D., a nephrologist on staff at South Chicago Community Hospital (SCCH), by Dr. Crawford's brother, who happened to be a colleague of Professor Smith's at Olive-Harvey College in Chicago. The 53-year-old math professor knew he needed medical attention, but he was worried he would have to give up his teaching career. In October 1988, Professor Smith was admitted to SCCH for treatment of a complex medical condition—a combination of hypertension, stomach ulcers, diabetes, and heart and kidney failure. Because of the care, he returned to his teaching responsibilities while undergoing kidney dialysis three times a week. With Dr. Crawford's guidance, Professor Smith and his wife, Emma, watch over his diet, medication and lifestyle so he can maintain a productive and rewarding life.

Corporate brochure for Sycamore Containers. Demonstrates capabilities in testing, design development and service. *Above*

Identity and awareness program for San Mateo Plaza. Introduces the first development in the state of California. *Left*

Siemens Historical Nuclear Medicine brochure. Celebrates 50 years of nuclear medicine technology and application. *Below*

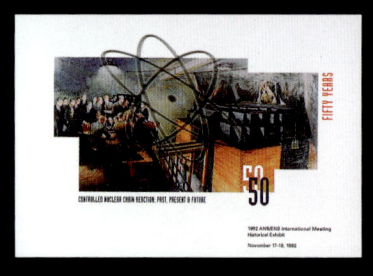

With a belief that being a designer and communicator means being driven by a passion to create and improve—one's self and everything one encounters—McMillan has built an organization of people who exemplify his philosophy.

McMillan Associates understands that designing and living are processes. Having the creative insight, knowledge, and experience to understand the rightness or appropriateness of each solution they create is earned through a consistent discipline and their passion for being the best.

Left to Right: Anne McMillan, Frank Marte, John Vieceli, Lisa Johnson, Michael McMillan, Julie Brown, Miki Racine, Colleen Dahlberg.

Corporate image brochure for Bruce Offset Company. Creates awareness; demonstrates film and printing capability. *Above*

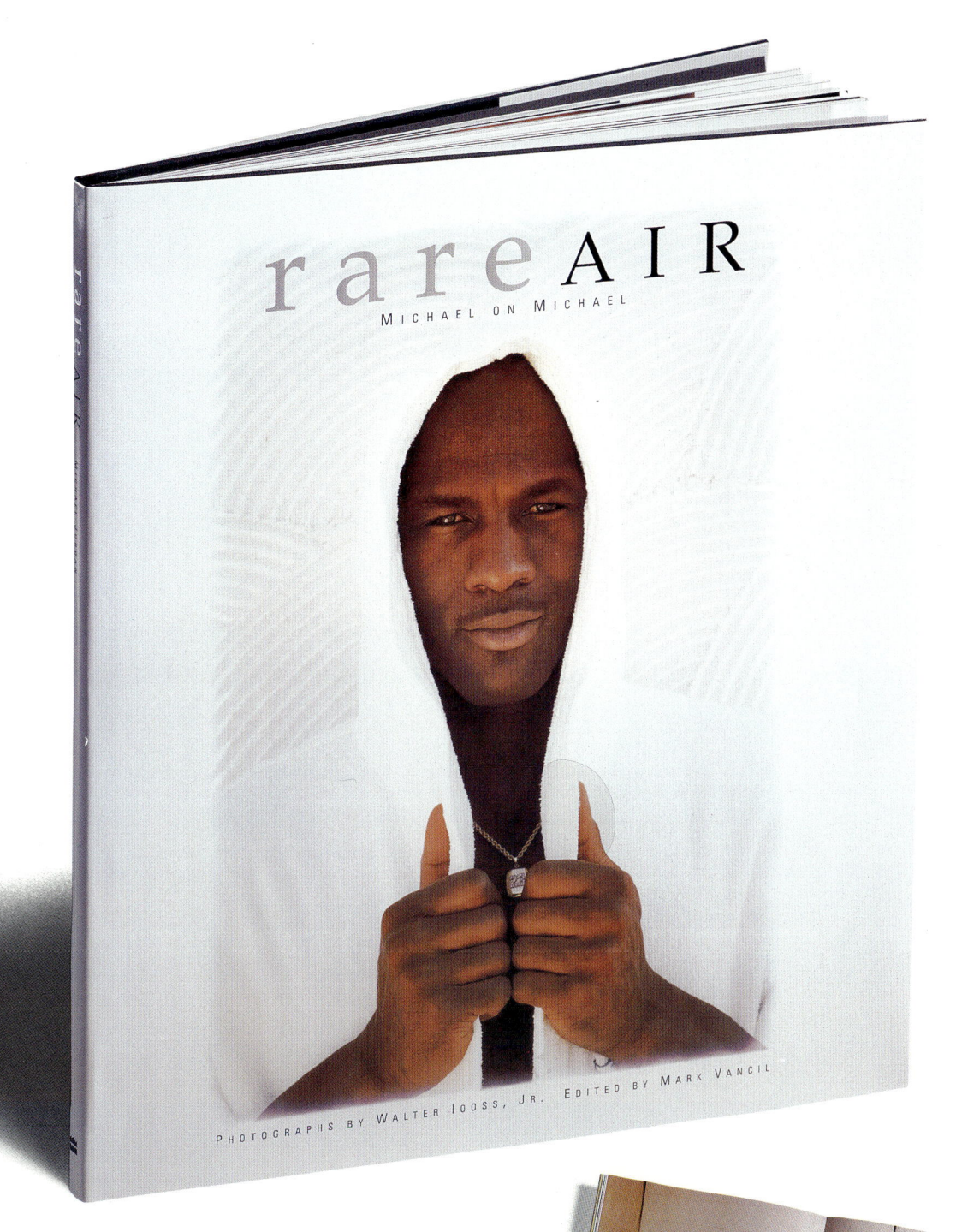

Pictorial autobiography for Michael Jordan. Coffee-table book gives a unique insight into the superstar's life on and off the court.

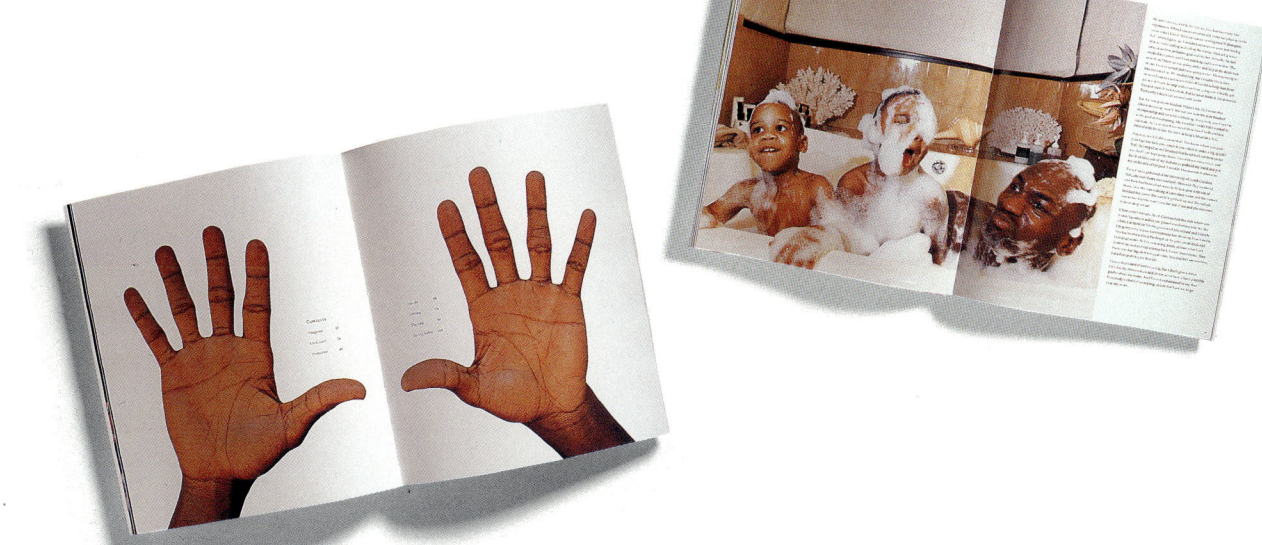

McMillan Associates

Annual Report for Tellabs, Inc. Communicates Tellabs' vision and the importance of investing for the future. *Above*

Global information brochure for A.C. Nielsen Company. Communicates to international markets the power of information. *Left*

Information kit for Micro Solutions, Inc. A multifaceted marketing tool including company history, product and service inserts. *Below*

McMillan Associates

155

Annual report paper promo for Hobart/McIntosh. Interactive package informs designers of inventory, services and paper selections. *Above*

Bilingual capabilities brochure for Tenneco Automotive. Communicates the products and services to both American and Asian markets.
Above

McMillan Associates

Benefits program written and produced by Hewitt Associates for the employees of Boehringer Mannheim. *Top*

Transaction announcement for Sears Tower. Updates brokers and clients on leasing, special events and building progress. *Center Left*

Identity program for Sears Tower. Reaffirms Sears' status as a world-renowned landmark. *Center Right*

Accordion-fold mailer for Sears Tower. Designed to inform audience of past, present and future development plans. *Left*

Michael Stanard, Inc. One Thousand Main Street
Evanston, Illinois 60202
Telephone 708.869.9820

Michael Stanard

Principals:
Michael Stanard,
President
Lisa M. Fingerhut,
Vice President / Design

Date Founded:
1978

Size of Firm:
12 Employees

Selected Clients:
Information Resources
Kraft General Foods
Protection Mutual Insurance
Swift Adhesives
Beatrice Cheese
Quintessence, Inc.
The Ertl Company
Mindscape, Inc
Vienna Sausage
Priester Aviation
Tombstone Pizza
Open Court Publishing
Matchbox Toys
The Alter Group
Kraft USA

Michael Stanard, Inc.

It is rare when an individual possesses the talent, acumen, and inclination to move with authority, from the cultivated and urbane towers of corporate design to the bareknuckle, blue-collar aisles of consumer packaging. Michael is a unique individual. He knows both stockrooms and boardrooms.

"When I came into the business, they told me that design was about solving problems. I've discovered that it's not about problems at all, it's about opportunities. Design is about seeing and creating opportunities, for clients and for ourselves. Thinking about design as an opportunity, as distinct from a problem, makes an enormous difference in the process as well as in the result."

Mr. Stanard has built an international reputation through his innovative and entrepreneurial thinking on behalf of his midwestern, national and multinational clientele.

"I'm impressed with people from Chicago. New York is talk, L.A. is hype... Chicago is work."

–Michael Douglas,
Actor / Director

Michael Stanard, Inc.

Packaging exhibiting a unique blend of strategic design and marketing savvy. All visual elements clearly communicate the product's reduced fat and reduced calorie message.

Client: Tombstone Pizza
Glenview, Illinois

Trademark for an old-line south side tool manufacturing company. The mark was redrawn and moderized without tampering with the character and equity of the original.

Client: SK Hand Tool Corp.
Chicago, Illinois

Brandmark, packaging graphics and photography for a line of snap-together model cars and airplanes. Each blister holds assembly instuctions and special collector card.

Client: The Ertl Company
Dyersville, Iowa

Packaging engineering, packaging graphics and a corporate identification program for this pharmaceutical research and manufacturing company.

Client: TheraTest Corporation
Chicago, Illinois

We made bold decisions with Reddi-Wip. We kept the old logo, but we enhanced it. We kept the distinct look and feel of the Reddi-Wip can, but we created a new image. We replaced tired old graphics with vivid new colors, photography and type. It didn't look different. It felt different.

Client: Beatrice Foods
Waukesha, Wisconsin

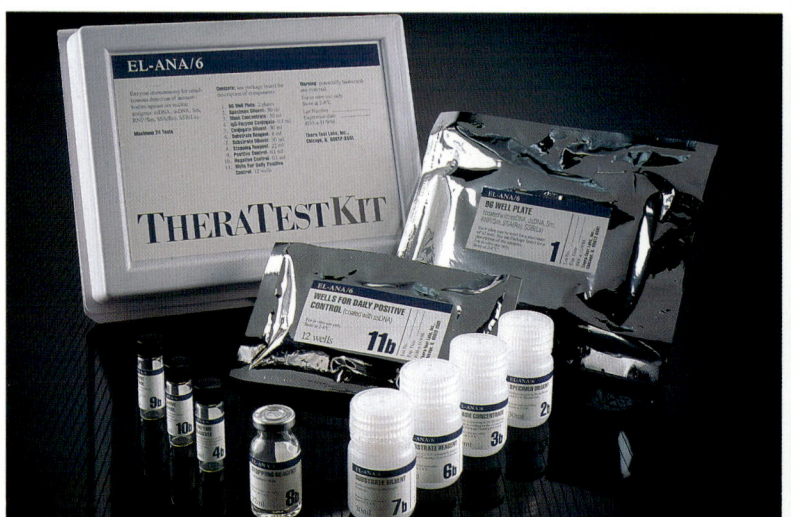

Kraft General Foods' first major publication on its environmental philosophy was a result of thoughtful collaboration with key staff members. The resulting publication communicates the dedication and commitment of the people of Kraft General Foods.

Client: Kraft General Foods
Glenview, Illinois

When Jovan introduced its famous Musk 20 years ago, it revolutionized the fragrance business. Twenty years later that revolution was celebrated with a package and merchandising program created by Michael Stanard, Inc. This compelling design recaptures the vision and excitement that changed the cosmetics industry forever.

Client: Quintessence, Inc.
Chicago, Illinois

Michael Stanard, Inc.

Corporate name development, trademark and identity system for Independent Retail Information Systems, a provider of sales data for retail opportunists.

Client: Iris Systems, Inc.
Hinsdale, Illinois

Name development, trademark, business papers, sales materials and retail packaging for manufacturer and distributor of pet care products.

Client: Pet Medic, Inc.
Chicago, Illinois

Trademark, business papers and promotional literature for the Couples Resource Center, a counseling service.

Client: Illinois Masonic Hospital
Chicago, Illinois

Trademark and business papers for importer and distributor of personal care products and fashion accessories.

Client: Paris Presents, Inc.
Wheeling, Illinois

One in a series of trademark parodies from American Trademark Parodies, a book featuring clever graphic interpretations and visual puns based on well-known corporate icons.

Client: Just Did It Enterprises
Evanston, Illinois

Name development, logotype, business papers and product applications, all based on this extraordinary visual interpretation of the word "earth," distinguishing the word "art" within.

Client: The Earth Art Institute
Evanston, Illinois

Our packaging graphics and unique structural designs capture the spirt of the Anasazi Indian philosophy. Sales materials and trade-show exhibitions work in harmony with a striking print advertising campaign.

Client: Anasazi, Inc.
Dubuque, Iowa

earth

Michael Stanard, Inc.

Open Court's special approach to mathematics education is captured and fully expressed throughout this handsome 16 page brochure.

Client: Open Court Publishing
Chicago, Illinois

Mama Tish, a one product company, necessarily relies heavily on packaging to favorably influence new customers. In Chicago, Mama Tish enjoys an almost cult-like following.

Client: Mama Tish
Chicago, Illinois

Print advertising and sales literature for Priester Charter delivers clients from among the most powerful and influential circles in Chicago and the midwest.

Client: Priester Aviation
Wheeling, Illinois

Brand name development, graphic design and packaging engineering services helped launch this line of exclusive salon products for men.

Client: American Crew, Inc.
Chicago, Illinois

In addition to print ads, employee communications and tradeshows exhibits, we have successfully completed thirteen consecutive annual reports, including this special Centennial Edition.

Client: Protection Mutual
Park Ridge, Illinois

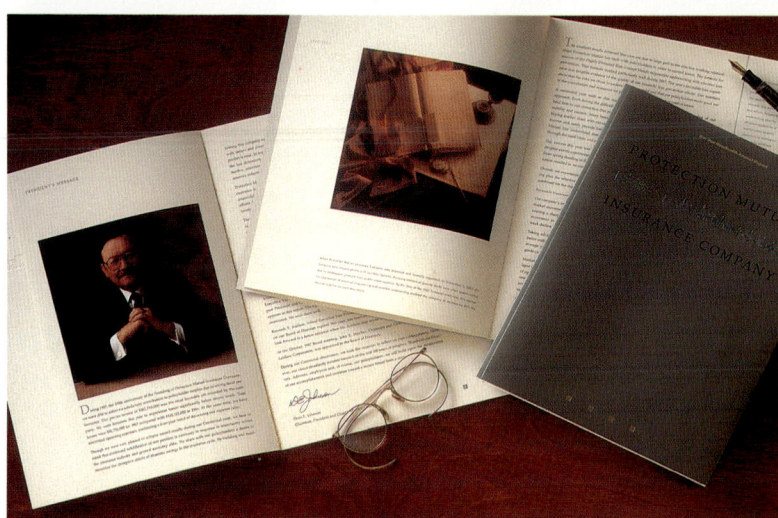

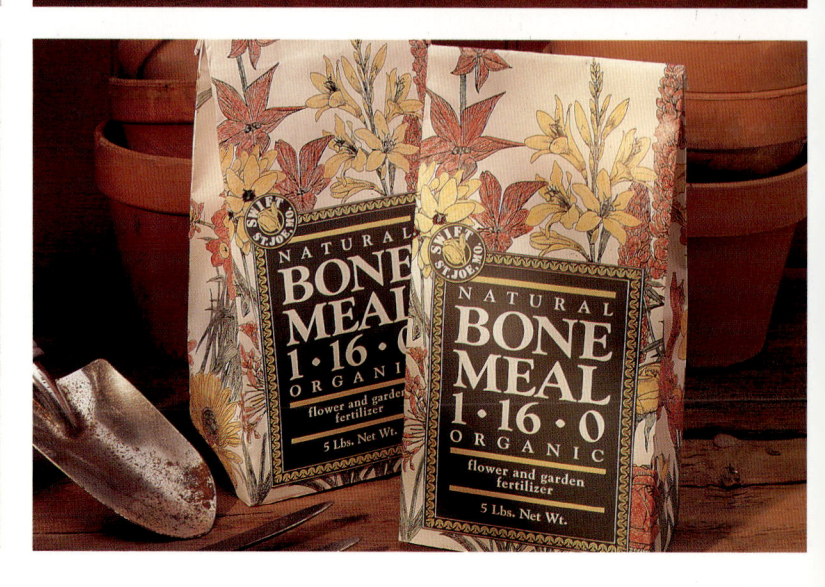

Packaging for Swift creates beautiful impressions for a sophisticated target audience. Effective use of graphic design helps create a compelling shelf presence supporting the premium position of a market leader.

Client: Swift Adhesives
Downers Grove, Illinois

Louisville Slugger has a name synonymous with baseball...it has an image money can't buy. When we designed today's Louisville Slugger trademark, we respected the history and character of the company. We are proud of our role in support and affirmation of this American classic.

Client: Hillerich & Bradsby
Louisville, Kentucky

166

Liska and Associates, Inc.

676 N. St. Clair
Suite 1550
Chicago, Illinois 60611
Telephone 312.943.4600

Principal:
Steven Liska

Date Founded:
1979

Size of Firm:
10 Employees

Liska and Associates, Inc.

Liska and Associates, Inc. has become well recognized for their intelligent design solutions that develop through an understanding of a client's business and its communication needs. The firm creates comprehensive identity programs, corporate and marketing communications literature, packaging and publication designs. Their clients are among a wide variety of industries including financial, retail, industrial and the applied arts.

Liska and Associates was founded fourteen years ago by Steve Liska who serves as the president and creative director. The firm's work, a collaboration of all employees, has been internationally acknowledged, widely published and has received virtually every major design award.

In an environment as diverse and exciting as Chicago, Liska and Associates has become an integral part of the city's graphic look. From the Hubbard Street Dance Company to the Chicago Mercantile Exchange, their work has made a significant impact on both cultural and business institutions.

VIEW
GALLERY
NEC
The Digital Video Advances of NEC.
Match your screen color to just about anything. With the AccuColor Control
system, MultiSync FG monitors let you match on-screen colors to closely approximate color reference systems. You can also match on-screen color to the hard copy color delivered by your color printer. Or by other monitors. Or simply adjust your display to the color you want to see. With this amazing advance in color accuracy, you can get the most out of 8-bit and 24-bit color capability.
Easy to use, too. The AccuColor Control System is also incredibly easy to use. You can hold a swatch of color from an output device or color reference guide up to the screen and use the digital control buttons to adjust the image and store your color settings in memory. Because it's done visually, you can match your screen color to virtually anything and your own eyes are the judge of accuracy.
The most detailed diagrams—even 3-D models
The AccuColor Control System is built-in on 4FG, 5FG and 6FG monitors and works independently from your video card and applications. With AccuColor, you can visually match your on-screen color to virtually anything.
The Mode Status LED turns on when the monitor is in AccuColor mode.
Red Decrease
CMYK
Fore
MultiSync 6FG
MATCH COLOR
Breakthrough display solutions for the Macintosh computer. Presenting the 15", 17" and 21" NEC MultiSync FG Display Solutions for the complete Macintosh® II family and the powerful new Macintosh Quadra™ series of computers. MultiSync FG monitors combine features that complement the Macintosh computer and advanced screen performance for brighter, sharper, more accurate images. The MacFG™ Color Display Interface card, engineered in conjunction with Radius,™ gives you flexible display capabilities seamlessly integrated with each of the MultiSync FG monitors. Together, the monitors and display interface create a total display solution that will meet virtually any application need.
Larger, more accurate images. Each monitor in the new FG line features a significantly larger active display area. The additional display area is a function of larger screen size, of edge-to-edge images provided by NEC's FullScan™ capability and of the custom display modes resident in the MacFG™ Color Display Interface card. That means you'll have larger images with no unused screen area between the image and the monitor bezel. And, each FG monitor's flat square screen surface is flatter both horizontally and vertically, which offers you a more consistent, accurate, edge-to-edge image.
Unprecedented color accuracy. The MultiSync FG line also introduces NEC's revolutionary AccuColor™ Control System, which allows you to adjust on-screen colors to meet your individual needs and preferences. At last, you can have WYSIWYG color accuracy without a lot of extra effort.
Advanced display performance for graphical applications. NEC MultiSync FG display solutions offer breakthrough display capabilities that take full advantage of the Macintosh computer's extraordinary graphic abilities.
To begin with, larger displays put more information on-screen, providing a larger desktop. And on NEC's flat square screen surfaces, images appear flat with less distortion at the edges. The high-contrast screen surface improves focus and displays colors more vibrantly. An advanced shadowmask made of heat resistant Invar alloy enables increased brightness with no loss of focus. And higher refresh rates produce flicker-free images, especially important for the white screen backgrounds found in many business applications.

Liska and Associates, Inc.

Through the development of strong client relationships, Liska and Associates gains an understanding of a company's true character, its business and its goals. This knowledge helps to create powerful design solutions which, among other objectives, work to further elevate each client's position within their industry.

MIRA
80# Miraweb

Mira
70# MIRAGLOSS

Liska and Associates, Inc.

Designing for the communications industry has given Liska and Associates an opportunity to collaborate with some of the country's best photographers, printers and paper manufacturers.

1991 Vehicle Selection Guide
Sponsor's Edge
the DIRECTORY
IEG DIRECTORY OF SPONSORSHIP MARKETING
CITY FESTIVAL
$175
IEG
FIFTH EDITION
NEW YORK

Liska and Associates, Inc.

The value of good design to any business is the competitive advantage that it offers the company. Liska and Associates' ability to understand the individual and unique needs of each client's business has enabled them to consistently develop effective design solutions for a diverse group of clients.

Nick Vancenti

Business As Usual

perception is not reality.
(and vice versa.)

in the community

where practice is a profession, however,

the day's events seem

often beyond control.

history occasionally eludes design's process

176   by Rick Valicenti, principal of thirst

An editorial on the state of modern graphic design

HeY!

phase I the call comes in

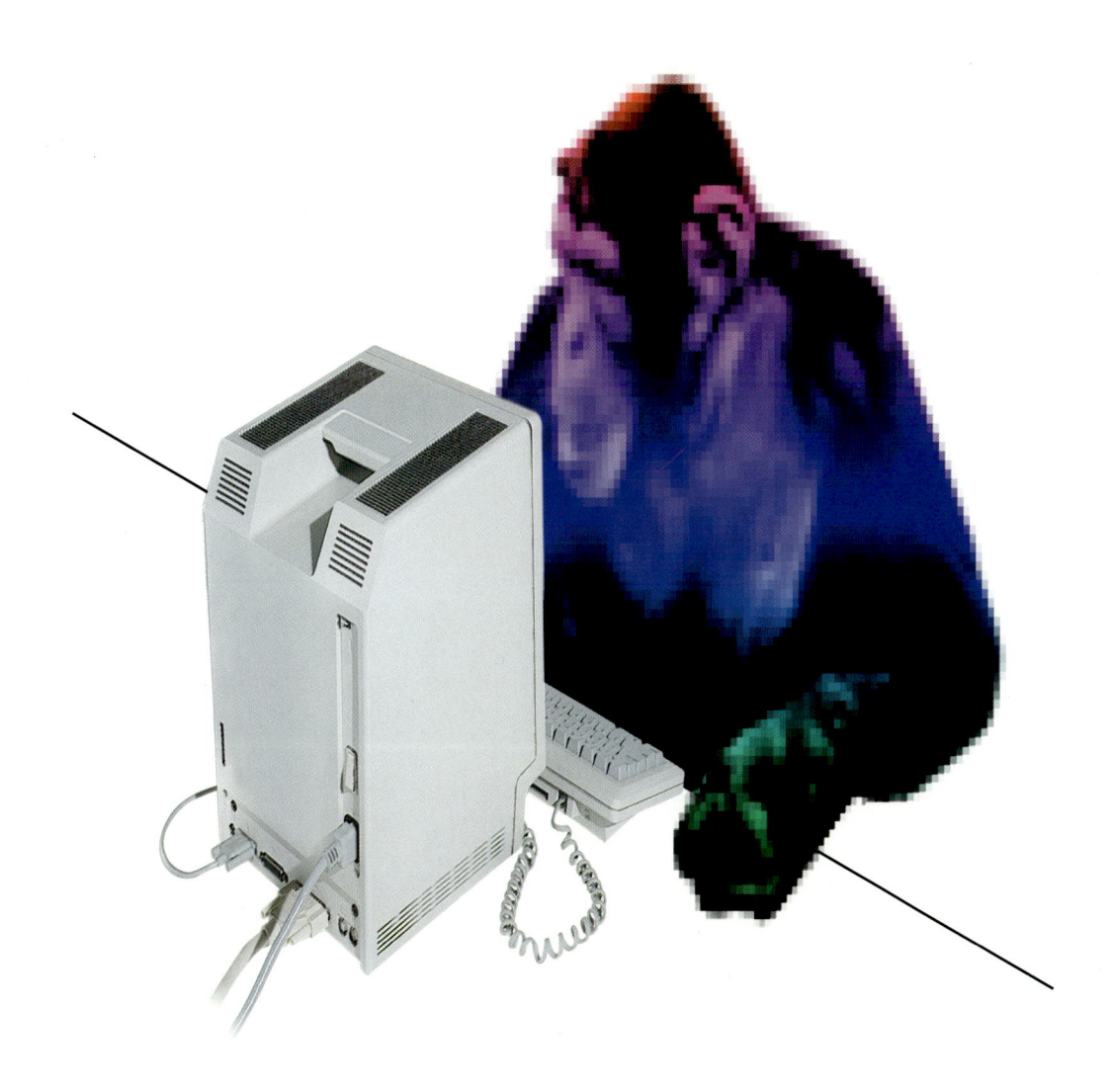

phase II the designer engages and the process begins

phase III the perception is manipulated and ready for transport

phase IV the presentation is delivered to an enlightened audience

photo Hedrich Blessing

Chicago, Illinois 60610
Telephone 312.337.4674
Fax 312.337.3687

Jackie Chan
Karen Goldschmidt
Jeffrey Heidekat
Mark Heitzman
Jerry Lenz
Joan Link
Mary Morvis
Wayne Webb

For our clients' management

It seems that every year our clients' business decisions depend on more complex and often more subtle issues. But decisions must be made faster and communicated to more people.

Designing ways for our clients to see sequential or conceptual pictures of complexity, and finding ways for clients to provide those pictures to their customers, employees or investors, is a category of important work.

Northern Illinois Gas, *Top* Wheelabrator Technologies,

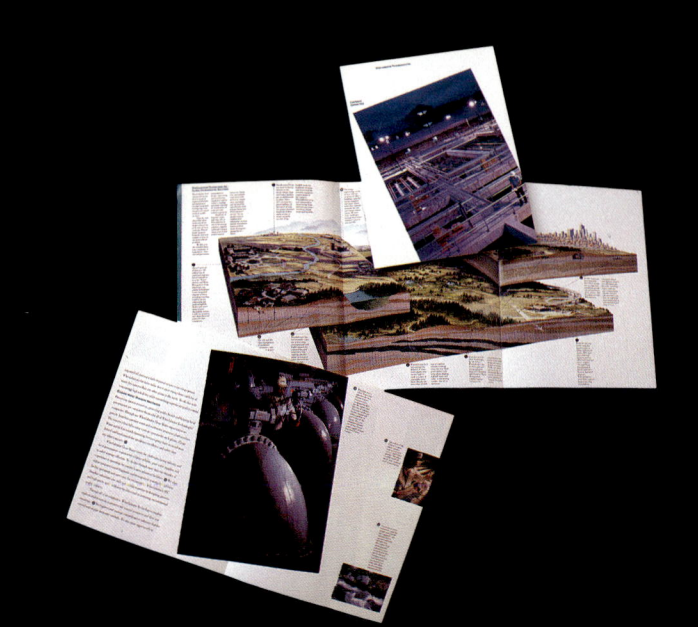

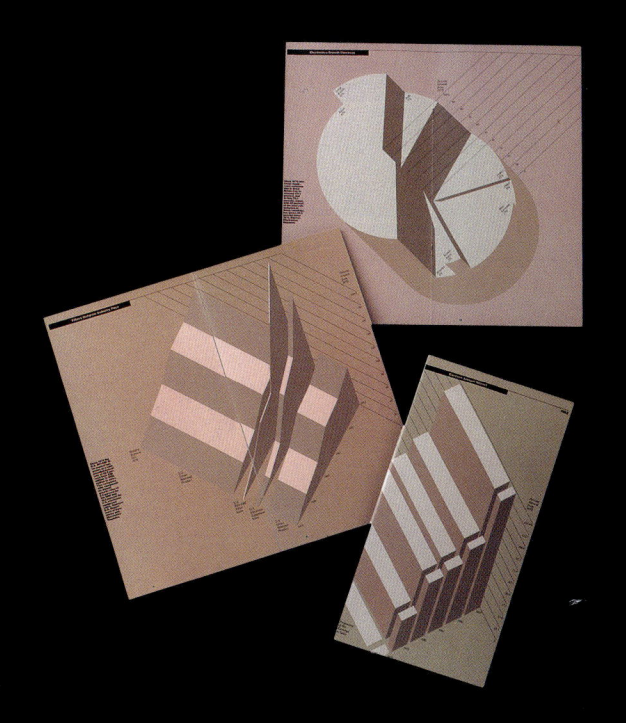

Meta-4 Incorporated

While planning for Meta-4 in 1989, it occurred to us that we often were surprised by the results of our work. Some projects that seemed really successful to us and our clients never made much difference to our clients' businesses. And other projects that seemed relatively unimportant became very useful. The scale or intensity of the projects often had little to do with their real value to our clients' businesses.

Doing work that is important to our client's business has become the focus of our efforts. Clearly the issues center around providing messages that the audience really cares about. This apparently routine goal actually requires worrying a lot more about the needs of the audience and considering a wider range of message strategies.

So, when our work has been important to our client's business, it's because our client encouraged the added work it took to prepare messages that the audience cared about. Thanks to our clients, we have made some headway.

For our clients' customers

In this "quality management" era of business, we think clients should create communications to help their customers rather than to brag about their products. Developing helpful communications is much more difficult, but the reward for getting it right just may be an entirely new, proprietary product—certainly important work.

Household Commercial, *Top*
Continental Bank, *Bottom*

Thrall Car, *Top*
MacNeal Hospital, *Bottom*

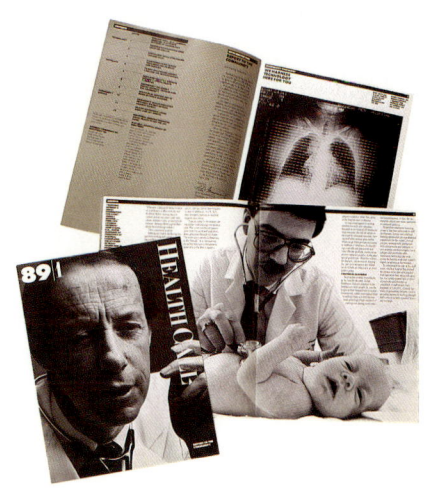

183

For our clients' shareholders
We think it is more difficult to set specific objectives for an annual report in these days of program-traded securities, more militant shareholders and employees anxious over restructuring and downsizing.

But all audiences will benefit from better anticipating the company's future. Using the annual report to shape future expectations in meaningful ways makes the report important work.

Sara Lee Corporation, *Top Left*
Waste Management, *Top Right*
Corcom, *Center Left*
CBI Industries, *Center Right*
Sara Lee Corporation, *Bottom*

Rockwell Graphic Systems,
Top Left
CBI Industries,
Top Right
Household International,
Center Left
Sara Lee Corporation,
Center Right
Rockwell Graphic Systems,
Bottom

185

For our clients' organizations

The identity goals for organizations are often confused with the identity goals for products.
The product marketing goal of instant and persistent public recognition is only a part of the identity story for organizations.

In fact, identity for an organization can be very powerful even if it is secret—although, being famous is usually even more powerful.

Designing identity to reinforce a new mission or demonstrate shared cultural values is important work.

Beatrice Company, *Top Left*
Labe & Company, *Top Right*
Household International, *Center Left*
Aetna, *Center Right*
Entertainment Marketing, *Bottom*

SPX, *Center*
Hamilton Investments,
American Hospital Supply,
Household Relocation,
United Charities,
Bottom, Left to Right

187

Tanagram, Inc.

855 West Blackhawk
Chicago, Illinois 60622
Telephone 312.787.6831

Principals:
Anthony Ma
Lance Rutter

ASPIRE
identity for high school program

the cool surface
movie title for a murder mystery

Barcelona
event identity for Stone Container Corp.

salsa
clothing store identity

symbol for 1st Chicago

group identity for the Kemper Executive Council

identity for an exhibit design firm

for an art exhibit

MG DESIGN

After viewing the work of Tanagram, Inc., one might guess that the firm finds Chicago to be a perfect home. Anthony Ma and Lance Rutter create a melting pot portfolio as diverse as each of their cultural origins. Originally from Honolulu, Ma was fortunate to have been raised in an environment of rich racial and cultural influences. Rutter spent most of his youth in a small Illinois farm town from which he draws a sense of value and respect for his visual surroundings. Their philosophies found common ground immediately, and their clients' varied problems and businesses have benefited ever since.

And while they attribute their fresh visual approach to keeping in tune with current culture and education (Anthony instructs part time at the School of the Art Institute of Chicago), neither has forgotten their common educational roots of good design methodology at the University of Illinois, Urbana-Champaign. Tanagram's goal is to reach rational conclusions in the most surprising ways, but they insist that they will never forsake grace and clarity for obligatory culture shock.

54th international conference identity and event poster for Stone Container Corporation, 1992. *Above*

Brochure highlighting reprints of Inland Steel Company's research and development. *Below*

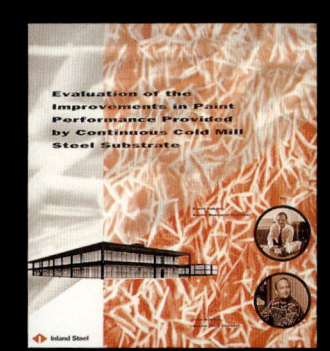

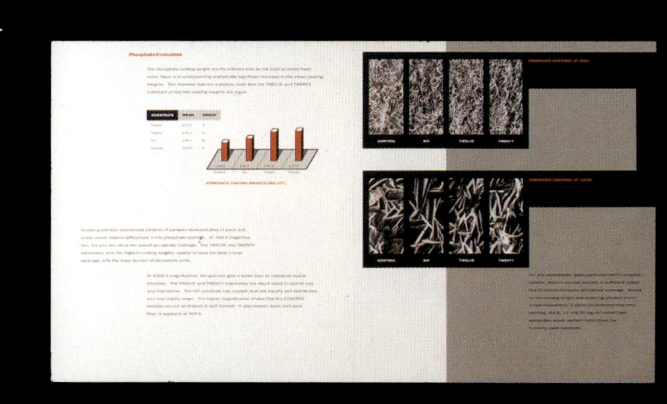

190

Manifesto for Visionary 1: The Deems Consultancy, a consultant to commercial film directors.

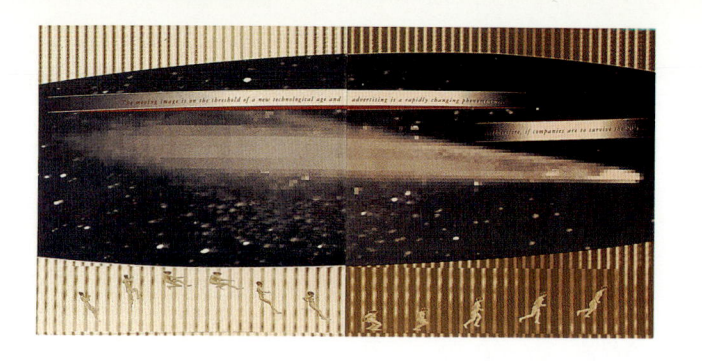

Recruitment package for the Kemper Executive Council, a select group of top producing bankers and broker/dealers selling Kemper products.
Opposite Page, Top

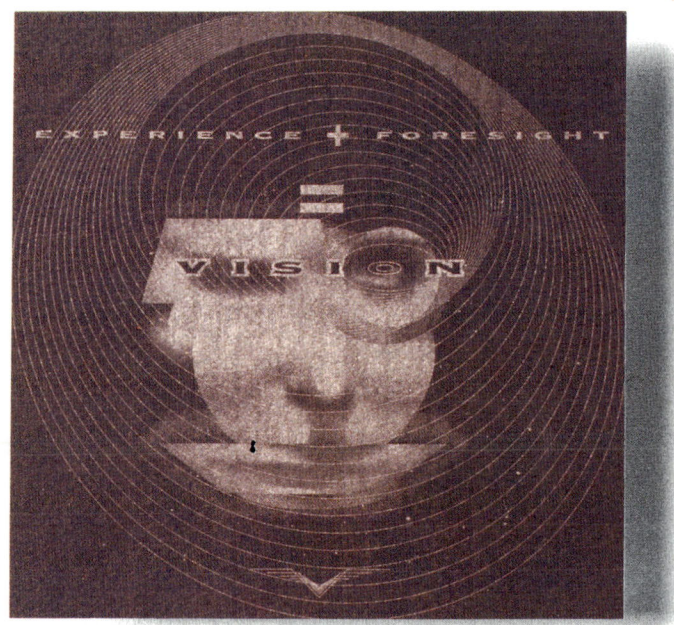

Tanagram, Inc.

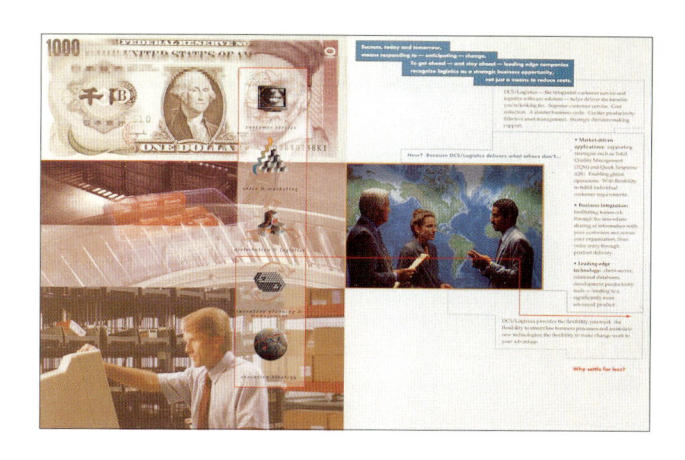

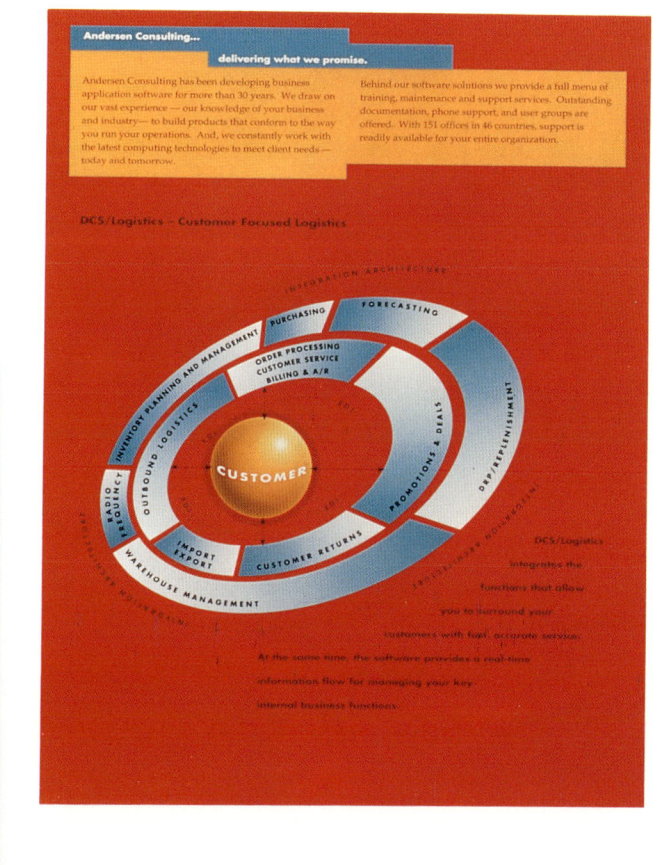

Capabilities brochure for logistics software package developed by Andersen Consulting.

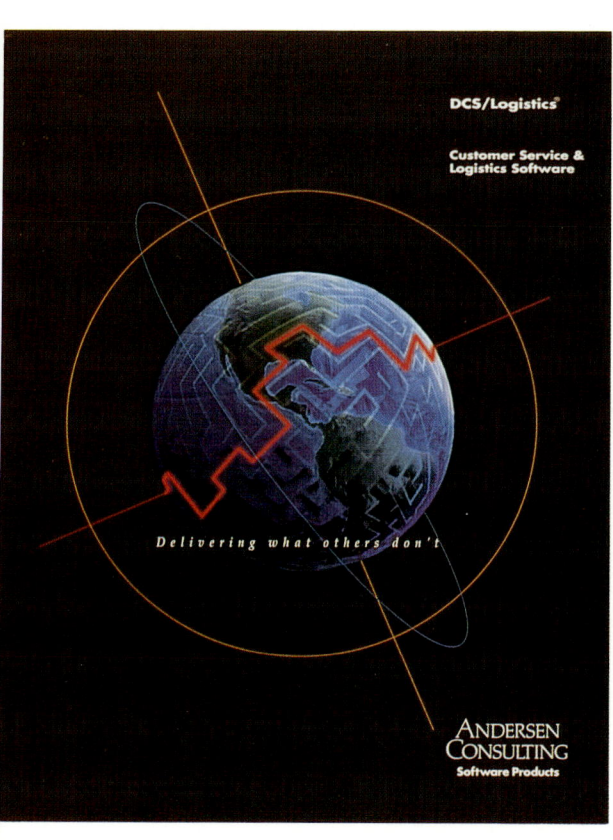

192 Tanagram, Inc.

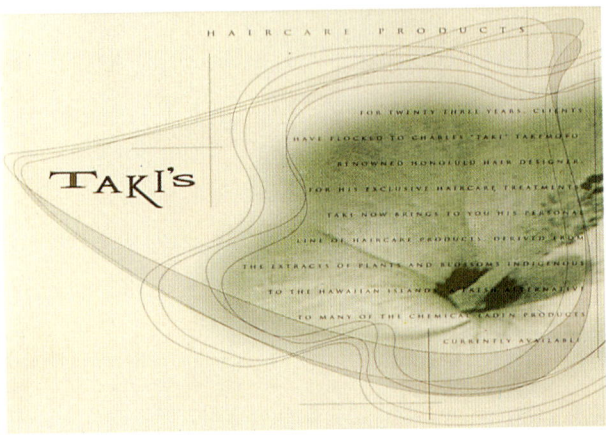

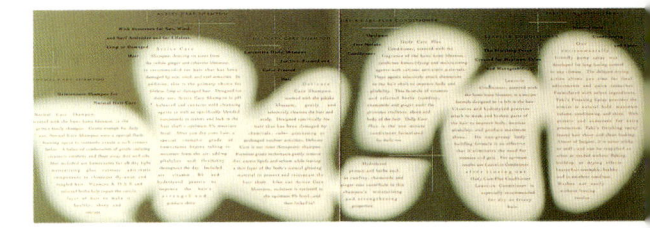

Corporate identity for Taki's of America, Inc., producers of Hawaiian hair care products.

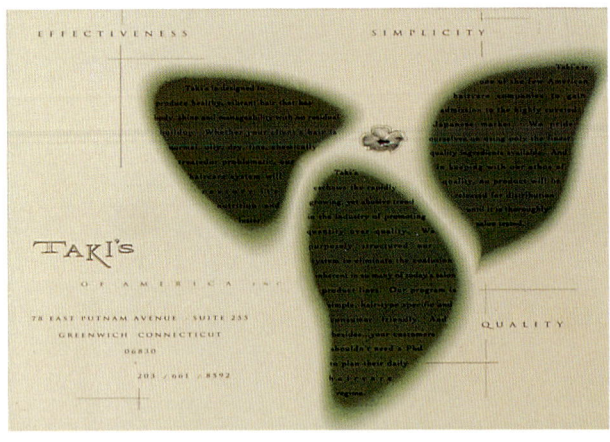

Package for "blah teau", a collection of designer napkins produced for the American Center for Design.

"My Kind of Town", the Chicago watch and packaging produced for the Chiasso stores.

194

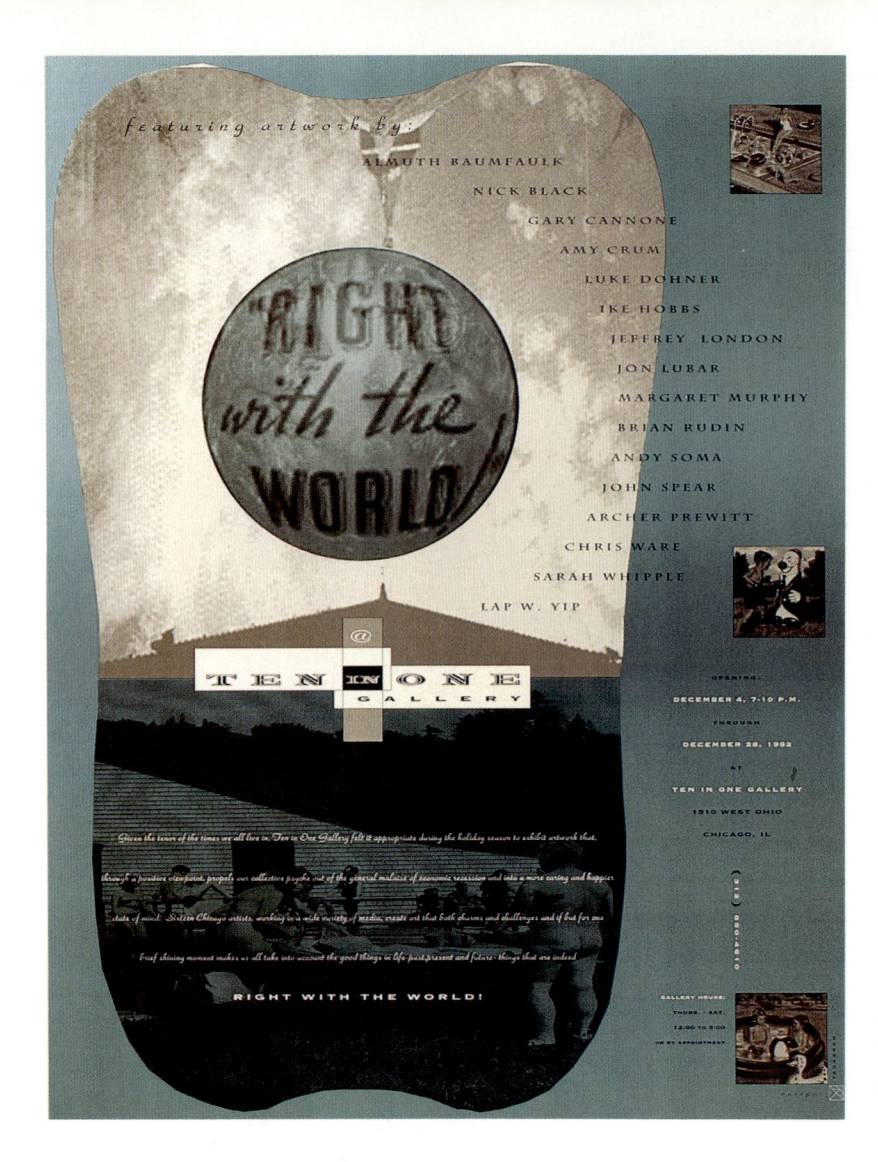

Poster announcing a show of various artists (generally associated with dark subject matter) promoting holiday cheer at the 10-n-1 Gallery.

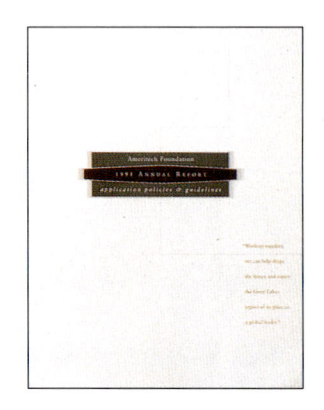

1991 Annual Report for the Ameritech Foundation, the philanthropic arm of Ameritech Corporation.

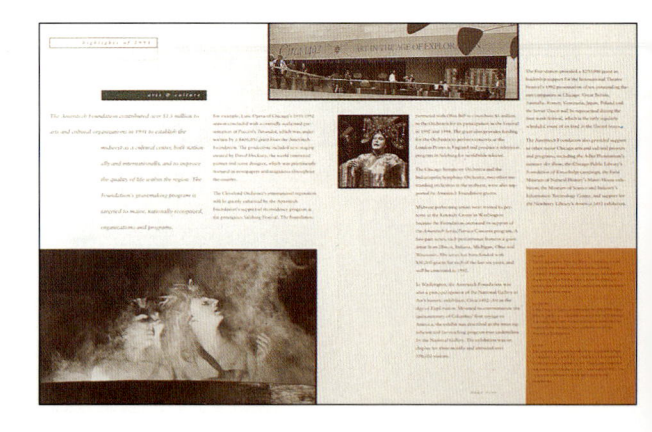

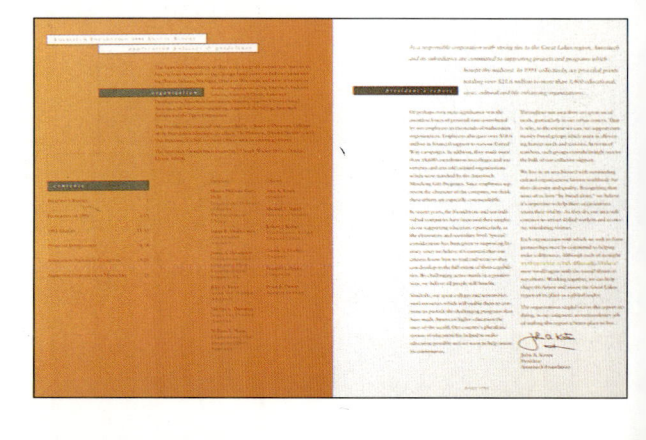

Tanagram, Inc.

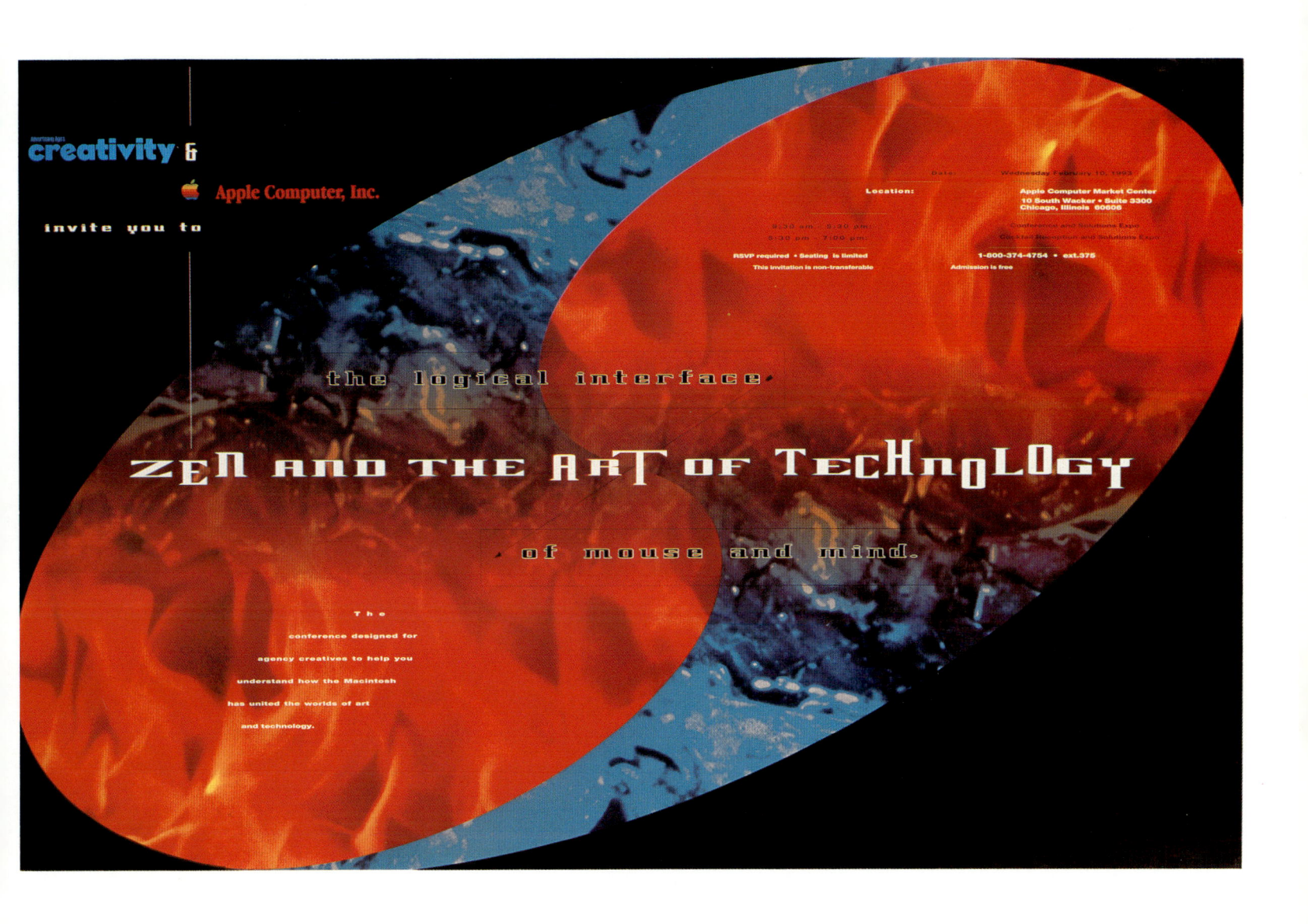

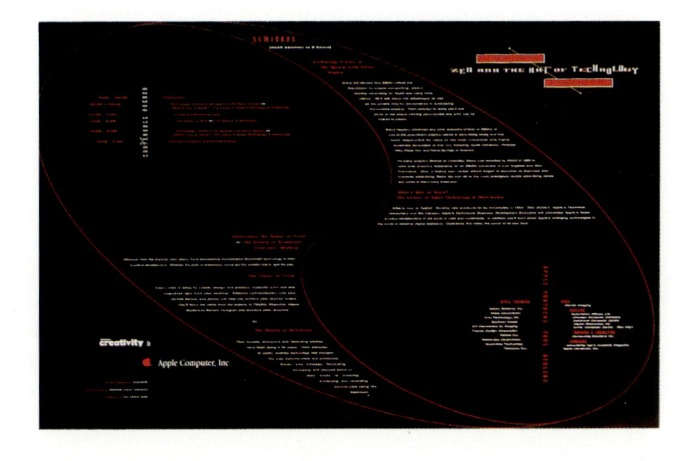

Conference theme
and poster/invitation for
Apple Computer, Inc.

Strandell Design   218 East Ontario
Third Floor
Chicago, Illinois 60611

Sometimes the process leads to self-expression. New product—new company. Great fun!

EYETHINK

Principal:
Don Strandell

Date Founded:
1976

Strandell Design

Strandell Design's distinctive style is derived from the philosophy that no two solutions are ever the same. Whether two or three dimensional, design should communicate clearly as well as dramatically.

Strandell designers believe that the process of fulfilling client needs always involves discovery and imagination in addition to skill. The result is work that is unexpected and effective.

For 17 years Strandell Design has worked with national and international clients in corporate identification, communications, packaging and exhibits. It's these varied, cross discipline projects that keep Strandell Design's solutions fresh and innovative.

CHICAGO HORTICULTURAL SOCIETY *Annual Report 1991*

MEMBERSHIP

Chicago Botanic Garden

Strandell Design

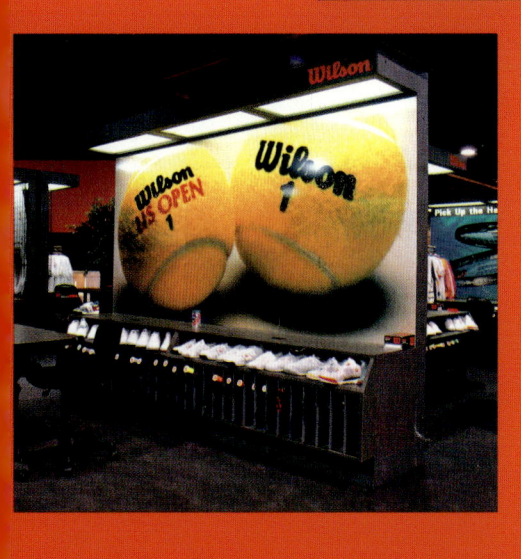

A communication program for one of the country's preeminent Botanic Gardens that reflects its quality and sensorial appeal. *Opposite Page*

A long standing relationship with an international sporting goods company nurtures innovative communication at all levels. *This Page*

Strandell Design

Many years of mutual support continue to allow for the development of materials that are as exciting as a child's imagination.
Opposite Page

In the totally digital "who has the most toys" world of film and video production, an identity that supports the one difference between the competition—it's people.
Below

MUSIC STUDENT WORKSHOPS

Squares and Circles
Three-Day Workshop
For Grades 4-8
VICKI MOSS uses dance and music to inspire a greater understanding of traditions in America's folk culture.
Day 1 – Dancing: students participate in dance and music activities that help them identify unique family traditions.
Day 2 – Talking: students discuss how dance is an example of a cultural tradition and learn dances that reflect these traditions.
Day 3 – Expanding: students learn a more complicated dance, building on previous lessons.
580
$650 for three days – 9 workshops

Squares and Circles
One-Day Workshop
For Grades K-8
VICKI MOSS teaches American folklore and traditions through dance and music. While listening to fiddle music, students learn clogging steps, the Appalachian Big Set dance, and the Virginia Reel.
327
$250 for one day – 3 workshops

STUDENT WORKSHOPS LIMITED TO 30 STUDENTS EXCEPT WHERE NOTED

202

Strandell Design

Light, shadow, color, shape and natural materials are among the tools used for the AIGA Communication Graphics traveling exhibit in Chicago. *Opposite Page*

An annual report should embody the mission of the institution. *Below*

Kym Abrams Design 213 West Institute Place
Suite 608
Chicago, Illinois 60610

Doctronics, a repair service owned by Montgomery Ward and Mobil, provides first aid for electronic appliances.
Client:
Montgomery Ward
Mobil Corp.
Art Director/Designer:
Kym Abrams

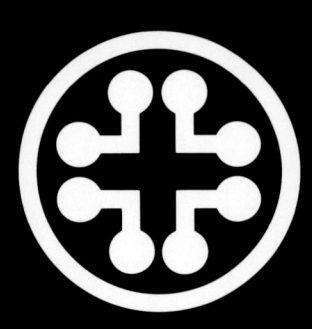

A writer's identity.
Need we say more?
Client:
Ink, inc.
Art Director:
Kym Abrams
Designer:
Kym Abrams

The logo created for IDA Advisors, specialists in market-neutral investment, conveys the ability to profit whether the market is bull or bear.
Client:
IDA Advisors
Art Director/Designer:
Kym Abrams

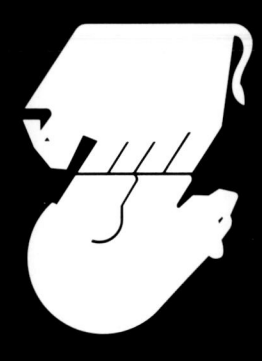

The logo for Chicago's public radio station shows exactly where to find it.
Client:
WBEZ 91.5 FM
Art Director/Designer:
Kym Abrams

Principal:
Kym Abrams

Date Founded:
1983

Size of Firm:
8 Employees

Kym Abrams Design

For Kym Abrams, the purpose of design is to communicate clearly. She starts with a thorough understanding of her client's business, then oversees all creative work to ensure that it supports her client's objectives. In her office, words are as important as pictures; copy and design are integrated to communicate strong concepts. Kym develops long-term relationships with clients, collaborating on projects ranging from stationery systems to marketing communications programs. Her understanding of the business as well as the art of design is reflected in the steady growth of her own client base, exclusively through referrals and word-of-mouth. Kym Abrams Design has won more than 50 national and international design awards.

BE A DESIGN MANAGER

YOU CAN HAVE AN EXCITING, WELL-PAYING DESIGN PRACTICE IN LESS THAN 6 MONTHS!

Train at home in your spare time...
No prior experience necessary

Corporations, not-for-profit institutions, retail, and consumer businesses are buying graphic design from salespeople with proven abilities right now. We guide you step-by-step with proven home study methods. Nationally Accredited Program. Diploma and pin included. Write or call for FREE information NOW (123-456-7890).

ATTENTION DESIGNERS

Don't go broke with Baroque selling techniques. Get the latest and greatest graphic selling tips. You'll never fail, you'll learn to curtail an ineffectual flail of a lackadaisical sale. A tale of mastery, mastered by you. Rhyme design with business sublime.

Get in the pink without a shrink. Turn that "SOLD" into GOLD. Lose your perplexion; improve your complexion! Order now.

SALES TIPS WITHOUT WHIPS
BY MUHAMMED ALI AKBA SALES

Do You Desire A HAPPY OFFICE

Unite the members of your staff more closely; establish common goals. Help overcome faults of character and develop dormant talents. Use the simple teaching of an age-old philosophy. Write for FREE sealed book of details (Not a religion). Address: Mr. Wizard, Toonville, Hollywood, CA.

Bring in bigger pay

HOME-STUDY™

Don't be caught napping when Opportunity knocks. Prepare for advancement and more money by training NOW for sales activities ahead. *Planning Your Sales Strategy* gives you fail-safe tips for... selecting sales strategies... forecasting sales...allocating resources...developing self promotions...working with real salespeople...and much more! Register NOW for this exciting Design Management Seminars program, February 3, 1990 at The Graham Foundation.

Write or call:
American Center for Design
233 E. Ontario, Suite 500
Chicago, IL 60611

CALL TOLL FREE
312/787-2018

Learn How to SELL!

Develop your personal selling power! NOW ...revealed for you...the secrets of **successful** *salesmanship*...that strange compelling force by which you can bring clients under your power. Learn to sway customers at will... virtually cast a spell over prospects. This sensational knowledge is not available anywhere else. Amazing lessons in simple, easy-to-learn language. How to make money selling design...how to sell on the telephone... how to use **MODERN** selling techniques...how to open and close a call...how to win a job. Clear, helpful visuals show best positions and movements. Attend *Fundamental of Sales: A Training Program*, March 24, 1990, at The Graham Foundation. For more information, or to register, call 312/787-2018.

DESIGNERS!

DO YOU WANT TO ATTRACT MORE CLIENTS?

Mystery Training Seems to Drive Clients Wild!

Designers! All ages. Even if you are considered "unattractive" or a poor salesperson to clients, you could be the most popular designer in town. New DESIGN MANAGEMENT SEMINARS 1990 teach you magical powers that naturally attract clients of all ages. These mystifying techniques seem to arouse clients' innermost desires and drive them WILD. This could change your life completely!

Get a new lease on your professional life. Sign up for the DESIGN MANAGEMENT SEMINARS 1990 today!

Write or call for details:
American Center for Design
233 East Ontario, Suite 500
Chicago, IL 60611

"I WAS A POOR DESIGN SALESPERSON"

I know the misery from the curse of poor design salesmanship; the agony to loved ones; the loss of happiness, money, health, career...BUT I know how to break the spell of failed sales. Get the answer. **Write: Designer's Genie**
P. O. Box 456, Kodiak, Alaska

CREATIVE IDEAS IN A CAN!

WIZARD

Design Solutions

GET A 12 OZ. CAN OF WIZARD FOR ONLY $1.99 AND SATISFY ALL YOUR CREATIVE NEEDS. COMES IN FIVE FLAVORS: BROCHURES, NEWSLETTERS, IDENTITIES, POSTERS, AND POP-UP SIGNAGE.
SOLD AT GROCERY AND HARDWARE STORES.
WHILE SUPPLIES LAST.

Corporate Logos Direct to You

$9.95 and up
Easy Terms

Genuine, Beautiful, CORPORATE LOGOS. They've worked before; they'll work again. For a FREE catalog, write to:

LOGO-A-GOGO
P.O. BOX USED, REPEAT, CA

Read This Ad Only If You Want MONEY, LOTS OF MONEY!

So Many People Have So Much Money It's Your Turn Now... GUARANTEED

Just hire this miracle design salesperson, that's all you have to do. Your luck will change overnite to bring you **MONEY, LOTS OF MONEY.**

SIT BACK AND WATCH YOUR MONEY COME IN!

HOW WILL YOU SPEND YOUR NEW FOUND MONEY?

- **A brand new house**
- **A long vacation**
- **A new car, maybe 2**
- **A CD player and color TV**

ANY WAY YOU WANT!

We all know how important a good salesperson is. We all need it...we must have it...without it a career can be no fun at all, sometimes downright miserable.

THE MIRACLE DESIGN SALESPERSON WILL WORK FOR YOU AND BRING YOU MONEY, LOTS OF MONEY!

The Miracle Design Salesperson is not an ordinary design salesperson. This born sales leader can convert even the most skeptical, the most ornery, prospects into tame, paying customers. Every call turns into gold, every client into a saint.

You'll change your life with the Miracle Design Salesperson. Just send $1,000,000 plus handling to: We Got You Sucker, P.O. Box 666, Chicago, IL. and get MONEY, LOTS OF MONEY!

Don't Look Now—He's Actually Smiling!

• Where's that deep frown and curt growl you've grown accustomed to? Gone! Yes sir, now even your most difficult prospect won't be able to resist the charms of your sales pitch with NEW Design-A-Way.

Design-A-Way is the safe, effective method guaranteed to produce design solutions that clients just can't resist!

How Does This AMAZING Product Work?

Years and years of rigorous scientific research led to this amazing discovery. Stated simply, **Design-A-Way** takes any communications problem and resolves it to reflect the clients own taste. That's right—no matter how visually illiterate your client may be, **Design-A-Way** will give him exactly what he is looking for, *or your money back!*

Does Mr. Calhoun live for plaids? **Design-A-Way** will help astonish him with the first recorded plaid brochure in history. Does Mrs. Excessive insist upon using 15 different typefaces all on one page? Don't worry—with **Design-A-Way** you'll find a way!

Unsolicited Testimonial

"...Ever since I started using **Design-A-Way**, there isn't a client I can't sell. My designs come out right first time—every time. Even the Japanese are jealous! It's made me the success I'd never dreamed I'd become."
Romeo T., NY, NY

Designers across the nation are buying up shelves of this incredible product. Don't be the last designer on your block to suffer the grumpy barks of a dissatisfied client. Get **Design-A-Way** in your neighborhood store today!

Guaranteed to work every time or your money back.
Batteries not included.

Be Your Own Boss

I WILL SHOW YOU HOW TO START A DESIGN BUSINESS WITHOUT CAPITAL

FULL OR SPARE TIME

J. Q. Smith, President
National Design Institute
Our 13th Year of Training Men For Success in Graphic Design

Let me show you facts about rich opportunities in Communications Design. See how knowing Design can give you security, a prosperous future, and let you name your own hours as your own boss in your own Communications Design business. Send the coupon for a FREE 64-page book, "Win Rich Rewards in Design." Read how you practice thumbnails, layouts, computer designs, and production with SIX BIG KITS OF PARTS I send you.

Future for Trained Men Is Bright in Design, Layout, Production

The Communications Design business is booming NOW. In your own spare time or full time Design business you'll make good money fixing designs, plus a good profit on production, and put yourself in line for more profits selling new designs of your own creation.

Trained Designers also find wide-open opportunities in Sign Painting, Grocery Store Packaging, Window Displays, etc. And greater opportunities are coming when space travel is available to the public. Send for the FREE book now!

Many Beginners Soon Make $5, $10 a Week EXTRA in Spare Time

The day you enroll I start sending EXTRA MONEY JOB SHEETS to help you make EXTRA money on production in spare time while your learning. You LEARN Design principles from my easy-to-grasp lessons—PRACTICE what you learn by designing real communications projects with the pieces I send you—USE your knowledge to make extra money in your spare time.

Find Out What N.D.I. Can Do For YOU

Mail Coupon for FREE 64-page book. It's packed with facts about opportunities for you. Read the details about my Course. Read letters from men I trained telling what they are doing and earning. Just MAIL COUPON in an envelope. **J. Q. Smith, President, National Design Institute, Generic Design Home Study School, Washington, DC**

You create this 16-page ANNUAL REPORT that gives you valuable experience. Provides photography and copy for experimental purposes.

LEARN GRAPHIC DESIGN BY PRACTICING IN SPARE TIME

with 6 Big Kits of Graphic Design Parts I Send You

I TRAINED THESE MEN

$250 A MONTH IN OWN SHOP
"I am now operating a Graphic Design shop for myself and own all my equipment. Right now I only do mailers for local stores, because there are no big companies in my town, but I average $250 a month."—J. M. SCRIVENER, Aberdeen, Missouri

FIXING DESIGNS PROFITABLE HOBBY
"I am doing Communications Design work in my spare time, and find it a profitable hobby. My extra earnings run about $10 a week. I certainly am glad I took your N.D.I. Course."—FERDINAND ZIRABEL, Chaseley, North Dakota

$50 A WEEK FROM MY OWN SHOP
"Am making over $50 a week profit from my own shop. Have another N.D.I. graduate working for me. I like to hire N.D.I. men because they know Design."—NORBERT MILLNER, Hebron, Nebraska

$50 A MONTH IN SPARE TIME
"I have a spare time Design and Production business of my own which has been profitable due to the efficient training I received from your last Course. Last year I averaged over $50 a month."—FRED H. GRIFFIE, Route 3, Newville, PA

64 PAGE BOOK FREE

J. Q. SMITH, President
Dept. 6C,
National Design Institute,
Washington, D.C. 30303
Mail me FREE, without obligation, your 64-page book about how to win success in Graphic Design.

Name
Address
City State
(Please include Post Office Zip Code)

DESIGNERS!

Take prompt steps to protect your creative ideas. Delays are dangerous. Get a new FREE book, "Protect and Sell Your Mediocre Ideas." Preliminary information free. Conscientious counseling. Learn to protect and sell your ideas. Write us today.

SODOM AND GOMORRAH
Registered Patent Attorneys
135-N Palestine Rd., NY, NY

We were IN A FOG

until we attended THE DESIGNER/CLIENT RELATIONSHIP

NO DESIGN MANAGER SHOULD MISS IT!

To most design managers, sales calls and efforts put them into a fog. This seminar removes that fog by revealing the essence of the designer/client relationship in straightforward, easy-to-understand language. Helpful advice and simple facts. Real clients will voice their views and respond to your questions. New and experienced design managers alike will benefit from this singular exchange.

DON'T MISS
THE DESIGNER/CLIENT RELATIONSHIP,
MAY 5, 1990,
AT THE GRAHAM FOUNDATION IN CHICAGO.
CALL 312/787-2018
FOR MORE INFORMATION.
ASK FOR "HELP."

Everyone CAN and SHOULD Have All the MONEY THEY WANT
That's our credo.
If it is yours,
write for
FREE information

Me Too
15 Self-Made Blvd.
Tampa, Fl

DRAW for MONEY!

Be A DESIGNER!

Trained Designers Are Capable of Earning $100, $1,000, $10,000 A Week!

Use Your Spare Time To Prepare For A Profitable Career

It's pleasant and interesting to study graphic design the DBN way. Graphic design...layouts... production...all in one *complete* home study course. No previous art experience necessary. We teach you step-by-step. Hundreds have profited by our practical method. FREE BOOK: *Graphic Design for Pleasure or Profit?* tells all. Write to Design By Numbers, 225 This Way, Chicago, IL.

Now...

The Continuing Saga of Justine and Carlos in the New Best Seller

The Client Who Wanted To,
The Designer Who Would

Damien Steele outdoes himself in this dire romance of a client who finds the perfect designer...the designer who understands, without words... the designer who shows uncompromising sensitivity...the designer who who stands up for the rights of all good communications. Don't miss this outstanding tale of success, glory, and romance.

Available at bookstores everywhere.

When PRAYER FAILS...

The prayers of the most talented designers often fail, while the unworthy often have the greatest health, success, riches, and happiness. The best, smartest, and most creative people often have only pain, poverty, and sorrow. Why? Three years ago, a young, saintly communications designer travelled to Tibet and found the answer. Poor then, he acquired wealth and worldwide professional acclaim. Now he wants to share his word with you. It is SALES. Take a first step to Power and Knowledge by ordering his 9,000 word treatise on this revolutionary science. There is no obligation. Write for YOUR FREE COPY of "Angel in My Pocketbook" today.

INSTITUTE for
PSYCHOKINETIC SELLING
373 Crystal Rock, Sedona, AZ

DO YOU WORRY?

ABOUT WHERE THE NEXT PAYCHECK WILL COME FROM?

Why worry and suffer any longer if we can help you? Try an American Center for Design patented Design Management Seminar. This marvelous series is GUARANTEED to bring you heavenly comfort and security—day and night—at work and play—by teaching you how to sell and gain more business! Three programs to choose from. Invaluable information. Thousands happy. Not sold in stores. Beware of imitations.

Write for your FREE brochure:
American Center for Design
233 E. Ontario, Suite 500
Chicago, IL 60611

USED Correspondence Courses

Complete HOME STUDY courses and self-instruction books on becoming a design sales wizard. Slightly used. Rented. Sold. Exchanged. Satisfaction guaranteed. Full details and 53-page illustrated bargain catalog FREE. Write now.

ABUSED BOOKS
1111 S. 4th Ave., Chicago, IL.

Kym Abrams Design

American Girl magazine, for 7-to-11-year-olds, was redesigned to give each department a distinctive look, with clear beginnings and endings to stories, and pacing that's a lot more fun.

Client:
Pleasant Company
Art Director:
Kym Abrams
Editors:
Nancy Holyoke
Michelle Watkins

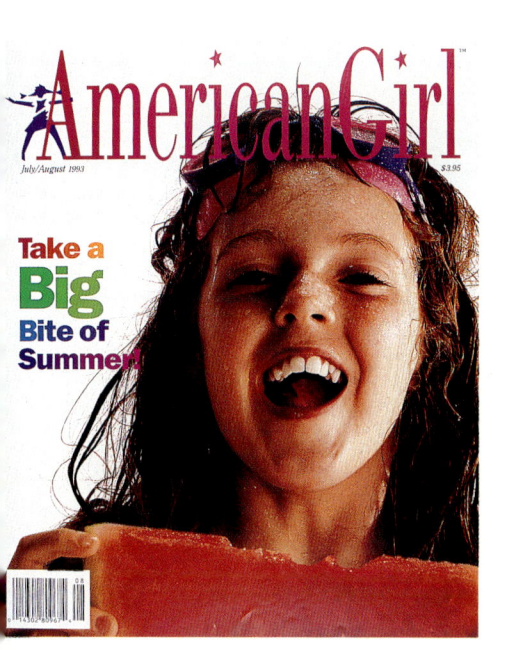

207

The cover for a mailer on a "Selling Design" conference drew an unprecedented response from members of the American Center for Design.
Client:
American Center for Design
Art Director:
Kym Abrams
Designer:
Mike Stees
Copywriter:
Lisa Brenner

For maximum "kid appeal," ScottForesman wanted the titles in its "Celebrate Reading" series to look like bookstore books, not textbooks. The brand identity and format unifies 48 reading books, plus marketing materials and a variety of ancillary products, including "Design Your Own Animal" shuffle cards.
Opposite Page, Bottom
Client:
ScottForesman
Creative Director:
Anne Lepley
Art Director:
Kym Abrams
Designer:
Mike Stees

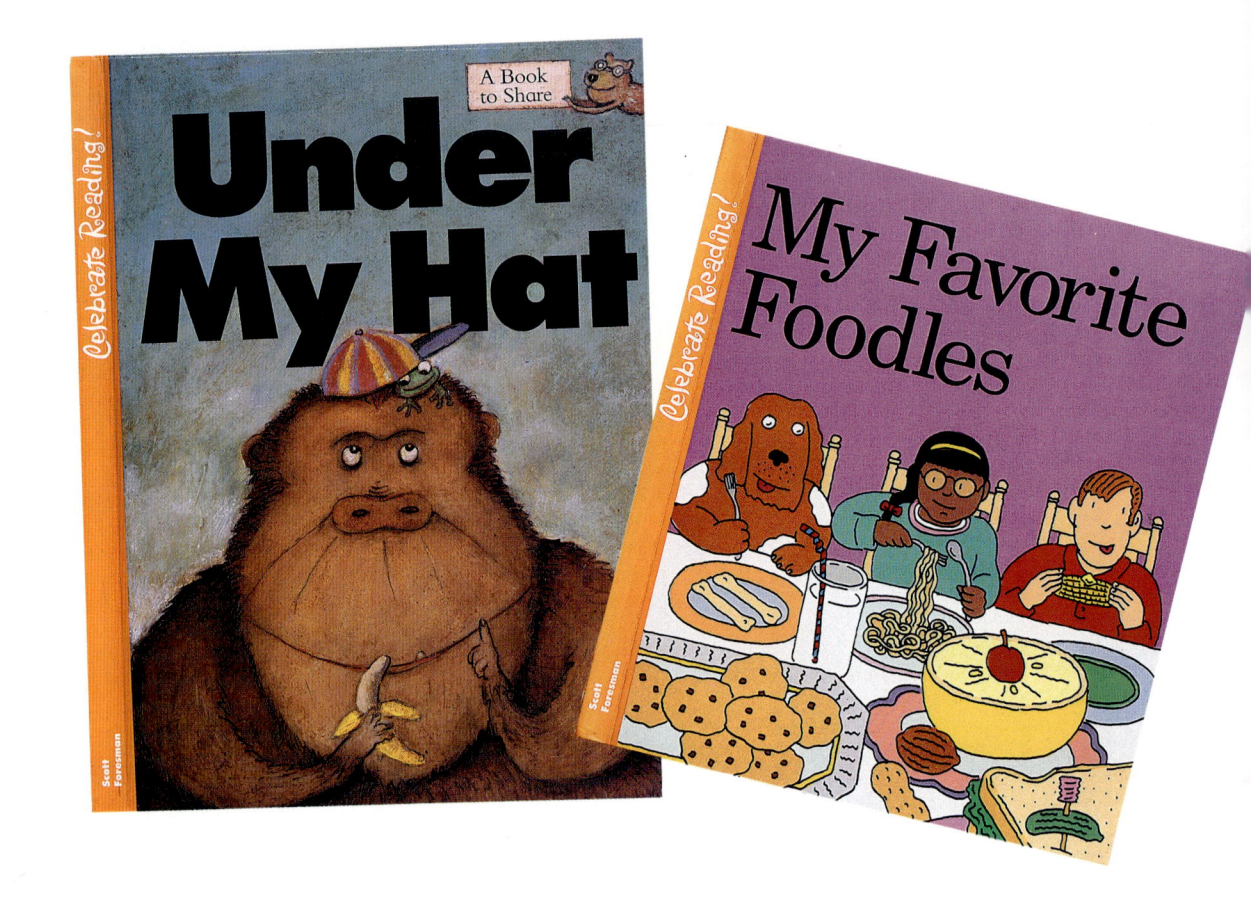

Celebrate Reading!

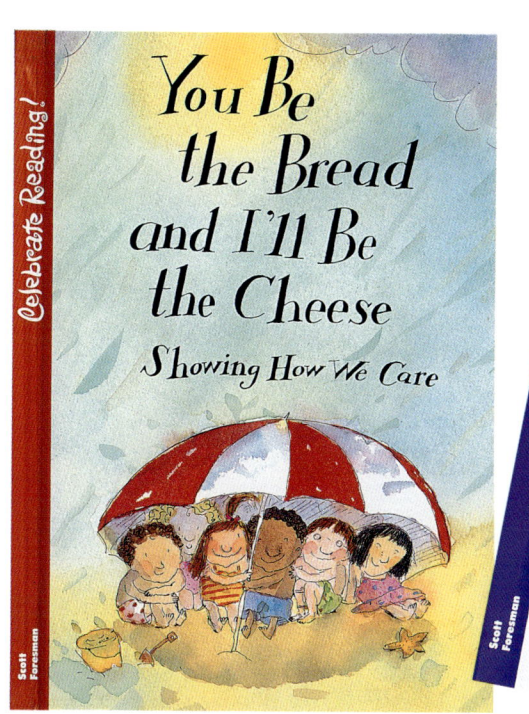

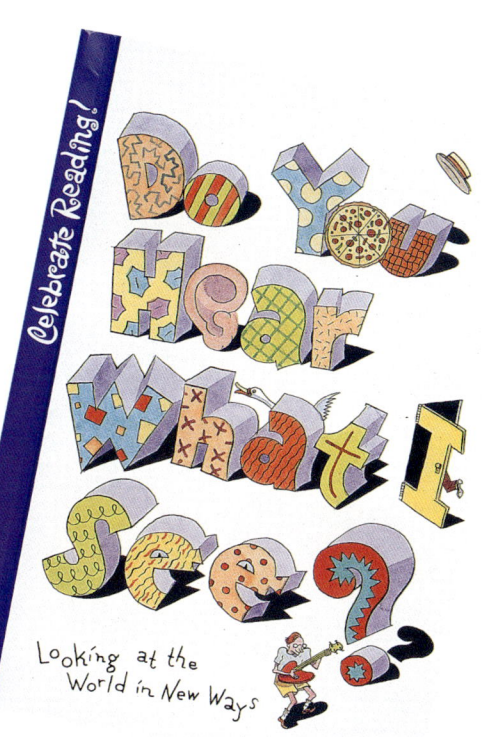

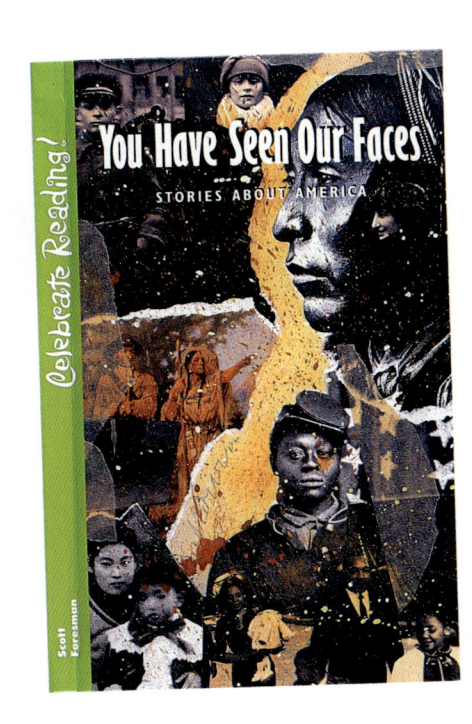

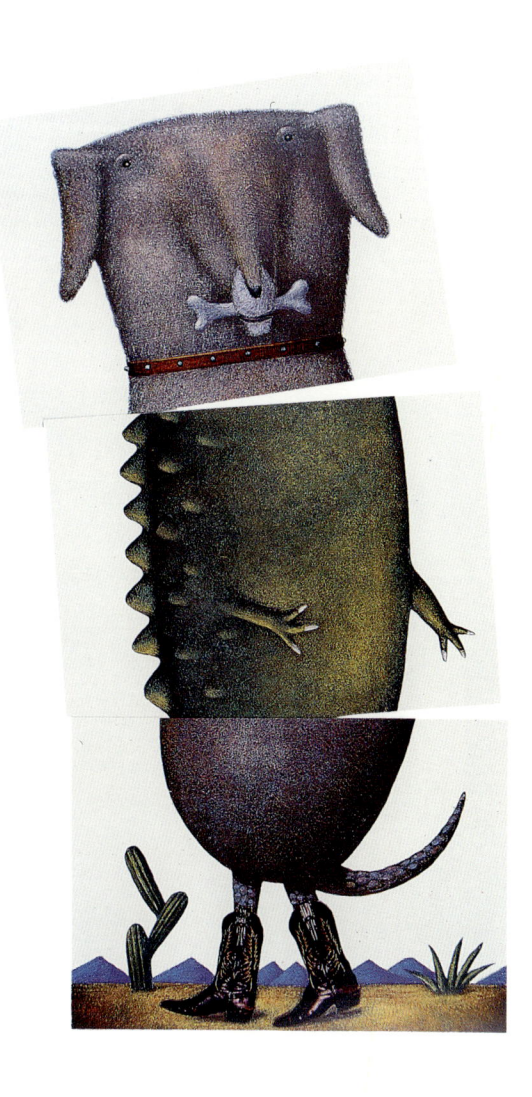

Kym Abrams Design

"Critical Issues," a business-to-business series on health care policy published by Lutheran General Hospital.

Client:
Lutheran General Hospital
Art Director:
Kym Abrams
Designer:
Barry Deck

A highly visual, compact guide to Chicago contains a weekend's worth of city highlights for designers attending the AIGA National Conference.

Client:
AIGA Chicago
Photographer:
Alan Shortall
Art Director/Designer:
Kym Abrams/Sam Silvio

Kym Abrams Design

A location guide for the Illinois Film Office was designed to attract producers and filmmakers to the state.

Client:
Illinois Film Office
Art Director:
Kym Abrams
Designer:
Mike Stees
Photographers:
Various

Celebrating the richness of ethnic and cultural diversity at Loyola University Chicago was the theme of this brochure, which we wrote and designed for the school's undergraduate student recruitment program. *Right*

Is an artist's voice colored by where he or she lives? We designed a single-color poster to promote a lecture series that addressed that very question. *Below*

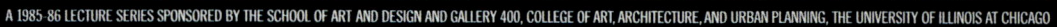

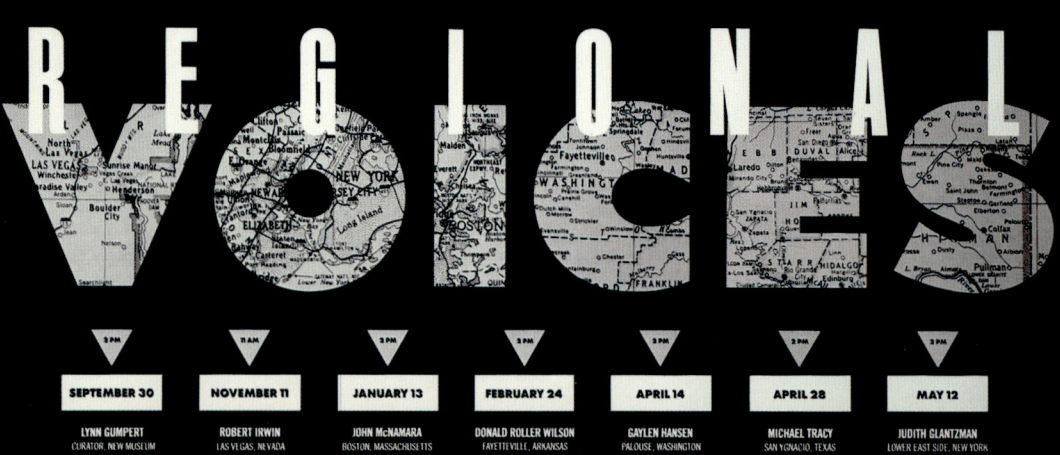

AMIA

Hafeman Design Group brings an added dimension of communications effectiveness to every client project. In addition to high quality, result-oriented graphic design, the firm also offers its clients in-house expertise in marketing consultation, communications planning, copywriting, and complete project management. In every project it undertakes — from corporate identity programs, annual reports, and corporate brochures to product literature, direct mail, and advertising — Hafeman Design Group emphasizes not only the esthetic qualities so important to effective communications, but more importantly the quantifiable results the client wants to achieve. At Hafeman Design Group, success is always measured in client satisfaction.

Immediacy. Strength. High impact. Those were the visual qualities that the American Medical Informatics Association wanted to embody in this new service mark that would convey its member's primary interest — computer applications in medical technology. *Above*

A direct mail campaign that featured this poster, generated for our client — Warzyn, Inc., an environmental management consulting firm — a 70 percent increase in awareness, among prospective clients, of the firm's new air quality management services. *Right*

The quality of air colors the quality of life. **WARZYN** Warzyn Inc. *The perfect balance between technology and creativity.*

The power and impact of this poster proved itself in a slightly unorthodox way — students insisted on continuously "borrowing" the posters as soon as they were put up on the walls of the university. Perhaps these students recognized that a poster promoting a series of artistic lectures represents an ideal marriage of form and function. *Right*

"One of our most successful publications ever," was the way our client at Booz·Allen & Hamilton described this marketing piece. Written in a "how to" style, it was designed to feel like an owner's manual to prospects for the firm's business process redesign consulting services. *Below*

A consistent inconsistency in corporate identity? For this Chicago typographer's service mark, we changed the type style of the letter "f" on each piece of corporate communications material. It seemed perfectly consistent with their image, considering their line of work. *Below Right*

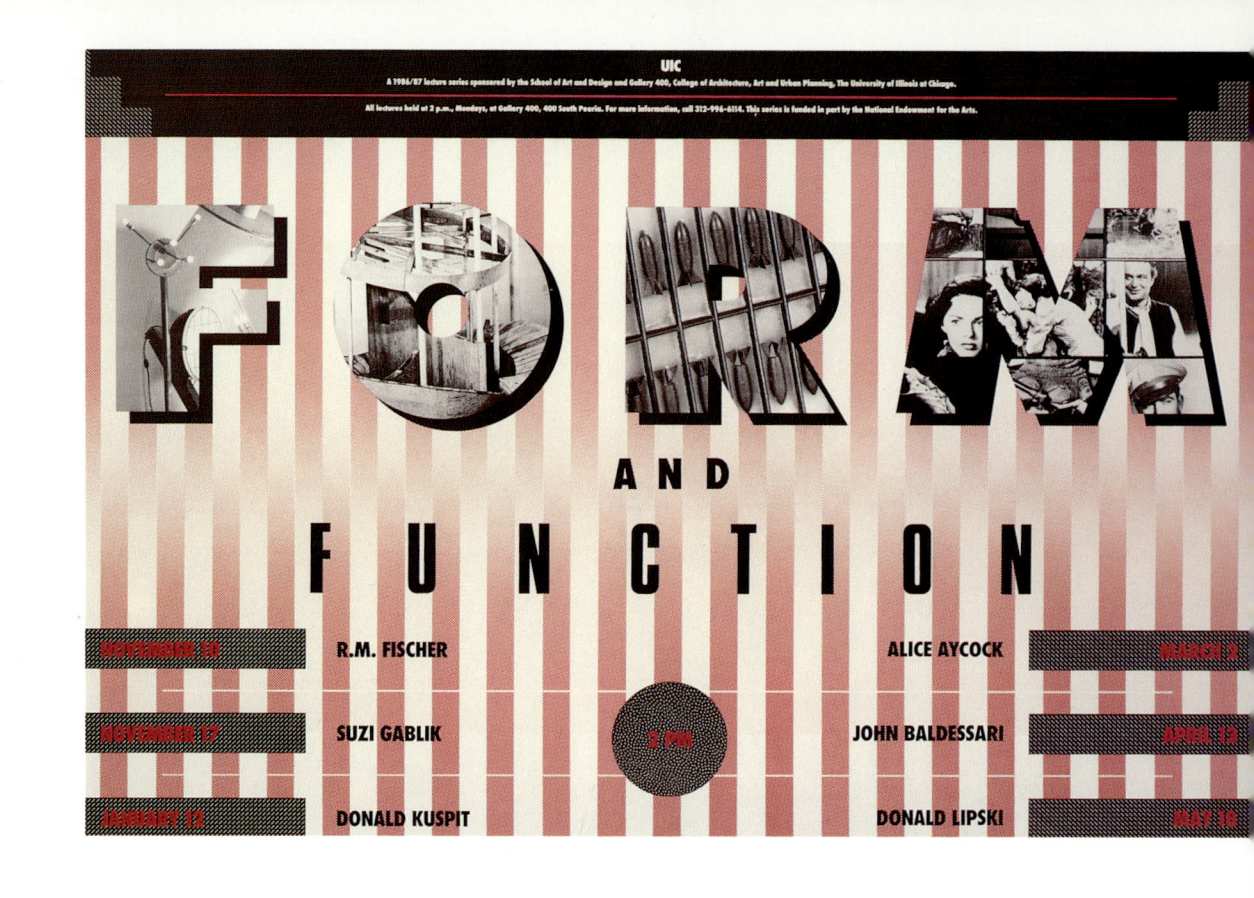

Hafeman Design Group

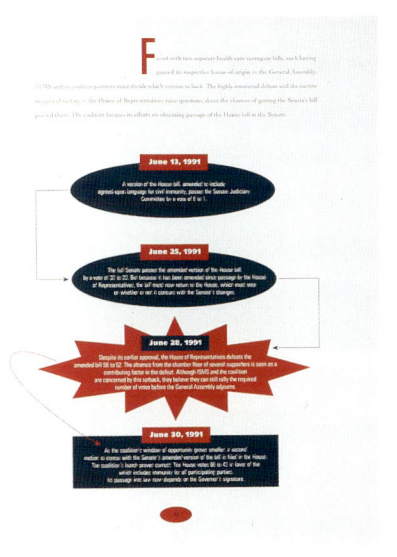

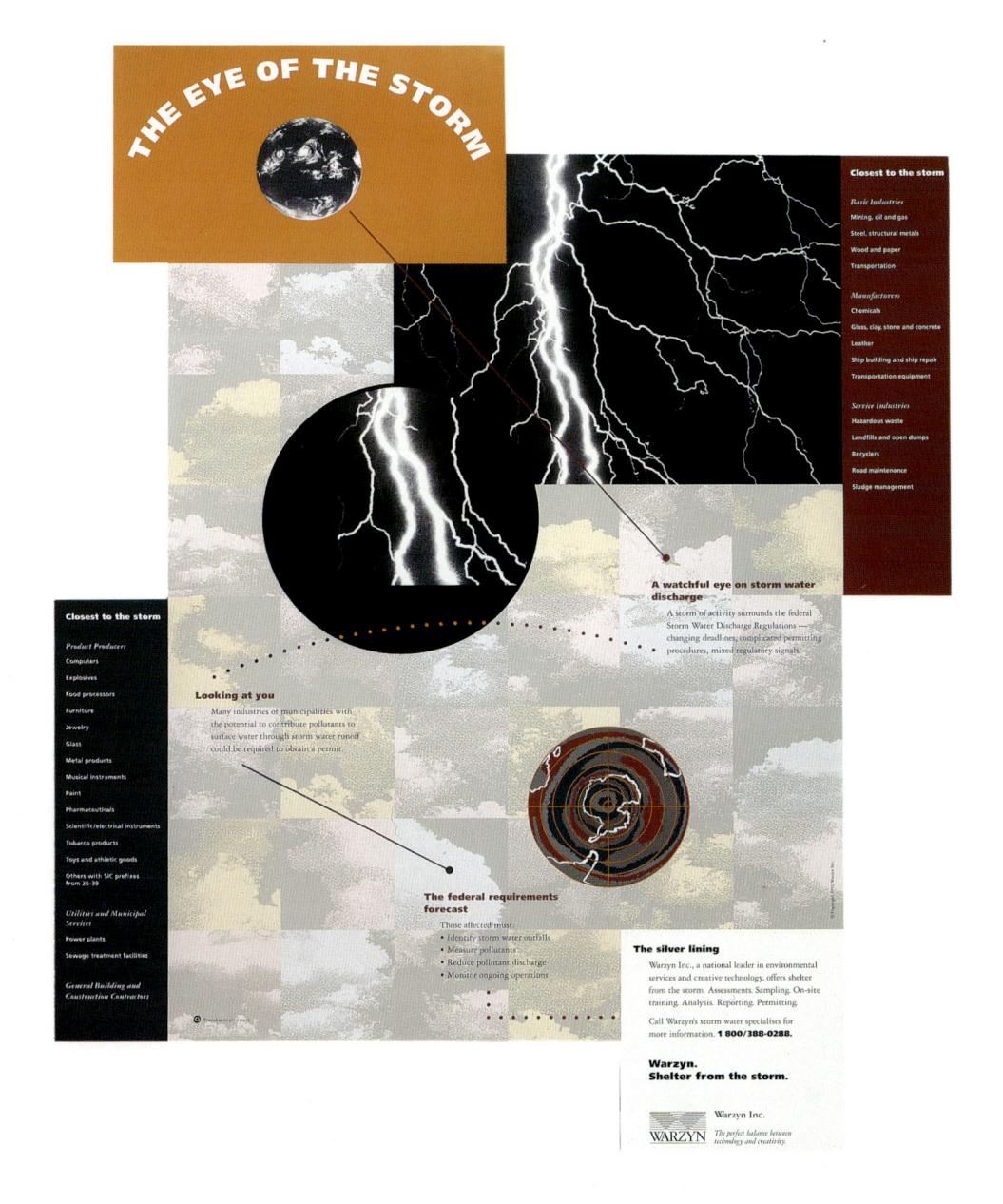

Graphic energy infuses the story of how the Illinois State Medical Society and its members help shape important health care legislation. In this annual report, we used vibrant language, evocative quotations, and a dramatically different visual platform on each spread (including sixteen different type styles) to create a highly readable and visually engaging publication. *Left*

To create a whirlwind of interest in Warzyn, Inc.'s environmental services relating to storm water discharge, we wrote and designed this electrifying poster, part of a direct mail campaign that also included a direct response mechanism for additional technical information. The result? A deluge of replies (a full five percent) from qualified prospects. *Below Left*

The international exchange of ideas was the theme established by the Fulbright educational exchange program. For our entry in this national competition, we choose to concentrate on the concept of interaction, avoiding the visual cliches that so often create conflict in a multi-cultural context. *Below*

Unifying and focusing the image of the American Medical Association has been the goal of our long-term assignment to help implement a new corporate identity program. Under that common banner, we have written and produced the identity program's standards manual, provided ongoing consultation, and designed — and often written — an enormous variety of consumer brochures, books, product promotions, campaign graphics, banners, flags, and exhibits.

Hafeman Design Group

Quality. Quality of care. Quality of life. Quality sets apart the excellent. Many try. Those with a plan succeed.

1991-92 Annual Report

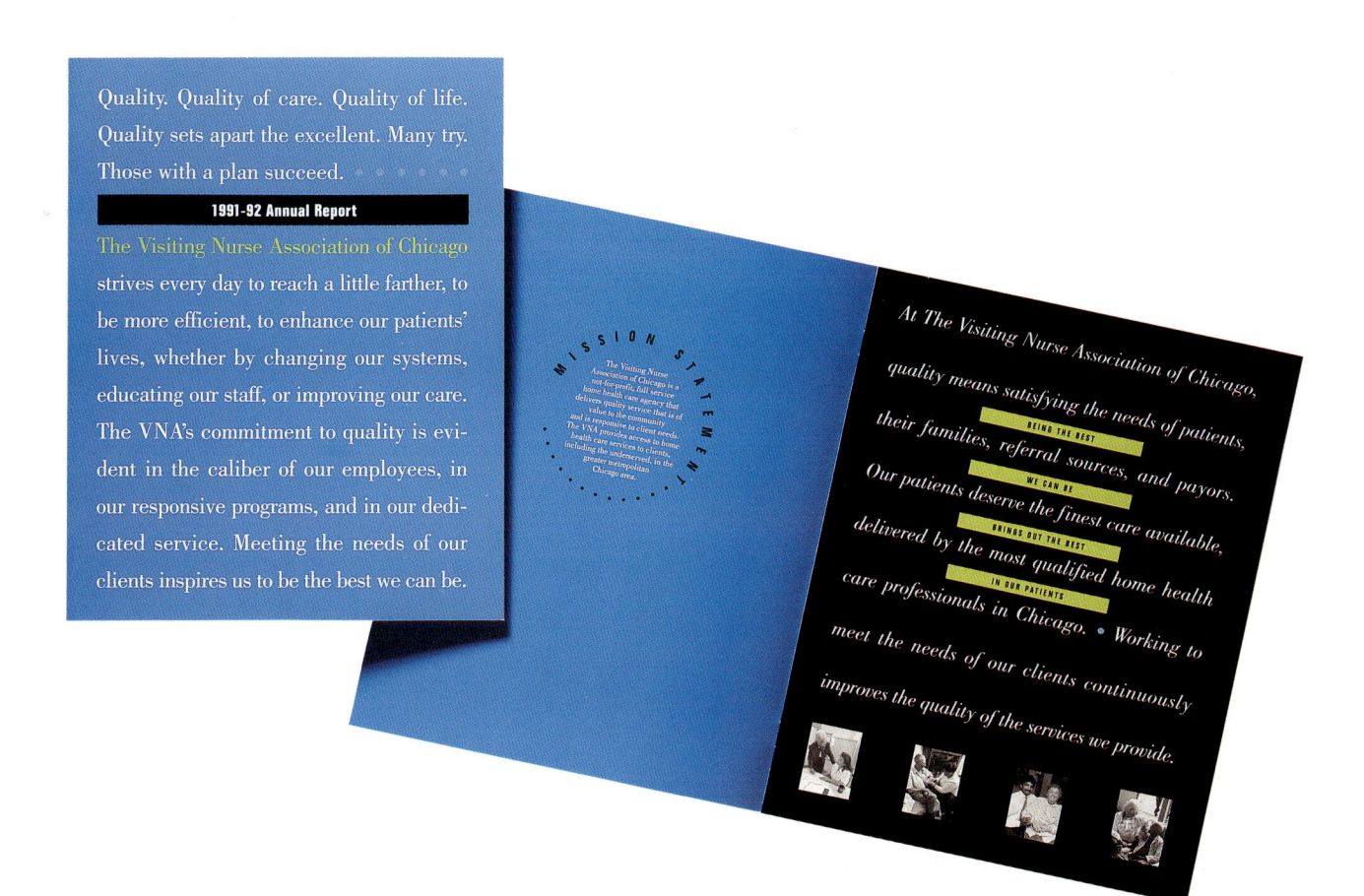

The Visiting Nurse Association of Chicago strives every day to reach a little farther, to be more efficient, to enhance our patients' lives, whether by changing our systems, educating our staff, or improving our care. The VNA's commitment to quality is evident in the caliber of our employees, in our responsive programs, and in our dedicated service. Meeting the needs of our clients inspires us to be the best we can be.

At The Visiting Nurse Association of Chicago, quality means satisfying the needs of patients, their families, referral sources, and payors. Our patients deserve the finest care available, delivered by the most qualified home health care professionals in Chicago. • Working to meet the needs of our clients continuously improves the quality of the services we provide.

BEING THE BEST
WE CAN BE
BRINGS OUT THE BEST
IN OUR PATIENTS

The challenge of creating an exciting, informative, and budget-minded annual report for the Visiting Nurse Association — a one-hundred-year-old Chicago home health agency — led us to this boldly colored solution highlighting their activities and achievements. *Above*

The service mark for the Community Economic Development Law Project symbolizes the cooperative efforts of the three organizations that founded this program for recruiting volunteers for redevelopment projects in low-income communities. *Left*

Getting the audience involved — literally — was the goal of this make-it-yourself poster announcing an exhibit at the University of Illinois at Chicago titled "Ingenious Fabrications." To construct the poster, recipients detached the word "fabrications" and wove it through the sheet. *Right*

A visual pun on an architectural feature — the spire — brought another layer of meaning to this service mark for the Real Estate Brokerage Council, a national association which uses the acronym ASPIRE for its program titled "A Sales Potential Inventory for Real Estate". *Below Right*

The archives of the American Medical Association proved a fertile source for the images we used in this tongue-in-cheek calendar that explored the history of medical quackery and fraudulent remedies. *Below*

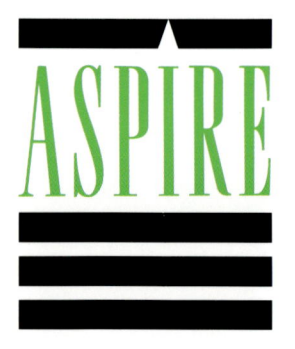

Hafeman Design Group 219

The high-tech orientation of the audience — potential corporate funders of research projects — inspired the look of this capabilities brochure for the University of Illinois at Chicago's College of Engineering. *Left*

The service mark for this developer of computer applications for business plays out boldly in stylized bits and bytes. *Below*

Vivid colors characterized this campaign celebrating the centennial of the Visiting Nurse Association of Chicago. Their brightness visually and thematically linked all the elements of the two-year celebration — brochures, a history book, calendars, street banners, and T-shirts. *Bottom Left*

Chicago's bold, yet familiar, skyline inspired this distinctive, stylized interpretation — the new service mark for the Sales and Marketing Executives of Chicago. *Bottom Right*

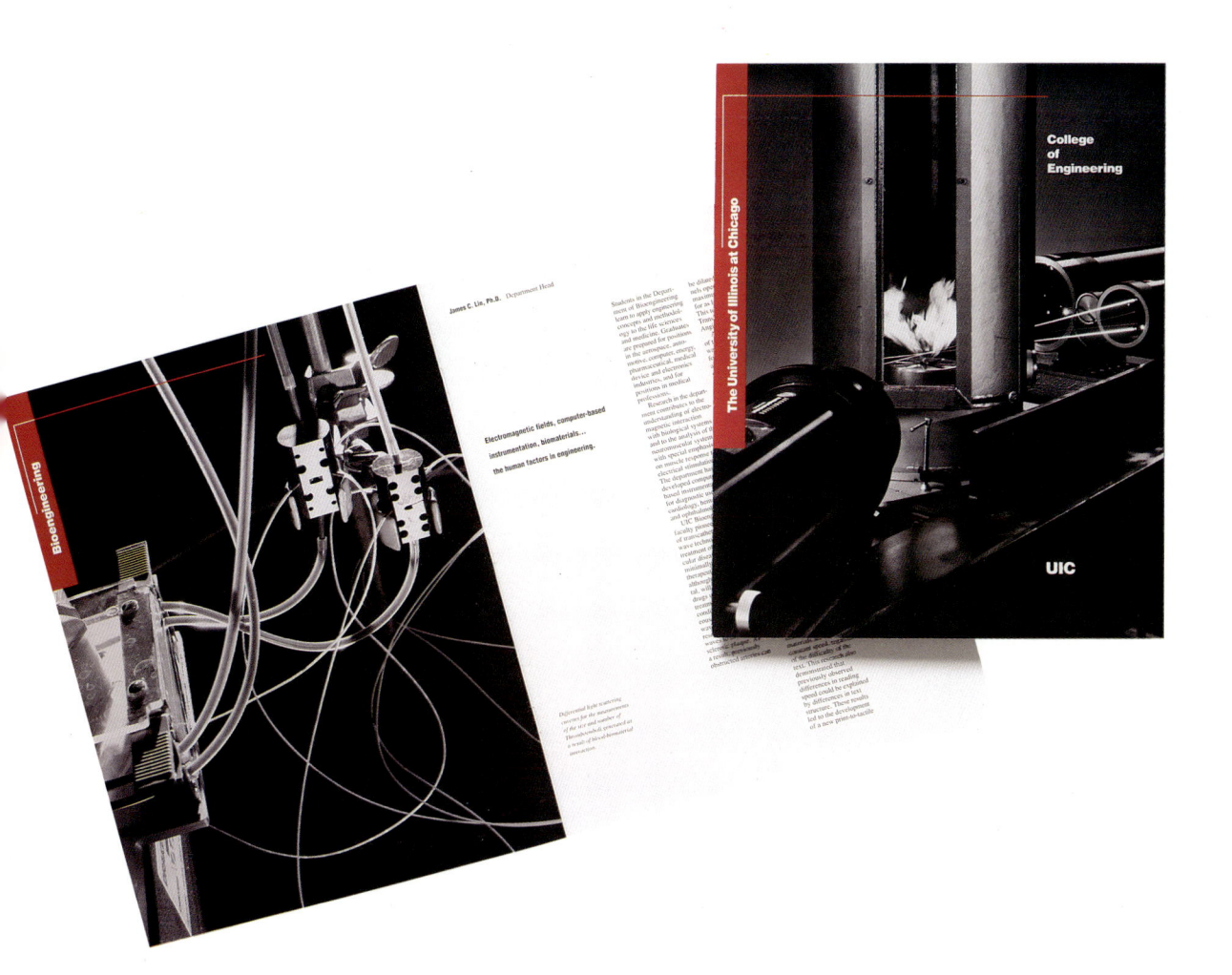

220

Gerhardt & Clemons, Inc.

848 West Eastman Street
Chicago, Illinois 60622
Telephone 312.337.3443

Principal:
Kristie Clemons

Date Founded:
1974

Size of Firm:
8 Employees

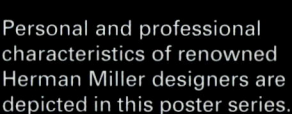

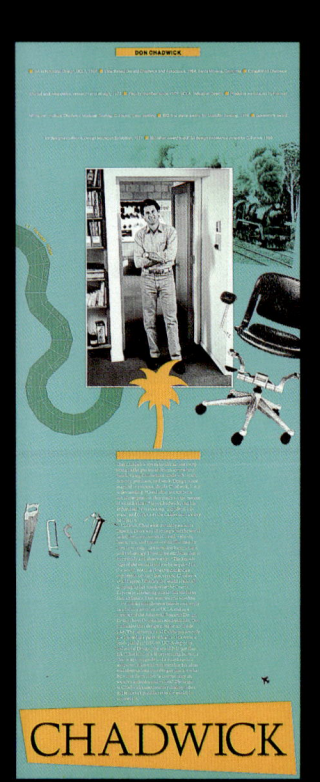

Personal and professional characteristics of renowned Herman Miller designers are depicted in this poster series.

Selected Clients:
Adler Planetarium
Chicago Board Options
    Exchange
Herman Miller, Inc.
The Investor Relations
    Company
LaSalle National Bank
Lyric Opera of Chicago
Quaker Oats Company
Schwab Rehabilitation
    Hospital
Scott Foresman
Sears Financial Services
St. Paul Bancorp
Sub-Zero Freezer Co, Inc.
Systems Lighting Products
Tang Industries
University of Chicago

Gerhardt & Clemons, Inc.

Successful design distinguishes a client while it solves a marketing or communications problem. Solving a problem without making a distinctive impression is a partial solution, at best.

At Gerhardt & Clemons, distinction doesn't require gimmicks. It requires listening, thought, knowledge and creativity. And it requires the experience to know that there are no shortcuts to the best.

Gerhardt & Clemons has been in business for twenty years. While trends have come and gone, the firm has continued to distinguish its clients, and itself, with fresh and thoughtful ideas.

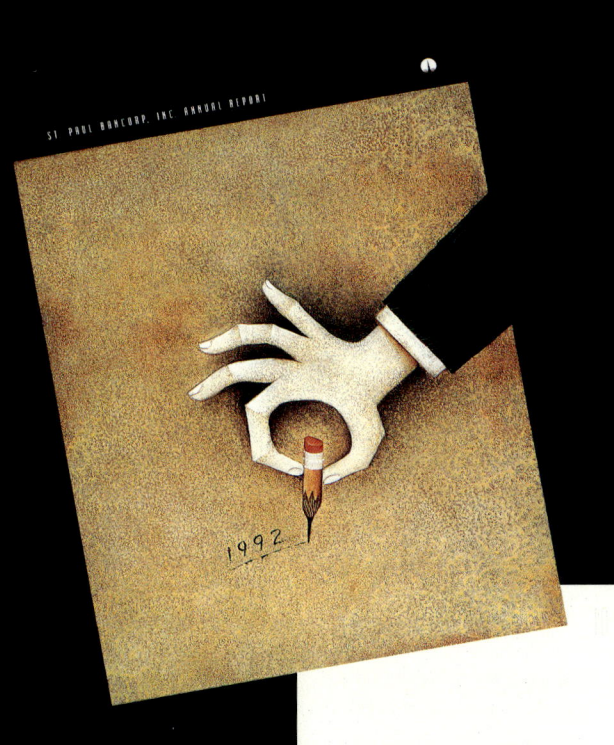

The "hands on" approach to management and service at St. Paul Bancorp is the basis for their 1992 Annual Report. *Above*

Exuberance is the emphasis for the Jamnastics Aerobics Center logotype. *Left*

222 Gerhardt & Clemons, Inc.

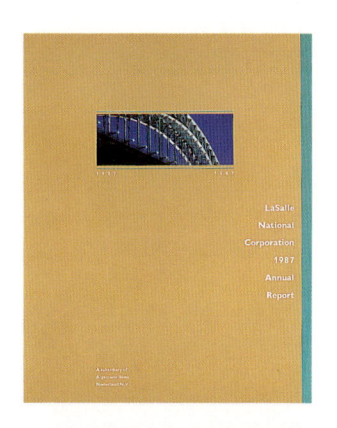

LaSalle National Corporation's 1987 Annual Report reinforced their "Banking Bridge" ad campaign. *Above*

Dramatic photographic perspectives give an overview of services in the 1991 St. Paul Bancorp Annual Report. *Below*

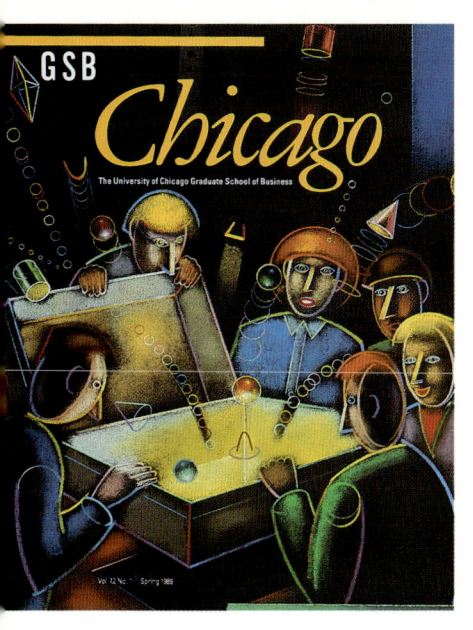

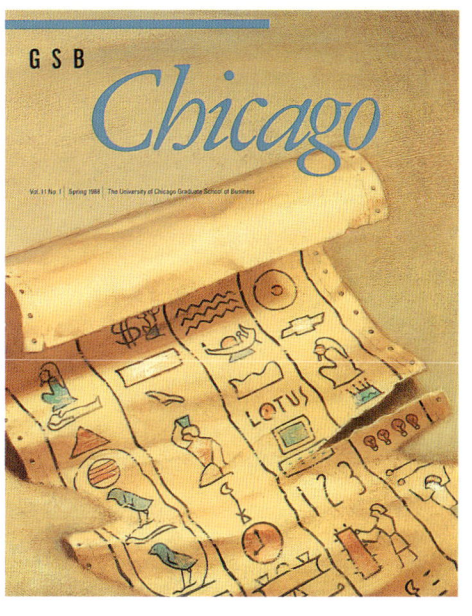

Conceptual illustrations help the University of Chicago Graduate School of Business Magazine attract the attention of alumni. *Top and Left*

The concept of food and the energy it provides is the focus of this logo identity for Nutrition Learning Centers franchises. *Below Right*

Product packaging for Eli's Cheesecakes gives hometown identity to a Chicago favorite that is marketed nationwide. *Bottom*

Humorous illustrations and elegant photos combine to present the superior quality of Sub-Zero refrigerators to the consumer.

The National Materials capabilities brochure utilizes studio and location photography to explain the scope of their industrial holdings. *Above*

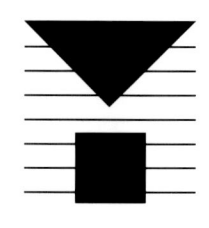

Right, Top to Bottom:
Logo for T2, a subsidiary of Thomson Furniture Company.

Logo for Milcare, a modular healthcare furniture manufacturer.

Children's Memorial Hospital's new logotype was highlighted in a full-page newspaper advertising campaign that showcased patients and their success stories.

Center Right, Top to Bottom:
Logo for Delnor-Community Hospital.

Logo for Schwab Rehabilitation Hospital and Care Network.

Gerhardt & Clemons, Inc.

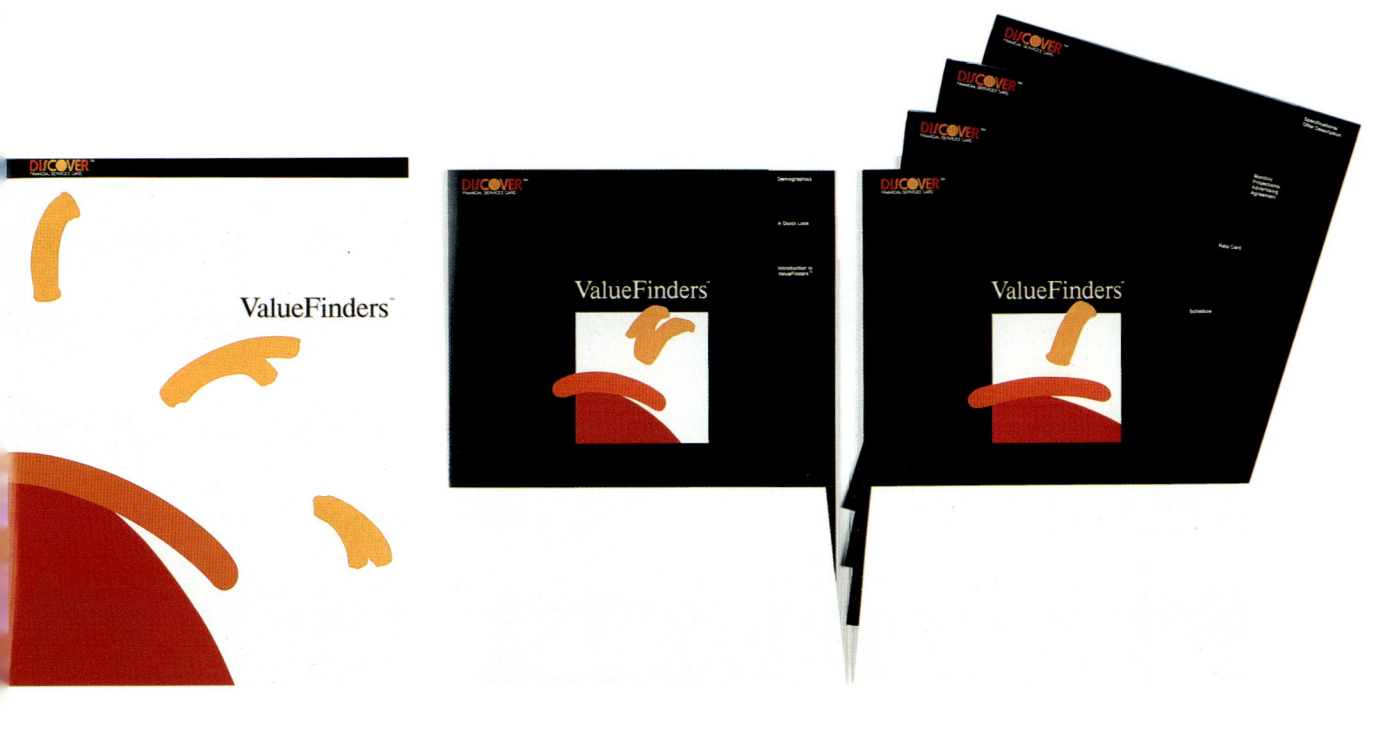

Graphic sunrise reflects the Sears Discover Card identity in the Value Finders direct mail sales kit. *Top*

Distinctive corporate identity repositioned Charlotte, Inc. in the contract furniture industry. *Left and Below*

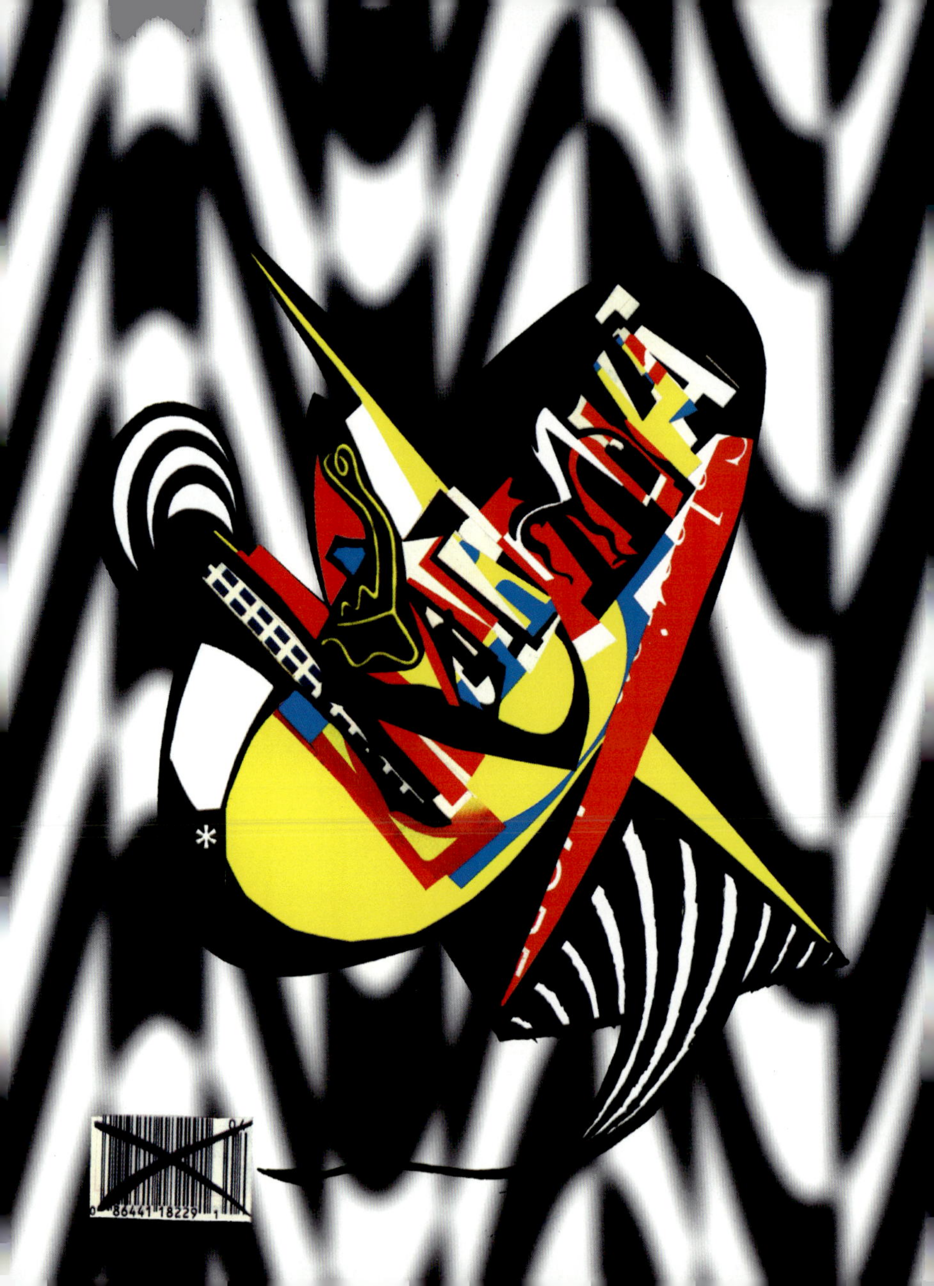

Cool

230 thirst The Color Center
Boston Chicago Los Angeles

Gilbert Paper
USA

thirst Kartell SpA
Milano

233

thirst

Elektra Entertainment
New York

Cooper Lighting
USA

Increase in shelf impact resulted from the redesign of Fisher product line. Procter & Gamble, Cincinnati, Ohio. *Above*

PDC Showcase Call for Entries. Coordinated communication materials were produced. Package Design Council, New York, New York. *Right*

Restage of Raid included brandmark update and redesign of graphics. S.C. Johnson & Son, Inc., Racine, Wisconsin. *Below*

Principals:
Stevan Lipson,
Howard Alport and
Allan Glass

Date Founded:
1947

Size of Firm:
80 Employees
(Combined Offices)

Selected Clients:
Baxter International
Dean Foods
FMC Corporation
ITT Sheraton
Keebler Company
Kraft General Foods
Marriott Corporation
Miles, Inc.
Morton International
S.C. Johnson & Son, Inc.
The Pillsbury Company
Procter & Gamble
The Quaker Oats Company
Thermos Company
USG Corporation

Lipson·Alport·Glass & Associates

The partners of Lipson·Alport·Glass & Associates have shared a common belief...service the client with great creative solutions based on solid marketing principles. This premise has resulted in their many long term business associations.

Recognized internationally for their work in package design and corporate identity, the firm is also an important resource for nomenclature development, consumer research and structural design.

With its expanded facilities and experienced professional staff, LAGA has developed a growing global communications business. In addition to offices in Chicago, Cincinnati, and New York, LAGA has formed an alliance with one of Europe's leading design firms.

While operations expand to meet clients' needs, the partners have not forgotten the ingredients that act as glue for client relations...personal service, strategic thinking, innovative design solutions and direct involvement in projects by directors of the firm.

Left to Right: Stevan Lipson, Allan Glass and Howard Alport.

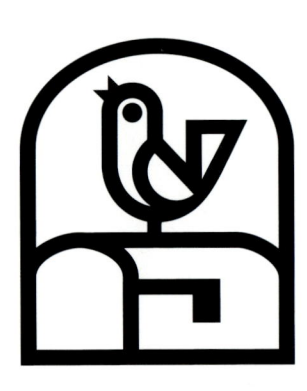

Continuous shelf presence created for Chiquita natural fruit juices. Chiquita Brands, Cincinnati, Ohio. *Above*

Corporate and brand identity preserved and modernized existing equities. Dean Foods Company, Franklin Park, Illinois. *Left*

Package design for a line of all natural peanut butter. The J.M. Smucker Company, Orrville, Ohio. *Right*

Design for a favorite of kids everywhere…Goober. The J.M. Smucker Company, Orrville, Ohio. *Below*

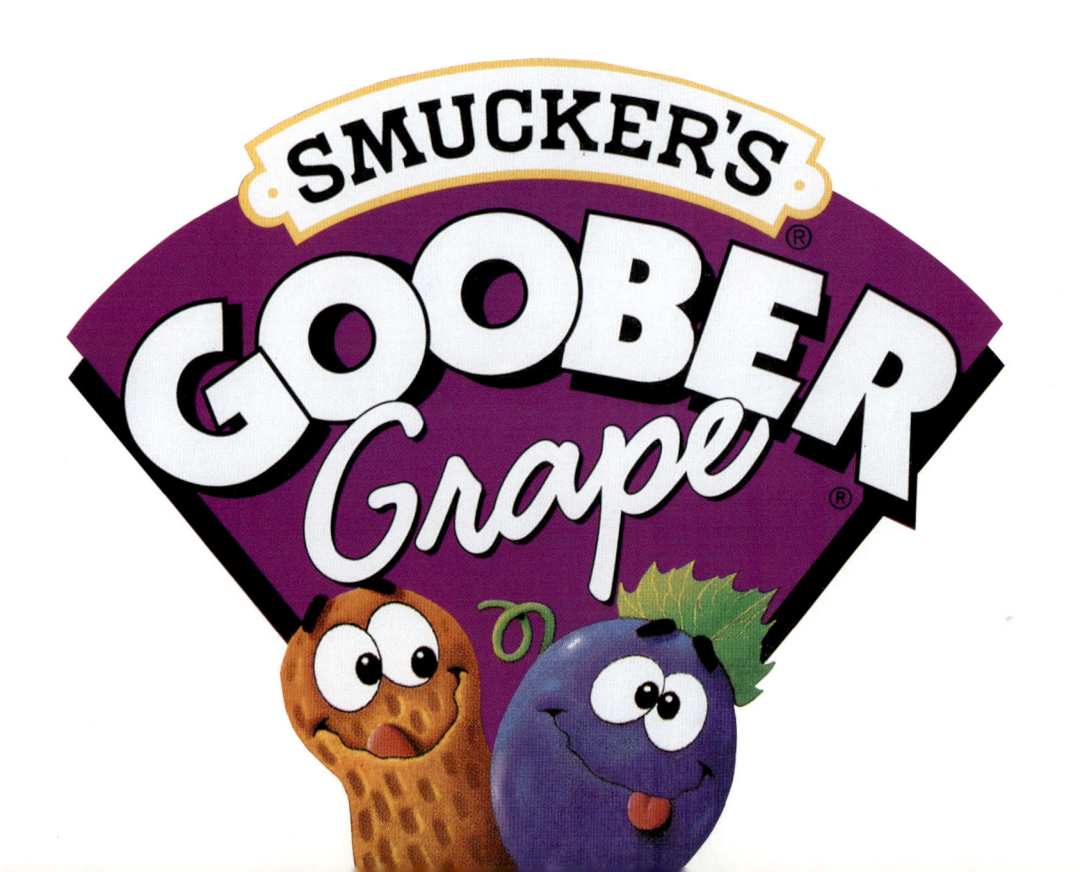

Since its opening in 1947, Lipson·Alport·Glass & Associates has provided package design services to national and international clients. Winning its share of design recognition, the office focus, in addition to creating excellent design, is to ensure that the creative solutions meet marketing and communications objectives. The office's strength is rooted in its staff skills in brand and corporate identity, package design, industrial design, nomenclature development and strategic research.

Brand identity and package design for a line of over 500 SKU's. Express, (The Limited) Columbus, Ohio. *Above*

Corporate identity for Kraft General Foods, Glenview, Illinois. *Right*

Packaging for building products include the creation of brandmarks. USG Corporation, Chicago, Illinois. *Below*

KRAFT GENERAL FOODS

Packaging, brand and corporate identity. Stefani's, Inc., Chicago, Illinois. *Above and Left*

Redesign of the popular game UNO, including anniversary tin. International Games, Joliet, Illinois. *Right*

Packaging for Agree. S.C. Johnson & Son, Inc., Racine, Wisconsin. *Below*

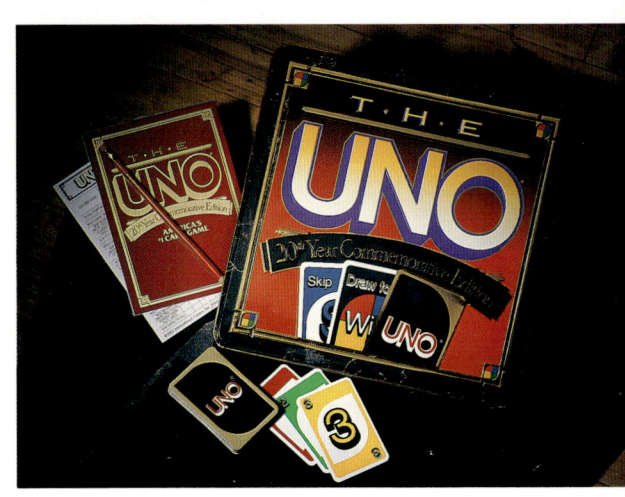

Lipson·Alport·Glass & Associates

Dominick's

Preserving equities and visually strengthening the Dominick's name were part of the assignment that included the creation of a Dominick's house brand, resulting in package design for over 1200 products. The Dominick's identity was implemented on vehicles, signs, in-store graphics as well as marketing materials. Dominick's Finer Foods, Northlake, Illinois.

The Dominick's program represents the combining of the office's strength in package design with the office's skills in corporate identity. From development of the word-mark and creation of the packaging system, Dominick's identity was adapted to exterior signs for 100 stores, vehicle fleet graphics, in-store bags and displays.

Lipson·Alport·Glass
& Associates

Brach's candies, holiday, seasonal and core products received new look.
E.J. Brach Corporation, Chicago, Illinois.

Lipson·Alport·Glass
& Associates

LAGA has developed identity programs for entrepreneurial startups as well as international organizations. The firm has significant corporate identity experience in lodging, food and health care.

Marketing collateral for a company that plans and produces company picnics. Rosie's Kitchen Picnics, Wilmette, Illinois. *Above*

Nomenclature development and identity system for Courtyard by Marriott. Marriott Corporation, Washington, DC. *Top Right*

Development of symbol and creation of graphic standards for Marriott. Marriott Corp., Washington, DC. *Top Right*

Creation of an identity system for a division of ITT Sheraton. ITT Sheraton Corporation, Boston, Massachusetts. *Top Right*

Symbol and graphic guidelines for the parent of Morton Salt. Morton International, Chicago, Illinois. *Center Right*

Annual reports and publications for Marriott, FMC, Baxter & Tellabs. *Bottom Right*

Clockwise from Lower Left Hand Corner: Deb, Marc, Reneé, Cindy, Helen, Amy, Karen, Jim, Verity, Grant, Tony, Megan, Woz, Debe, Larry. *Above*

Communications package consisting of brochures, worksheets and enrollment materials informing employees of individual benefit choices for GenCorp, 1992. *Top right*

Annual report for a regional trucking company focusing on less-than-truckload freight transportation, 1993. *Right*

LaSalle Partners
Motorola Inc.
Rand McNally
Square D/Schneider
  North America
Security Capital Group
Underwriters Laboratories
TNT Freightways

ComCorp, Inc. is a 20-member design/communications firm. Founded in 1982, we provide a full range of services for our clients. Our scope of work includes design conceptualization, planning, development and execution in the areas of corporate identity, corporate collateral, annual and quarterly reports, employee communications, print advertisements, customer communication literature, point of sale collateral, packaging, target market collateral, computer-aided 2-dimensional and 3-dimensional illustration and rendering, and computer systems consulting.

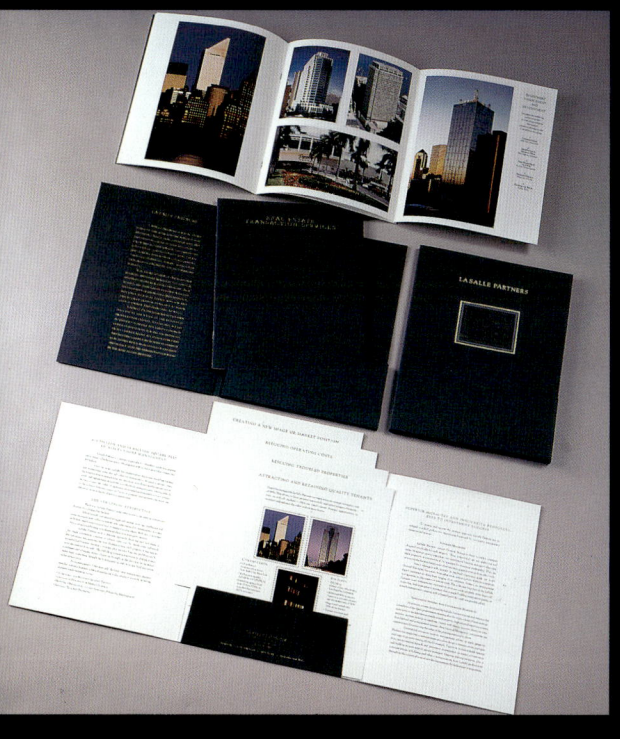

Capabilities brochure developed for a major corporate real estate firm describing the areas of company expertise and involvement throughout the United States, London and Mexico, 1991. *Above*

Labels for a complete line of custom color paint products manufactured and distributed in Mexico, 1992. *Right*

Series of individual pages used both as section dividers in a Chicago Sourcebook and as promotional mailers for RPP Printing Enterprises, Inc., a commercial printer, 1991. *Bottom*

246 ComCorp, Inc.

Promotional literature for the worldwide introduction of a new Motorola flexible wireless Local Area Network system, 1992. *Right*

Corporate identity, annual report and promotional materials for a national organization founded to prevent child abuse, 1991–1993. *Below*

KidsPeace
The National Center for Kids in Crisis

Wiley House
Treatment Centers
For America's Kids in Crisis

National Hospital
for Kids in Crisis
Ending their pain

ComCorp, Inc.

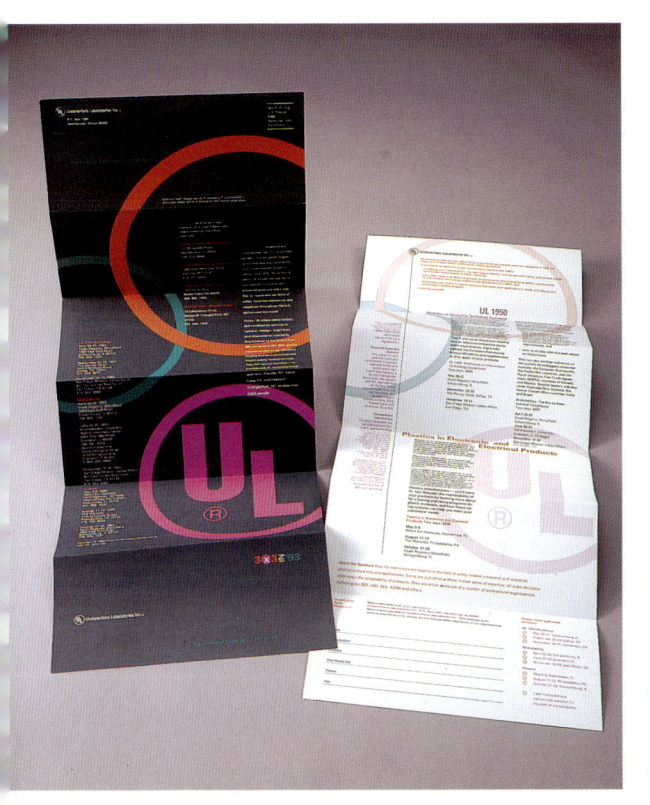

Seminar announcement and registration form for a non-profit safety organization, 1992. *Top Left*

Series of promotional mailers targeted at real estate brokers announcing space available in a New York office building, 1992. *Top Right*

Pedestrian barricade and exterior signage for a Michigan Avenue construction site, 1992. *Bottom Right*

ComCorp, Inc.

MOTOROLA CYCLING TEAM

Series of newsletters addressing the combined benefits packages of two companies joined through a corporate merger, 1990. *Below*

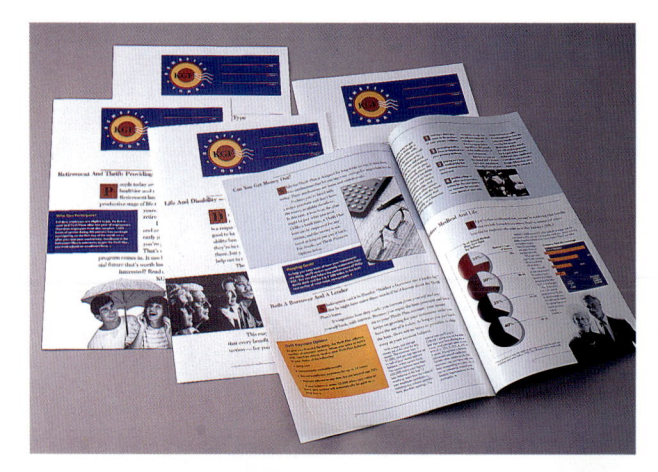

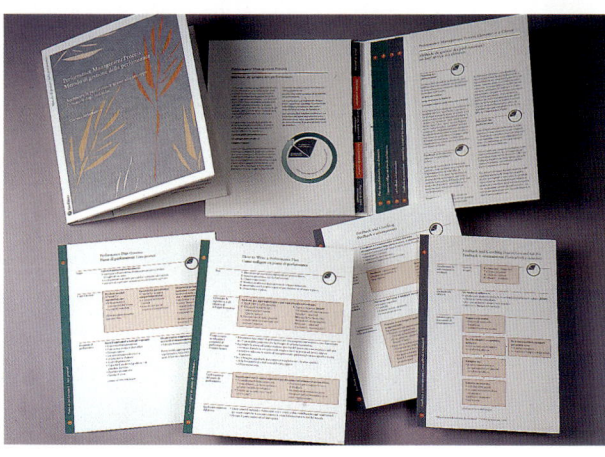

Logo development, application and various promotional materials created for the Motorola Cycling Team, 1990, 1991. *Above*

Communications package outlining the Performance Management Process for a major chemical company, 1992. *Left*

Series of brochure and folder covers representing logo and project development within the corporate real estate markets, 1990–1993. *Right*

ComCorp, Inc.

249

ENERGÉS

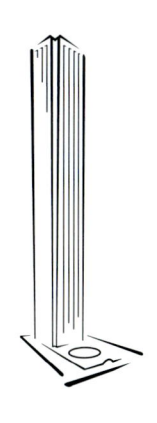

+EMerge

Christmas card. All employees contributed a personal interpretation of the word "peace", 1991. *Left*

Representation of informational and promotional material produced for a cellular phone company. The program identification was developed and implemented throughout all levels of communication materials, 1990–1993. *Above*

Label, packaging and instructional manual for an electronics science kit used in high school classrooms, 1991. *Right*

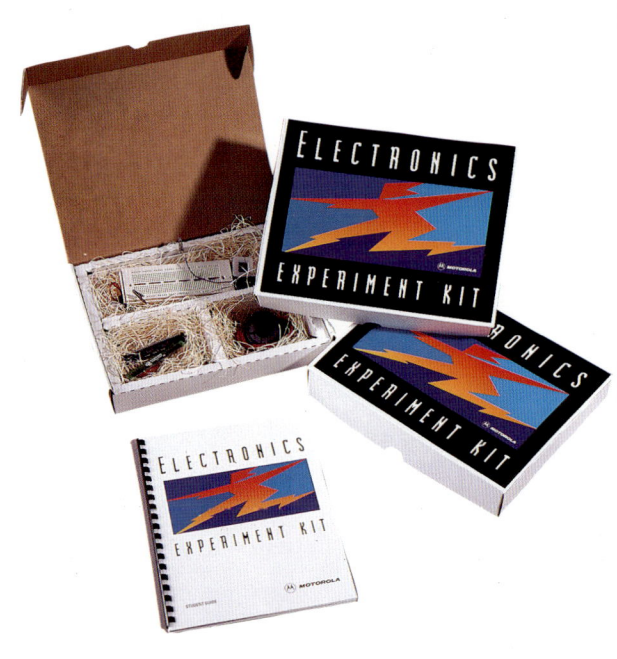

ComCorp, Inc.

Brochure created to market and support leasing efforts for a Fifth Avenue, New York office building restored to full Art Deco grandeur,1990. *Left*

Sales literature and product ads for a navigational device developed with state-of-the-art electronics, 1992, 1993. *Bottom Left*

Streetfinder maps with supporting transit information and regional attractions for six major cities within the United States. All cartography was created on the Macintosh, 1991–1992. *Bottom Right*

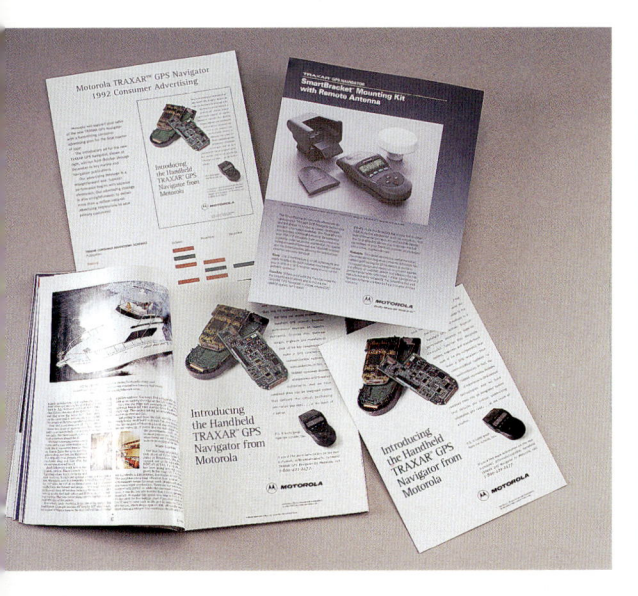

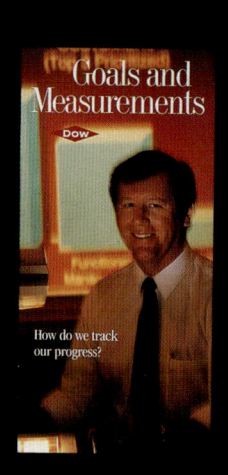

Essex Two Incorporated
116 South Michigan Avenue
Chicago, Illinois 60603
Telephone 312.630.4430

This literature system was created for Dow Chemical Company to convey, to its employees, the depth of Dow's commitment to quality performance and the ways in which they can help support that goal. Midland, Michigan. *Left*

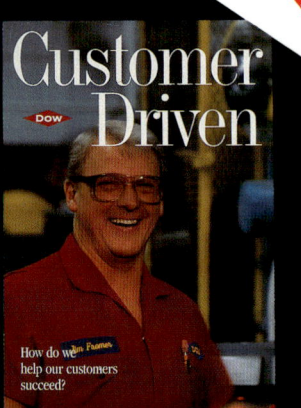

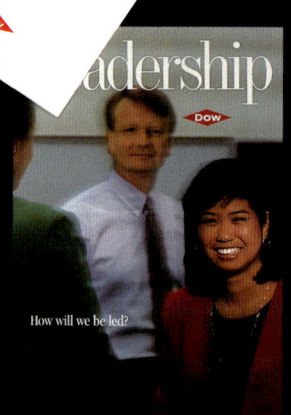

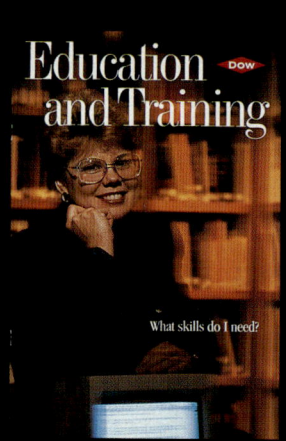

Nancy Denney Essex
Joseph Michael Essex

Essex Two Incorporated

Principals:
Nancy Denney Essex
Joseph Michael Essex

Date Founded:
January 1989

Selected Clients:
Ameritech
Borg-Warner
Dow Chemical Company
Harpo Studios, Inc.
Haworth, Inc.
Illinois Institute of Technology
Lettuce Entertain You Enterprises
Lutheran General HealthSystem
Methodist Hospital of Indiana, Inc.
McDonald's Corporation
Miller Brewing Company
Motorola Inc.
The NutraSweet Company
Pillsbury Corporation
Sandoz International
Sears, Roebuck and Company
Spiegel, Inc.
Unilever International

Nancy Denney Essex and Joseph Michael Essex know what it means to work together: they're married and they're business partners. Together, they are Essex Two Incorporated.

They help their clients identify and then visualize the qualities, values and personality traits that define the character of their goods and services. The result is a constituency, a team, of customers, suppliers and employees that all share the same vision of the company.

Essex Two translates business objectives into emotional understanding through the implementation of their Design By Objectives℠ process. This process consists of combining the results of strategic interviews and careful analysis of possible messages and positionings. They can then prepare images that promote understanding and attract the empathy of the client's collective audiences. This process is not one of visual manipulation or decoration, but one of clarification and discovery.

The work of Essex Two is focused in three primary areas: publication design and positioning; corporate and product identification and naming; and issue oriented corporate advertising. Each area shares the same premise: the presentation of the client's personality traits and values to its audiences. In this way, Essex Two serves as the conduit between their clients and their clients' customers, using candor, intelligence and a sense of humor, to make meaningful connections.

The Latin School's recruitment brochure was created to entice parents and intrigue potential students to one of Chicago's premier private schools. Chicago. *Above*

This brochure/invitation was developed to display the portfolio of furniture designer and manufacturer David Alan Robbins. Chicago. *Right*

254   Essex Two Incorporated

Chicago Times Magazine is a bi-monthly consumer publication positioned for people who would appreciate in-depth articles on issues affecting Chicago: people who read. Chicago. *Right*

HealthWise is a magazine produced for the health conscious audiences of Methodist Hospital of Indiana. Indianapolis. *Below*

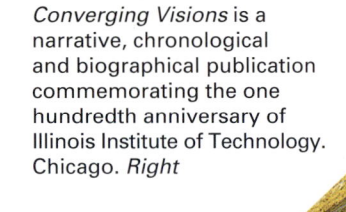

Converging Visions is a narrative, chronological and biographical publication commemorating the one hundredth anniversary of Illinois Institute of Technology. Chicago. *Right*

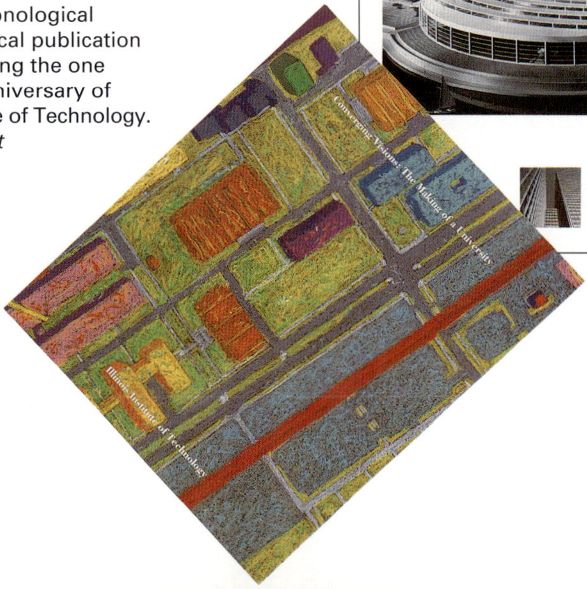

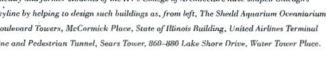

Essex Two Incorporated 255

Office Journal is a tabloid-size quarterly publication designed to present timely and technical information to corporate facilities managers from Haworth, Inc., a commercial furniture manufacturer. Grand Rapids, Michigan. *Top Left*

Chicago Bar Association Record focuses each issue on a different point of law, presenting the complexity and interdependence of continuing education and specialization, impacting the practice of law. Chicago. *Left*

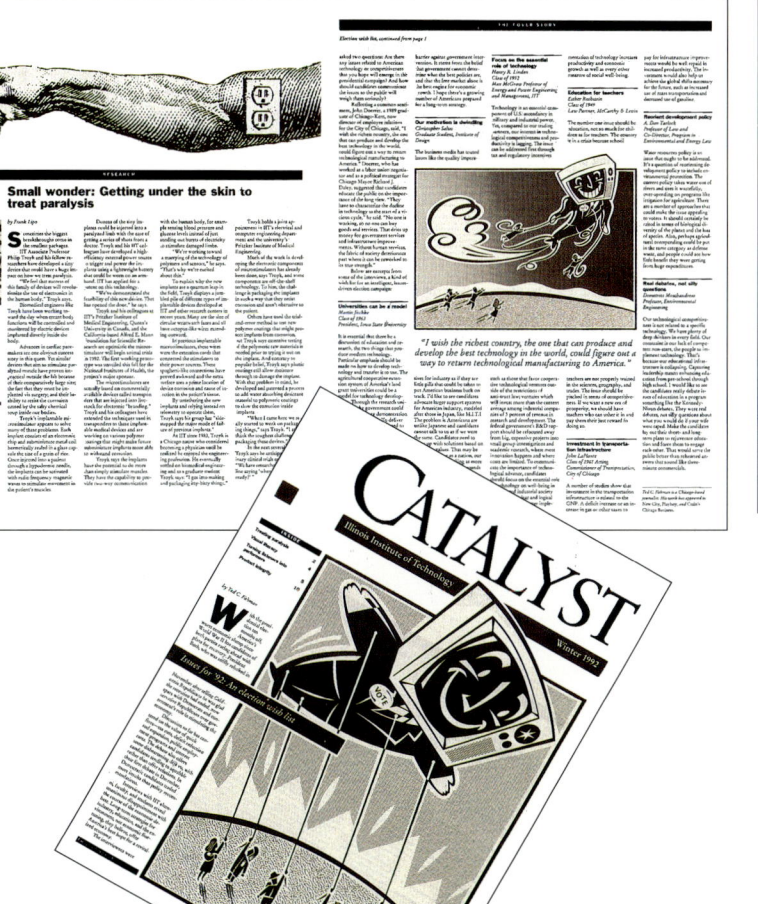

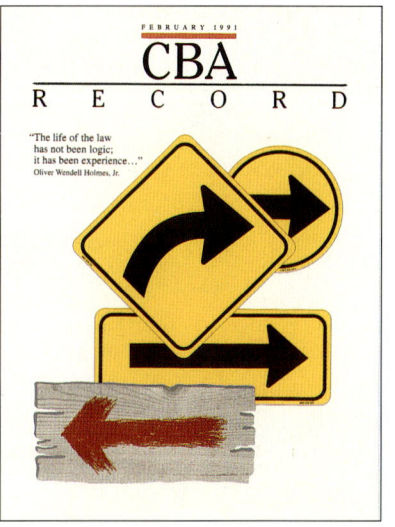

Catalyst is a quarterly newspaper for the alumni of Illinois Institute of Technology, and is prepared to focus attention on significant ideas and trends that affect technology issues. Chicago. *Bottom Left*

Essex Two Incorporated

High Jump: A high school preparation program for economically disadvantaged students. Chicago

Chicago City Theatre Company: A multi-disciplinary ensemble theatre company, dance troupe and training center. Chicago

Grossmen Plastic Tubing Co.: Manufacturers and distributors of plastic products. New York City

Laracris, Inc.: Designs and manufactures lingerie and intimate apparel. Chicago

Ronald McDonald Children's Charities. Oak Brook, Illinois

WellBridge Center: A facility to promote wellness for people over fifty, from the NutraSweet Company. Deerfield, Illinois

American Fiber Textile Apparel Coalition: Manufacturers' association identifying and promoting products made in the USA. Washington, DC

ITP Sport, Inc.: Contemporary sportswear manufacturers. NYC

Chicago Tourism Council. Chicago

Spiegel, Inc.: Upscale catalog company. Oak Brook, Illinois

The Big Bowl Café: An eclectic menu served in bowls from Lettuce Entertain You Enterprises. Chicago

Johnson Products, Inc.: Matching funds program with the Dr. Martin Luther King, Jr. Foundation. Chicago

Sears World Trade: International trading component for Sears, Roebuck and Company. Chicago

Essex Two Incorporated

United African Companies: Forty manufacturing, textile and distribution companies owned by Unilever. London

Methodist Hospital of Indiana: Twelfth largest not-for-profit hospital in the United States. Indianapolis

Pillsbury: Developed to identify products made for use in microwave ovens. Minneapolis

Alcohol Information from Miller: An informational service from Miller Brewing. Milwaukee

Masque: Retail women's clothing boutique with a southwestern flair. Chicago

InterCultura: International curatorial service organization of art and cultural exhibitions. Dallas

Chicago Sun-Times: Book and periodical publishing subsidiary of the newspaper. Chicago

Weaving Workshop: Retail store providing weaving products, supplies and instruction. Chicago

Oprah Winfrey: Personal identification for talk show host and actor. Chicago

Toshiro, Inc.: Importer and manufacturer of Japanese textiles and apparel. Chicago

Ben A. Borenstein and Company: International upscale general contractors and construction managers. Evanston, Illinois

The Who: Identification for a rock group tour sponsored by Miller Brewing Company. Milwaukee

Ace Chain Link Fence: Manufacturer and distributor of fencing materials. Chicago

Couture clothier Ultimo's advertising campaign focused attention on people with a *Natural Sense of Style*. Chicago. *Top Left*

The advertising for the National Junior Tennis Association was to create awareness and spark fundraising. NYC. *Top Right*

The campaign for National Surgery Centers was directed toward physician groups managing and operating their own clinics. Chicago. *Above*

1800 Clybourn is a retail shopping mall with a live theatre, restaurants, a day care center and one-of-a-kind retail stores. Chicago. *Right*

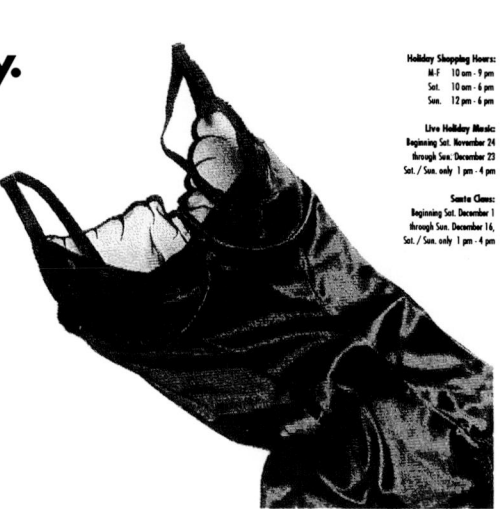

Essex Two Incorporated

259

The campaign for Apple Photography Group was to target client-initiated work, acknowledging the spoken and unspoken concerns of clients working directly with photographers. Appleton, Wisconsin. *Top Left*

The campaign for NASTEC was to present the idea of custom-tailored computer programs for specific functions. Southfield, Michigan. *Top Right*

The Kraft General Foods ad announces the availability of Kraft stock on the Nikkei exchange. Chicago. *Left*

Patrick Whitney
Kim Erwin

Is Theory of Any Use to Designers?

Within the context of a given profession, theories are used to organize sets of assumptions and established principles so as to understand and predict the results of practice. Itten's theory of color and Shannon's theory of communication are both frequently used in design. Theories are always incomplete and abstract compared to the reality they attempt to describe – qualities that make using theories both frustrating and, in a pragmatic field like design, seemingly irrelevant.

There are, however, two key advantages to using theory. Simplifying the explanation of a practice helps other people (including potential clients) understand what appear to be arbitrary actions and values. Advertising, marketing, economics, and psychotherapy are all less concrete than design, yet because designers often fail when explaining design to people who are not already "of the faith," design appears to be more mystical than other fields. The second, and perhaps less cynical, advantage is that the abstract quality of theory allows it to be manipulated so that when tried and true assumptions about practice begin to fail us, we can move quickly to develop new methods that will address the changes in practice.

Two current examples

As mentioned, new theories and methods emerge from observing changes in practice. The overriding change we observe in our field is a shift from a mass society to a de-massified society. Modern design and photography were born at the end of the last century in response to the emergence of mass markets, mass production and mass media. The current shift to segmented markets, interactive media and flexible manufacturing has ushered in a new age – one that is forcing us to practice design differently.

The result? Communication designers, once focused on printed mass media, must now embrace customized communication in all media. Product designers, who focused on single products used by millions of people, now must understand how to create multiple variations from one production line and to design for the interaction between a user and a complex, adaptable product.

Because both the structure of markets and the means of production have grown more complex, designers needs new principles and methods for a better understanding of users, and more predictable ways of conceiving new messages and products.

To accommodate this need and the growing interest in new ways of approaching design, the Institute of Design has formalized principles of human-centered design and design planning into courses for a new graduate program for communication designers and product designers.

Human-centered design

Four types of human factors constitute human-centered design:

Physiological human factors are not new; ergonomic theory has been applied for decades in the design of furniture and control panels. Obvious applications of other physiological factors in communication design include legibility – specifying the acceptable size and contrast of type. These issues are particularly acute for designers working on applications where the final information is presented on screens instead of paper.

Cognitive human factors offer principles for information design that match users' existing knowledge, abilities and preferences for using pictures, diagrams, math, text or other sign systems. The most often cited example of the absence of consideration for cognitive human factors is the incomprehensible VCR control panel.

Social human factors, or the principles of how to design for groups of people working together, is one area where perhaps the greatest amount of effort will be focused in the next 5 to 10 years. The need is compelling: facilities, products, furniture and software are all carefully designed to help individuals work better. Spend any time inside any large company however and you will notice that individuals no longer work alone on anything more complicated than a memo; virtually all the work is done in teams. There is probably no other area in design where the need is so great and the knowledge is so absent. Potential applications for social human factors work include easily adaptable furniture, page-making software for team-crafted documents and conference rooms that encourage team interaction.

Cultural human factors include principles that help designers create products and information that correspond to the different values of the groups and individuals who use their design. The principles of cultural human factors account not only for large-scale value differences among different regions in the world, they can give guidance about creating products and information that are responsive to individual values.

Students and faculty at ID are expanding the study of human factors because flexible manufacturing systems (including laser printers) and flexible products and media are offering unprecedented opportunities for tailoring messages and products to small groups and even to individuals. In order for design to do this, the field needs principles to describe the desired results.

Design planning

Faculty and students in this area work in communication planning, product planning and strategic design planning. Communication planners prescribe new content, presentation formats and channels of delivery. Product planners prescribe new product lines, alternative manufacturing processes and ways of using design to reposition existing products. Strategic design planners focus on the organization rather than individual products or messages. They prescribe new organizational systems that result in services and information systems, as well as products and messages.

In all three cases, the result of their work is not a detailed specification of information or products, but a written brief describing the forces influencing the users, competition, means of production and financial projections. These briefs are different from those that traditionally come from marketing because they focus on fundamental – not incremental – change. They are also different from those that usually come from strategic planning firms because the designers put proposed products, messages and services – rather than existing financial forces – at the center of the problem.

Audience-centered communications

Cognitive human factors
Physiological human factors
Social human factors
Cultural human factors

Current wisdom has it that the main challenge communication designers face is the shift to digital tools and digital media. This is an illusion. The truly major transformation in our industry is a shift from producer-centered media to audience-centered media. The key dimension – whether the medium is paper, computer screens or interactive television – is that each end user will assemble segments of information into a final presentation that is most meaningful to his or her immediate need. For designers, this means that instead of designing the details of the final presentation of information, we will be creating easy-to-use systems that allow innumerable individuals to create innumerable tailored presentations.

To design these systems, designers need to pay attention to the four types of human factors mentioned earlier.

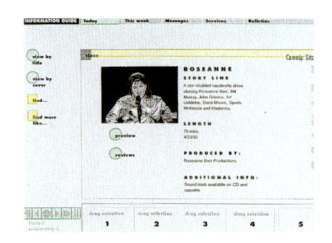

Cognitive Human Factors and the Future of Television

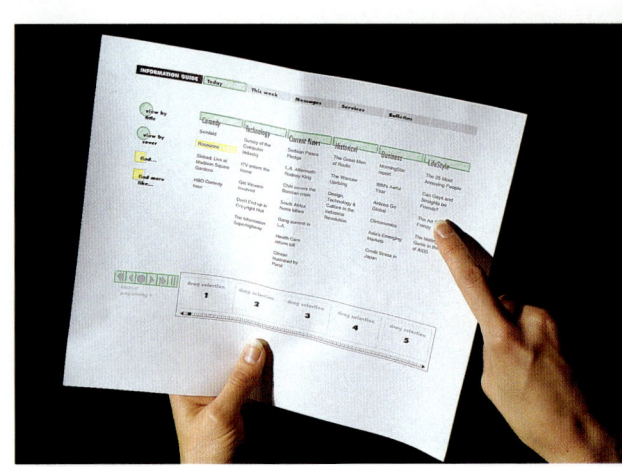

The transition of television to an interactive communication medium raises interesting questions about how we will choose our information from a sea of available options. In working toward a solution, these paper prototypes created early in the development process allow faster testing and reformulation of a preference-based information retrieval system. This method insures that by the time this project progresses to the electronic medium, the cognitive pit falls of the interface will have been identified.
Designer: Kim Erwin

Cognitive Human Factors and Customized Learning

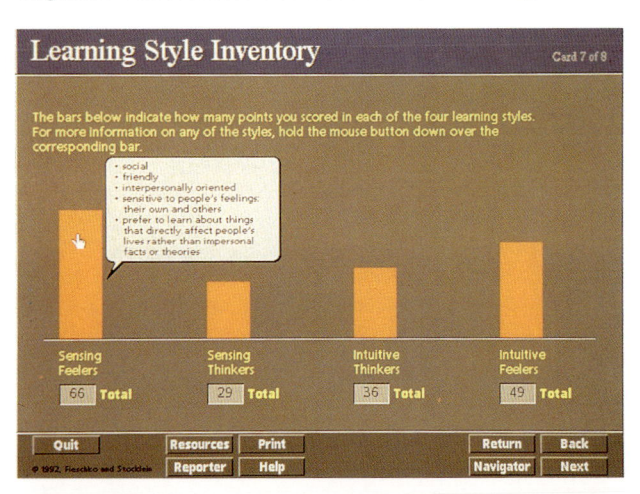

Recognizing that meaningful learning takes place when information is presented within a familiar context, this computer-based prototype explores using learning styles to better match the student to the information. This screen portrays one user's cognitive profile – the result of a personality-based assessment – used to identify the user's learning style.

Based on the cognitive profile, the ScienceNow program directs the user to a customized educational module crafted from standardized content, offering presentation formats, activities and assessments tailored to the information needs of that student. The next student would most likely be viewing a presentation quite different from this one.
Designers: E. Heidi Fieschko, Carl Joseph Stocklein

Cultural Human Factors and Inner City Learning

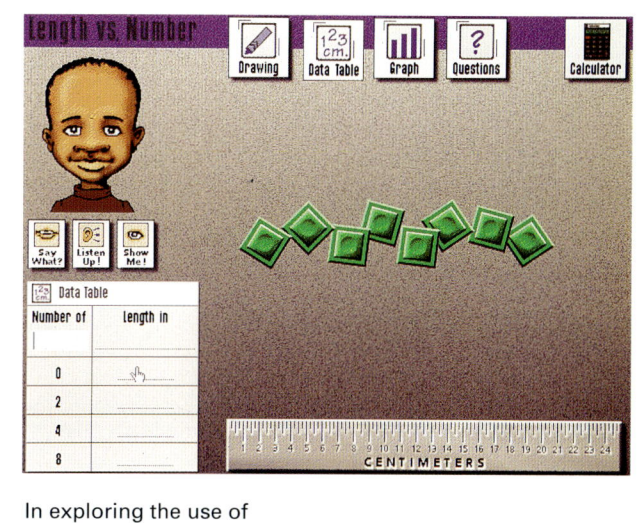

263

In exploring the use of electronic "peer" tutors to help young children, One on One offers six animated tutors from which children can choose to help guide them through their math session. Designed with input from a 7th grade class from McCorkle Elementary School in Chicago, the tutor shown here both speaks the kids' language and possesses a unique personality well-suited to encourage and assist children, as well as offer immediate error correction. Designer: Carl Joseph Stocklein

Social Human Factors and Corporate Acculturation

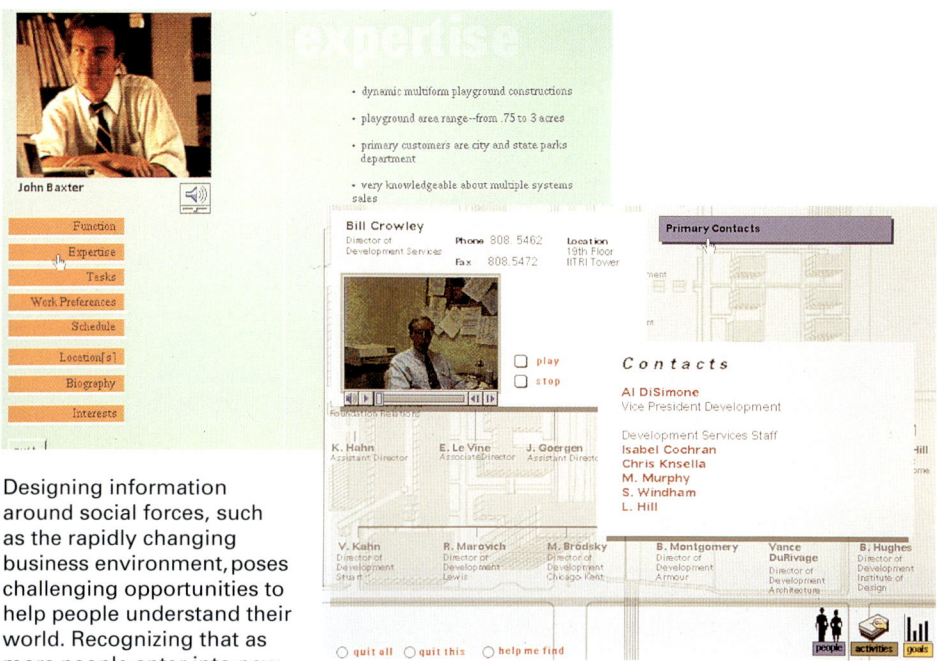

Designing information around social forces, such as the rapidly changing business environment, poses challenging opportunities to help people understand their world. Recognizing that as more people enter into new work situations with greater frequency, corporations are in need of tools to bring them up to speed quickly. CultureLink focused on making the informal aspects of corporate culture more accessible. By using interactive maps, diagrams and video, new employees can both "browse" the corporate environment and seek answers to specific questions.

The cognitive factors of orientation and navigation were addressed via an information landscape – making the whole screen active – as opposed to more traditional control panel-style interfaces. In this image, the background diagram, an interactive organizational chart of the departments of the Illinois Institute of Technology, functions as the interface. Designer: Jan Yeager

Social Human Factors and Team Dynamics

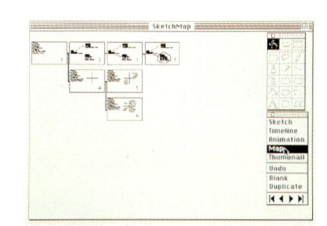

Creating tools that accommodate and enhance the dynamics of team interaction is a growing area for information designers. This project explored the advantages of maintaining a visual history of a team's progress. By building an archiving facility into the software, team members could check the interactive timeline, return to a previous idea and quickly branch off into a new direction.

This image captures the testing environment. Extensive user-testing and group observation play a large role in identifying and refining the tools and information display needed. Several iterations later, a strong working prototype emerged, demonstrating the effectiveness of visual histories when seeking consensus and building new ideas.
Designer: Steven Sato

Designers as Planners
Communication Planning
Product Planning
Strategic Planning

Companies are finding it increasingly difficult to plan new products and services. The cycle time for producing the next generation of products is being greatly reduced. Corporate competitors are forming strategic alliances to take advantage of each other's unique competencies. Consumers are becoming more demanding and less loyal, due in part to the increased choices offered by flexible technology and increased global trade. Changes within the context in which businesses make decisions are forcing executives to look for more reliable methods when planning how to serve volatile markets. Marketing methods which tend to focus on existing consumer expectations are proving insufficient in planning fundamental innovations. It is difficult to imagine, for example, a focus group in 1970 asking for "a small machine that is like a tape recorder that doesn't have to record, but has to play great-sounding music – and, by the way, we want to be able to walk around with it." Executives are also finding that being overly focused on finance or technological invention is as unreliable as being overly focused on existing markets. The emerging specialty of design planning is beginning to provide an answer.

Written briefs describing new products and communications, along with an analysis of the effect these innovations will have on a business, are providing persuasive evidence to executives for using design. Most of the following examples are from briefs written by students in planning classes. Student-developed interactive diagrams on computer are just some of the kinds of planning tools that can help designers analyze complex problems. This emerging type of analytical software tool will become as important for planners as the page layout tools have become for conventional graphic design.

Structured Planning and Communication Planning

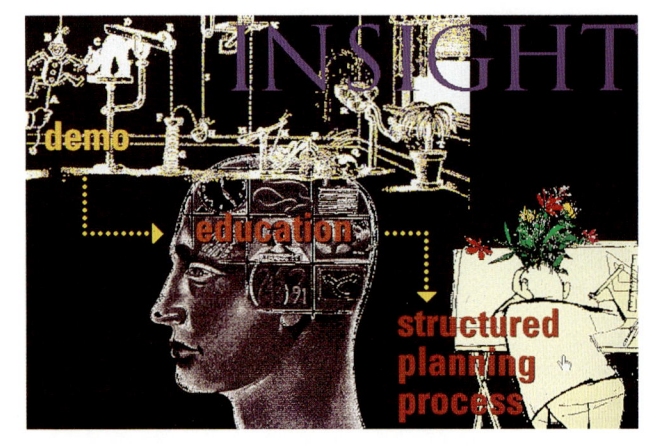

Structured Planning is a proprietary method developed at the Institute of Design for handling large-scale, complex design problems. InSight was developed as an on-line interface for the planning software. Because the Structured Planning method is complex, the interface offers access to a demo and an instructional module as well as the actual workspace.

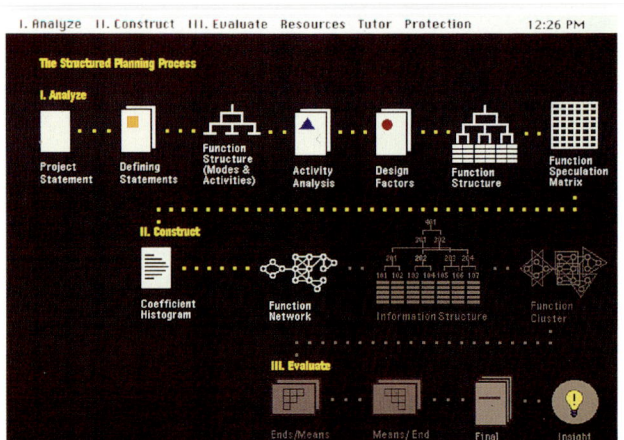

This interactive system diagram accomplishes three goals: it clearly defines and organizes the steps involved in Structured Planning; it indicates the current stage of work the team is focused on; and it functions as the actual interface, providing access to the "mini applications" that comprise the process.

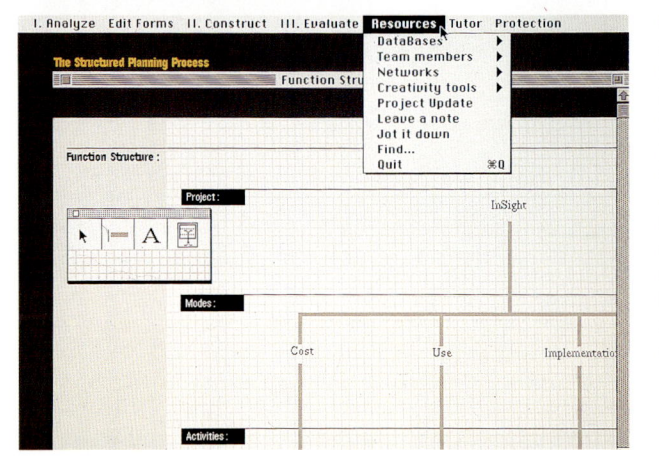

Once a user begins a new step, tools are provided to assist with conceptual block-busting, contact other team members and research pertinent issues. InSight was developed and prototyped by a team of designers using the Structured Planning method and Aldus SuperCard authoring system.
Designers: KuohShiang Chen, Kim Erwin, Heidi Fieschko and Tom Martino.

Strategic Design Planning and the Hospital Room of the Future

Planning documents are often of such a length that it makes more sense to present the information in modules. The Hospital Room of the Future focuses on three subsystems, each fleshed out in their own document.
Designers: Ewan Duncan, Doug Cooke, Jason Nims and Barry Shimelfarb

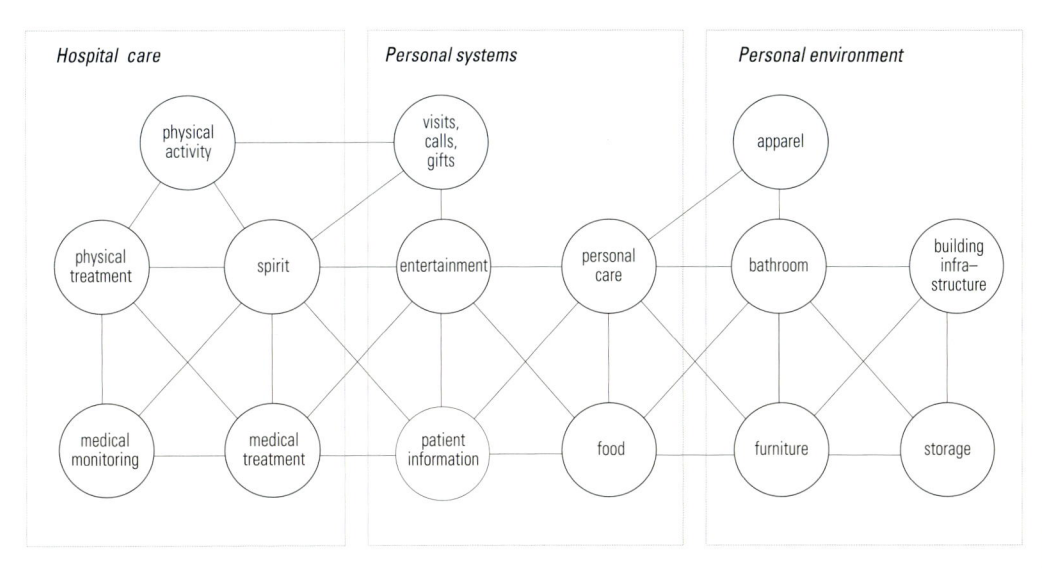

Strategic design planning focuses on information and product systems rather than artifacts. Because of the complexity and the sheer quantity of information involved in undertaking projects of this scale, diagrams are an appropriate and valid method for understanding the components of the design issue.

When planning the Hospital Room of the Future, this team used a network diagram to organize key elements and to provide focus for each of the three subteams.

The role of patient information in patient-centered care is just one of the communication issues this brief addresses. Using the network diagram, the teams identified subsystems that help provide new insights for the future of hospital care, all centered on a profound understanding of patient's behaviors and needs.

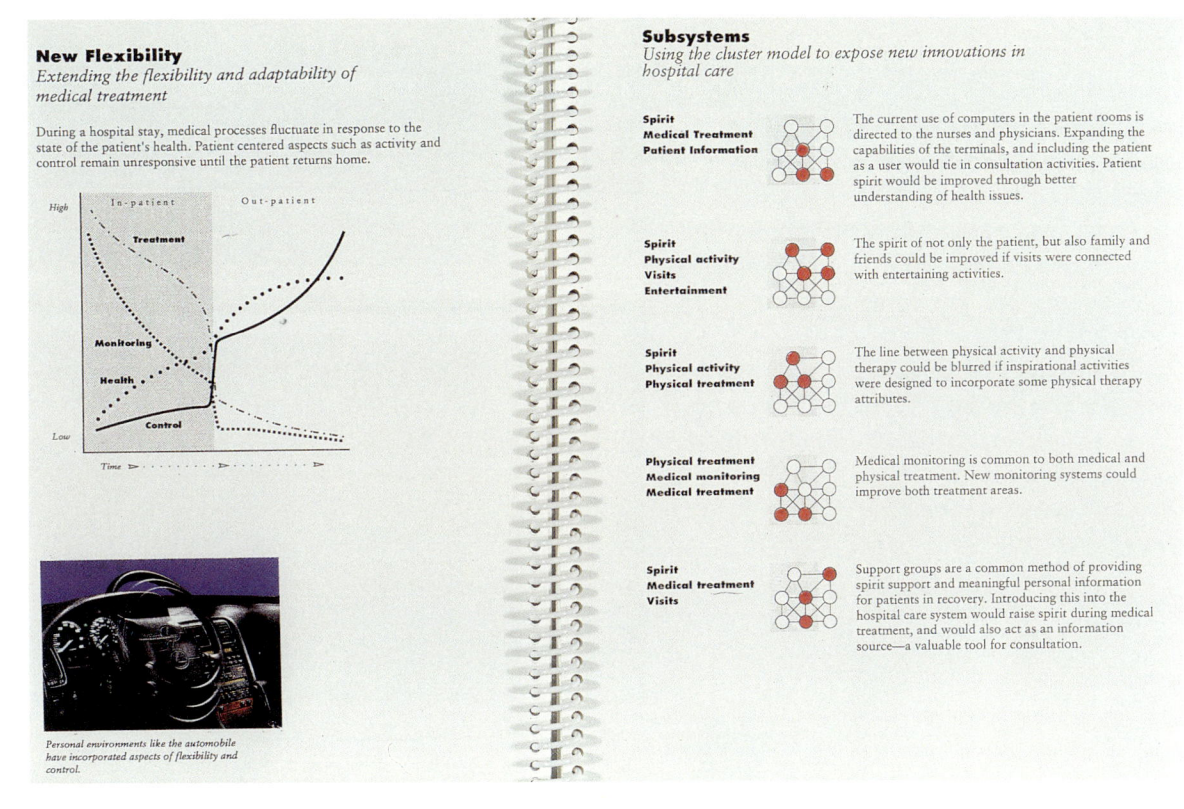

New Flexibility
Extending the flexibility and adaptability of medical treatment

During a hospital stay, medical processes fluctuate in response to the state of the patient's health. Patient centered aspects such as activity and control remain unresponsive until the patient returns home.

Personal environments like the automobile have incorporated aspects of flexibility and control.

Subsystems
Using the cluster model to expose new innovations in hospital care

Spirit
Medical Treatment
Patient Information

The current use of computers in the patient rooms is directed to the nurses and physicians. Expanding the capabilities of the terminals, and including the patient as a user would tie in consultation activities. Patient spirit would be improved through better understanding of health issues.

Spirit
Physical activity
Visits
Entertainment

The spirit of not only the patient, but also family and friends could be improved if visits were connected with entertaining activities.

Spirit
Physical activity
Physical treatment

The line between physical activity and physical therapy could be blurred if inspirational activities were designed to incorporate some physical therapy attributes.

Physical treatment
Medical monitoring
Medical treatment

Medical monitoring is common to both medical and physical treatment. New monitoring systems could improve both treatment areas.

Spirit
Medical treatment
Visits

Support groups are a common method of providing spirit support and meaningful personal information for patients in recovery. Introducing this into the hospital care system would raise spirit during medical treatment, and would also act as an information source—a valuable tool for consultation.

Where the Methods have Gone...

Carl Joseph Stocklein, interface designer at Apple. Joey received his MS from the Institute of Design in 1993; his BS in psychology came from the University of Wisconsin. His work has been published in I.D. Magazine and he hopes to be rich and famous real soon.

When asked about the focus of his work at Apple, Joey divulges what he can of the issues: "The next time you turn on your computer, what will it look like (menus, windows, icons)? How will it act (will it adapt passively or actively to the user)? How will you interact with it (speech/voice recognition, touch screen)?" His interface work at Apple calls on many of the methods taught at the Institute of Design – user-testing, scenario-writing of a user's experiences, developing story boards, exploring the requisite cognitive human factors, rapid prototyping and paper testing. "Apple is starting to think about the design process the same way people at I.D. do, in terms of their interest in an overall methodology."

Pamela Mead, interface and information designer and Vijay Sivasankaran, design methodologist for Doblin Group, a strategic design planning firm in Chicago.
Both Pamela and Vijay received their MSs from the Institute of Design.

Together they have developed a new dynamic diagramming tool for transforming data into visual form. Analysis and Transformations is a Macintosh-based software system that allows its users to enter lists of elements and to score the relationship between elements. For example, enter a set of seemingly unrelated solution options for a design problem and compare them to one another. The software evaluates the scores, sorts the elements and visualizes the relationships between groups. The resulting diagrams allow the users to detect patterns in their data and to probe the strength of the resulting relationships.

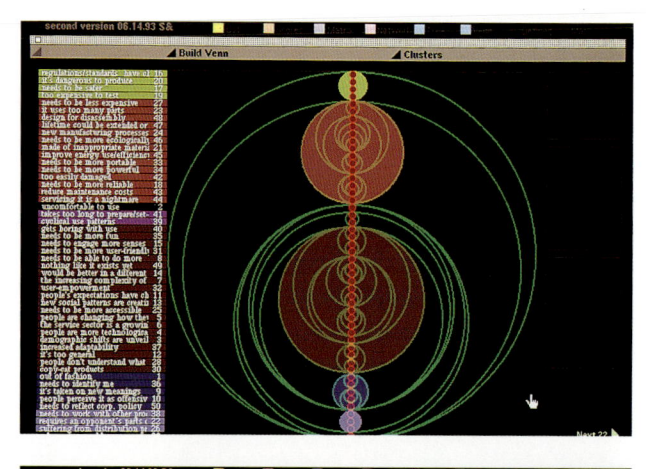

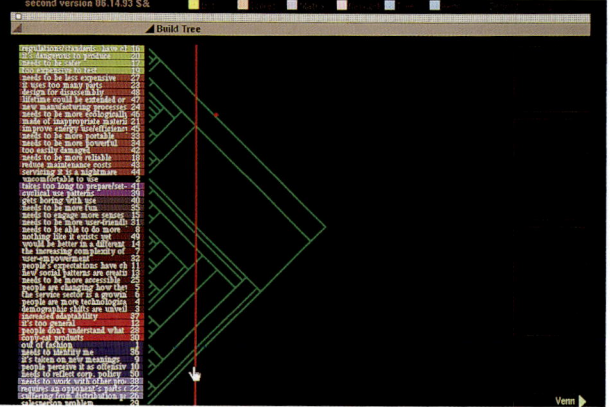

In designing an easy-to-use interface for Avocet's instrument's extensive list of functions, Peter and Jaoto identified key factors of use, including bad weather conditions and use while in motion or wearing ski gloves and formulated their interface elements around them. They tested their ideas using paper prototypes.

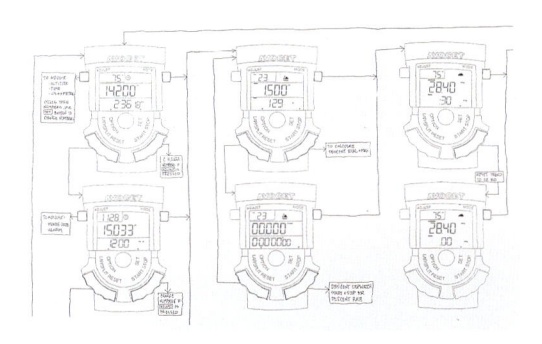

Peter Spreenberg, Director of Interaction Design, IDEO. Peter received his BS from the Institute of Design and went on to teach at the Royal College of Art in London, the Art Center College of Design in Europe, Sozosha College of Design in Osaka and to win design numerous awards from IDSA and I.D. Magazine.

His work at IDEO began in 1988, assisting in the establishment of interaction design at their London office. His work includes planning a user-interface design strategy for AT&T and exploring the use of graphical user interfaces to help shorten training time for systems operators at Tandem Computers. The project featured here, designed with IDEO industrial designer Jaoto Fukasawa, is an instrument that supplies skiers, runners and hikers with a large range of atmospheric information.

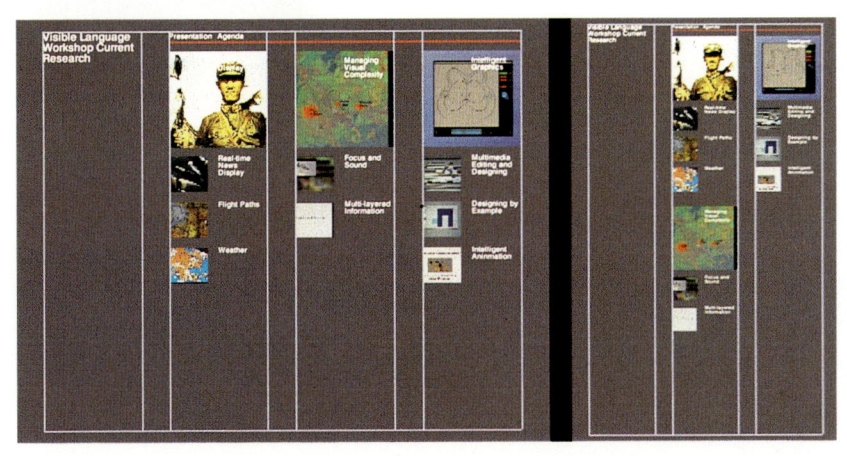

A new system-generated layout is presented in response to a user's desire to resize the display area.

Grace Colby, interface designer for Taligent, an IBM/Apple joint venture developing the next generation operating system. After receiving her BS from the Institute of Design, Grace fulfilled her desire for greater influence on technology at the Media Lab at MIT, where she received her MS in 1992.

Grace was sworn to secrecy about her work at Taligent, but she sees a definite connection between her experience at the Institute of Design and the path to Taligent. The title of her master's thesis, "Intelligent Layout for Information Display: An Approach Using Constraints and Case-Based Reasoning" hints at the level of logical complexity that she – and her computer program – needed to employ to examine text and generate layouts. The goal was to figure out how to embed design knowledge into software. Her program needed to operate at a detailed level; for example, the system determined the thickness of a graphic rule by the x-height of its associated text. Why should designers care? Grace answers: "Because these systems are already being developed. Designers may as well be there."

Index

Abrams, Kym *204*
Alport, Howard *236*
Arnett, Dana *44*
Biliter, Fred *180*
Blake, Hayward R. *76*
Blake, Simone L. *76*
Cagney+McDowell, Inc. *142*
Cagney, Bill *142*
Clemons, Kristie *220*
ComCorp, Inc. *244*
Concrete *84*
Crosby Associates Inc. *102*
Crosby, Bart *102*
Dewey, Rob *7*
Erwin, Kim *260*
Essex Two Incorporated *252*
Essex, Joseph Michael *252*
Essex, Nancy Denny *252*
Fingerhut, Lisa M. *158*
Gerhardt & Clemons, Inc. *220*
Gerhardt, Carol *220*
Glass, Allan *236*
Glass, Michael *36*
Goldammer, Dawn R. *76*
Greene, Howard *126*
Grillo, Maria *44*
H. Greene & Co. *126*
Hafeman Design Group *212*
Hafeman, William *212*
Hansen, James G. *68*
Hayward Blake & Company *76*
Heidekat, Jeff *180*
Hofeldt, Roger *94*
Kovach Design Co. *28*
Kovach, Ron *28*
Koval, James *44*
Kubricht, George *244*
Kym Abrams Design *204*

Lee, John *76*
Lienhart, Jim *20*
Lipson·Alport·Glass & Associates *236*
Lipson, Stevan *236*
Link, Joan *180*
Liska & Associates, Inc. *166*
Liska, Steven *166*
Ma, Anthony *188*
Margolin, Victor *12*
Mark Oldach Design *110*
Matjasich, Carol *134*
McDowell, Bill *142*
McMillan Associates *150*
McMillan, Anne *150*
McMillan, Michael *150*
Meta–4 Incorporated *180*
Michael Glass Design, Inc. *36*
Michael Stanard, Inc. *158*
Murrie Lienhart Rysner & Associates *20*
Murrie, Herb *20*
Nicholas Associates *60*
O'Connor, William J. *68*
Oldach, Mark *110*
Porter/Matjasich & Associates *134*
Porter, Allen *134*
Pressley Jacobs Design Inc. *118*
Pressley-Jacobs, Wendy *118*
Rutter, Lance *188*
Rysner, Shel *20*
Samata, Greg *92*
Segura Inc. *52*
Segura, Carlos *52*
Simons, Jilly *84*
Sinadinos, Nicholas *60*
Source/Inc. *68*
Speare, Ray *94*
Stanard, Michael *158*
Stoik, Ted *44*
Strandell Design *196*
Strandell, Don *196*
Stuetzer, Wayne *94*
Tanagram, Inc. *188*
Thirst *228*
Valicenti, Rick *174, 228*
Vogele, Robert *44*
VSA Partners, Inc. *44*
Webb, Wayne *180*
Werner, Deborah *244*
Whitney, Patrick *260*
Windy City Communications *94*

Acknowledgements

Chicago Graphic Design would not have been possible without the contributions of two people: Rob Pearlman of Resource World Publications, whose vision and perseverance set the effort in motion and kept it on track, and Robert Vogele, whose selfless energy and unflagging support of the Chicago design community enabled it to come to a successful conclusion.

The staff of VSA Partners, Inc., which took on the monumental task of coordinating the book's production on a very tight schedule, executed their work with unwarranted patience and humor. Geoffrey Mark, the book's production designer, moved mountains. Other members who deserve special credit is Curtis Schreiber for his design management and Tony Klassen for the photo-illustration on the cover.

Thanks to Victor Margolin, Greg Samata, Rick Valicenti and Patrick Whitney, whose editorial contributions are an invaluable part of the story told here. The publishers also wish to thank the American Center for Design, the University of Illinois at Chicago and the Chicago Historical Society for their interest in this project and for access to their resources.

Finally, special thanks must be given to the unique group of creative professionals who make up the Chicago design community. Their belief in the importance of this effort, their patience through the involved and vexing production process, and their remarkable talents truly made this book possible. They are the heart and soul of *Chicago Graphic Design*.